DOING
THE
DUNES

by Jean Komaiko
and Norma Schaeffer

Photographs
by
George Svihla

D1506926

Dunes Enterprises   Beverly Shores, Indiana

To Katie, who edited this book

Contents

Illustrations

DUNE TERMS

Dune. A sand hill formed through the steady accumulation of sand granules brought by the prevailing wind.

Foredune. A dune located closest to the water, usually a young and not too well developed dune, low and bare. The first stage in dune succession.

Live Dune. A dune on which the wind is accumulating sand and on which grasses and other cover have taken root.

Permanent Dune. A stabilized dune which is covered with vegetation and trees.

Bare Dune. (Also called a dead or bald dune.) A dune on which no vegetation is growing. The wind has blown away all its cover and the dune is open to steady erosion.

Moving Dune. (Also called a horseshoe dune.) An unstabilized dune whose leeward side is fed by blowing sand. Such a dune can travel sixty feet a year engulfing anything in its path.

Blowout. A saucer or bowl shaped excavation in a dune occurring wherever the protective covering of vegetation is broken and sand blowing proceeds rapidly. In the Indiana dunes, blowouts occur on the northern side of a dune.

Tree Graveyard. (Also called a tree cemetery.) Dead tree trunks and branches originally covered by a moving dune and later uncovered by the wind when the dune has moved further on.

Singing Sands. (Also called whispering sands.) Beach sands which when walked upon emit sounds. It is believed that the sounds are caused by the contact of a top thin layer of dry sand with a layer of moist sand.

Storm Beach. The area closest to the water upon which the waves cast up debris such as dead insects, fish and driftwood.

Climax Forest. The final stage in the evolution of a forest. In the Indiana dunes, a woods where beech and maple trees predominate.

Marsh. An area of low lying wetlands where grasses, sedges, cattails or rushes form the dominant vegetation. Usually treeless.

Swamp. An area of low lying wetlands covered with dense vegetation including trees.

Slough. A stagnant swamp, marsh or bog.

Swale. Marshy ground.

Swell. A rounded elevation. Usually occurring close to swales.

Bog. A marsh or swamp whose vegetation is composed of sedges, shrubs and moss and which characteristically has open water.

Acid sphagnum bog. A type of bog found in the Indiana dunes in which sphagnum moss grows on a sedge mat. The moss, the cold temperature of the water and the lack of water circulation contribute to the acidity of the bog. Though physically wet, this kind of bog is a desert-like environment for the plants which live in it because the acid waters make moisture unavailable to the plants.

Quaking Bog. A bog in which the surface vegetational mat, often of sedge, is anchored at its sides but not in the middle. The mat thus tends to quiver under foot.

Moraine. An accumulation of rock materials deposited by a glacier.

Virgin Prairie. Grasslands untouched by plow or overgrazing.

Succession. The progression from simple to complex in vegetation and animal life.

Habitat. A specific locale for birds, animals or insects.

Ecosystem. The pattern of relationships between vegetation and animal life and their environment.

Environment. The combination of physical and social factors affecting the growth and development of vegetation and animal life.

Introduction

In the autumn of 1972 the Indiana Dunes National Lakeshore was dedicated as the first urban park in the history
of the Department of the Interior. This momentous day
marked victory for a small band of conservationists who
had struggled for more than half a century. It was a day
which moved the authors of this guidebook to action.

"Wouldn't it be great," one of us said, "if someone
wrote about this park so that the thousands of visitors
could learn about dune formations and climax forests
and why orchids grow next to cacti!"

"Wouldn't it be even greater," said the other, "if
someone did a guidebook for all ages and tastes which
also told about interesting places outside, but near the
park."

"You mean like the orchards of LaPorte and the factories of the Calumet. . . ." ". . . and restaurants, and
off-beat shops, and places to fish. . . ." And so it began,
and it grew like the marram grass in the dunes. Friends
and acquaintances called to say, "do you know about
the little cemetery. . . .", or "have you visited the Indian
mounds", or "has anyone told you about the asparagus
fields. . . ."

From the beginning we had to establish some simple ground rules. First we decided to confine ourselves to towns and sights that lay within an hour's drive from the door of the National Lakeshore headquarters. Second, we never permitted any restaurateur to know that we were Mrs. Michelin and Mrs. Baedeker. We bought all our own meals; no freebies; no obligations either. We refused to list franchises and chains. While very few of the restaurants listed are great, at least as of our last visit all are clean, with good food—and some of the country ones are excellent.

From the beginning it was obvious that this book would be highly personal in point of view. Geographically we covered a large area: Lake Michigan south to the Kankakee River; the Indiana state line on the west to southwestern Michigan on the east. We crisscrossed roads and forded rivers and thumped over bridges, and each mile we explored, we disagreed about listings. One of us is a history buff with an advanced case of "historical marker disease," the other is a horticulture buff. All the way apricots competed with covered wagons, petunias with pioneers. We could agree on things like hunting: neither of us liked it, but we had to presume that you, our reader, might. But what about including discount stores? What antique shops go in? Which go out? So the judgments were always personal, necessarily arbitrary, often prejudiced.

In organizing this book, we decided that the first section should deal with the dunes and the Lakeshore itself: its geologic history, its botany and bird life. A score of specialists have helped to educate us on these matters. At the end of the section you will find a calendar of local flora and fauna, so you can watch for plants and birds most prominent at different seasons.

The second section of the book is a community-by-community guide, with towns listed in alphabetical order within counties. Each town has a brief history and a detailed account of what to do and see. Almost all towns are listed, with the exception of some very small ones. We begin this section with Porter County where the National Lakeshore is located, then fan west to Lake, east to LaPorte, on to St. Joseph, and finally to Berrien County in Michigan. The portion on the Kankakee River cuts across four or five counties, but the river is such an entity in itself that we've let it flow its own way. At the end of this section, there are listed a few special places which are beyond the hour's driving limit. These have been included because they have some unusual quality that makes them really special and worth a longer drive.

Some observations:

All attractions which charge admission are starred. (Obviously there are no free bowling lanes, restaurants or movies.)

Unless indicated, private homes can be viewed only from the road. Artists and craftsmen can be visited by appointment only unless otherwise indicated.

Fruit ripens at its own whim; the best we could do was list an approximate picking date.

All northern Indiana phone numbers have the area code: 219. Southwest Michigan is: 616. All other numbers outside these areas have the area code indicated. If you phone from Illinois and Indiana, there is a free Michigan vacation information line: 800-248-9610.

If you are crossing the Michigan line, remember that there is a time change. Indiana is an hour earlier than Michigan.

Section three lists all the galas and festivities together, the special days and events in various communities: ethnic parades, beauty contests, blossom festivals. We cannot vouch for the size of crowds, adequacy of plumbing facilities, kindness of weather—but we've given dates, times and events.

In the fourth section are some suggested outings for a day or half day, with ideas about a number of interesting places to visit, plus a good meal.

In the fifth and final section you will find a categorical guide. Here we have lumped all sporting stores under one listing, all artists under another. The architectural buff, the cemetery prowler, the museum gazer, the berry picker can, in this section, follow his special interest throughout the whole area, all under one heading.

To cope with this book a driver needs to understand Indiana county roads. There are two firm though imaginary lines bisecting each county down the middle: east and west, and north and south. From the place where the two lines cross, a person measures all east-west and north-south numbers. Thus, 350E is 350 blocks east of the imaginary line. Warning: make sure you are in the right county since the markings are the same in all.

Only two things are left to be said. One is that it is in the nature of guidebooks to become rapidly out of date; all things are subject to change, but this sort of information more than most. This book was accurate when it went to press.

Finally, a word of gratitude to the many friends and strangers who helped to get this book written—helped with advice and ideas, with cars, with time and knowledge and interest: Dorothy Ballantine, Beverly Barsy, Dr. William Beecher, Muriel Berkson, Richard Conklin, Olga Davidson, George Frerichs, Willis and Myrtle Grieger, Margaret Horner, Lois Howes, Marion Isaacs, Mary Lou Keeney, Dr. Carl Krekler, Irving Levin, Stan Locke, Hazel McKinnon, Ray Nordstrand, Kate Ollendorff, Nancy Padilla, Judith Parkhurst, Warren Reeder, Dr. Mark Reshkin, Esther Saks, Paul Strand, Robert Tweit, Kitty Wade, Jim Whitehouse. Our thanks to all of them! And most of all to our patient families. And our special thanks to Sylvia Troy and Charlotte Read and a hundred others including Dorothy Buell and Senator Paul Douglas: they SAVED THE DUNES. And in so doing they made possible a glorious park that will remain a rich heritage for all the people of the United States.

Indiana Dunes National Lakeshore

The Indiana Dunes National Lakeshore is America's first urban park. It is within easy driving distance of millions of Americans. Authorized by Congress in 1966 and dedicated in 1972, the Lakeshore provides a remarkable opportunity to examine man and his environment. Unlike America's famous western parks which stretch for hundreds of miles in the wilderness, the Indiana Dunes National Lakeshore is a mosaic park where giant industrial complexes, residential communities and a web of railroad tracks and highways are interspersed with areas of great physical beauty which remain substantially untouched by man. Though the Lakeshore's land holdings are not contiguous, they include the recreational, aesthetic and historical elements which typify all of our country's great parks.

In scale the National Lakeshore is small, so that, in effect, it represents a sheltered refuge. It requires the visitor to foresake modern transportation and go afoot to experience its delights. By tramping its dunes, walking its beaches, feeling its north wind, blowing sand, moist heat and biting cold, smelling its faint marsh sour and the perfume of its fields, and quietly examining its vast profusion of flowers, trees, insects and birds, the visitor

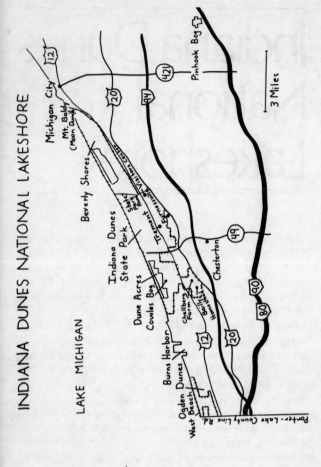

INDIANA DUNES NATIONAL LAKESHORE

LAKE MICHIGAN

Michigan City

Mt. Baldy (Moon Dune)

Beverly Shores

Indiana Dunes State Park

Dune Acres

Cowles Bog

Burns Harbor

Ogden Dunes

West Beach

Porter-Lake County Line Rd.

State Park

Tremont

Furnessville

Visitor Center

Chesterton

Chilburg Farm

Bailly Homestead

Pinhook Bog

3 Miles

12

421

20

94

49

90

80

20

12

can begin to reconstruct the world that existed before man intruded.

The Lakeshore's present 5,328 acres including almost ten miles of Lake Michigan shoreline—a quarter of Indiana's entire lakefront—stand as a testament to man's need to return to his natural environment amidst his technological wonders. The contrasts here are vivid and capture the whole panorama of the area's history. You can catch glimpses of the environment which predated man's settlement, the life of the first settler in northern Indiana, the farm life that existed for almost a century, and then see twentieth century industrialization so well typified by the nearby steel mills. The effects of air and water pollution and erosion and the material wealth which this century has brought are all here to witness.

Because of the location of the Lakeshore at the extreme southern shore of Lake Michigan, the effects of glaciers millions of years ago and the prevailing northwesterly winds, the Lakeshore is an ecological wonder. In fact, a part of the Lakeshore, Cowles Bog, was the site where the father of North American plant ecology, Henry Chandler Cowles, undertook his pioneering studies. Cowles first proclaimed to the world that here in the Indiana Dunes man could witness the succession of plant life which elsewhere might take centuries to perceive. He pointed out that in these changing dunes man could observe how plant and animal life adapted to a changing environment and the adaptations and modifications which change brought. Because the climate zones for birds, plants and trees mix and mingle here, the visitor can observe flora and fauna which are native to the tundra, the plains and the desert.

Location

By car, travellers from the east or west have two options:

1. The Indiana Toll Road (Rt. 80-90) to Exit 4 (Burns Harbor). Turn left (north) on Rt. 249 to Rt. 12. Continue east on Rt. 12 about ten miles to Kemil Road where the Visitor Center is located.

Visitor Center on Kemil Road and Rt. 12, headquarters for the Indiana Dunes National Lakeshore

2. Rt. 94 to exit 5 (Chesterton). Turn north on Rt. 49 to Rt. 12. Continue east on Rt. 12 about three miles to the Visitor Center.

From the south, drivers may take either Rt. 421 or Rt. 49 north to Rt. 12 and respectively turn west or east to the Visitor Center.

By train, the nearest stop to the Lakeshore on the South Shore Railroad is Beverly Shores. It is approximately 2 miles from the train station to the Visitor Center. The Michigan City cab companies will provide service if called from the Beverly Shores station or if notified to meet your train. The visitor without a car should plan for considerable walking. Car rentals are available in Michigan City, the next stop on the South Shore Railroad.

The South Shore Railroad will carry bicycles if previous arrangements are made.

By plane, the nearest scheduled service to the Lake-shore is the Michigan City-Chicago route via Joe Phillips Airlines.

Boundaries

The Lakeshore is a long, narrow park. At the present time, its boundaries extend from the Lake Michigan shoreline to the north, the Lake-Porter County Line Road on the west, the Michigan City limits on Rt. 12 to the east and a jagged line which runs between Rt. 12 and Rt. 20 depending on the specific location to the south. (See Lakeshore map.) The Park Service will provide you with a small map at the Visitor Center. Since some of the acreage included within the Lakeshore's boundaries has yet to be acquired, many other parcels are presently leased back to their former owners and Lakeshore land is not contiguous, it is important to check at the Visitor Center to make sure you are on Lakeshore land before you plan the route of a walk or a ride.

General Information

The Indiana Dunes National Lakeshore is operated by the National Park Service. Address all mail to R.R. 2, Box 139A, Chesterton, Indiana. The phone number is 926-7561.

The Lakeshore's Visitor Center is located at the corner of Rt. 12 and Kemil Road. The Center is open year round daily from 8 to 4:30. During the summer months extended hours of operation are usual. Guided tours usually begin from the Center and evening programs are given here. Park Rangers and other staff members are on duty at the Center to answer visitor's questions and to provide information about the Lakeshore. Bus and car parking is available at the Center.

The Lakeshore is a day use facility. That means no camping is permitted within its boundaries. Campers are advised to use the nearby Indiana Dunes State Park or commercial facilities. (See Categorical Guide for assistance.)

Picnicking on the Lakeshore beaches is permitted but open fires are not allowed. Only stoves and grills using charcoal, gas or manufactured fuel can be used by visitors, and for these a permit must be obtained at the Visitor Center. Charcoal must be removed and not buried in the sand.

Pets are also not allowed on the beach and must be leashed in all other Lakeshore locations. Hunting is not permitted within the Lakeshore boundaries. Fishing is permitted in accordance with federal, state and local laws. An Indiana fishing license is required for fresh water fishing and can be obtained from most sporting equipment stores. (See Categorical Guide for assistance.)

It's absolutely against regulations to pick flowers or to dig them for transplanting any place in the Lakeshore. With a permit from the Visitor Center you may pick mushrooms, nuts, berries and fruit within the Lakeshore. The Rangers will advise you where the bounty is most abundant. The permit is also for your protection; so the authorities know where you are and so they can keep you from trespassing onto private property.

Facilities

Beginning at its western boundary, the Lakeshore includes:

1. West Beach. This almost 600 acre section has a fine swimming beach on Lake Michigan near the Lake-Porter County Line Road. This beach is the primary swimming area of the Lakeshore. Lifeguards will be on duty and parking and bath house facilities are available.

This area also includes a heavily sand-mined section as well as a number of untouched permanent dunes and some interdunal ponds, such as Long Lake. Hiking here is excellent, bird life abounds and the wild flowers are abundant.

2. Dune Acres Beach. This section is accessible only by boat, not by land. The Lakeshore beach presently available to the public extends from fifty feet west of the

The marker at Cowles Bog in Dune Acres where the study of plant ecology in North America began

first visible house to the Northern Indiana Public Service Company plant. Visitors swim at their own risk.

South of the beach is a beautiful heavily wooded section of permanent dunes. There are no trails and experienced hikers will enjoy climbing up to the top of the dunes for spectacular views of the area as well as down to lovely Goose Lake where marsh birds and flowers can be found. The Crow Island blowout is an outstanding feature of the foredunes. Tours are conducted to this area. Check the Visitor Center for dates and times.

3. Cowles Bog. This 120 acre acid sphagnum bog, with its fascinating specimens of carnivorous plants and extensive variety of flora, is available on a limited access basis only. A National Landmark since 1966, it has remained almost virginal since its formation thousands of years ago. Check the Visitor Center for specific information about tours.

4. Bailly Homestead Area. This section which contains much of the land between Rt. 20 and Rt. 12 from Babcock to Wagner Roads contains the home and grounds of the Joseph Bailly family as well as their family cemetery. Bailly, a French-Canadian aristocrat, came here with his wife and children in 1822. For more than a decade they were the only settlers in northern Indiana. A fur trader, Bailly acquired 2,200 acres close to the Little Calumet River, in what was then a vast virgin wilderness inhabited by the tribes of the Potawattomi. In the next decade Bailly established a fur trading empire, buying skins from the Indians and selling them to the Astor interests on Mackinac Island and as far south as the Gulf of Mexico. He also became involved in shipping on Lake Michigan and planned a community, Baillytown, near his home. In 1834 he began building a two story home on a high knoll in a setting of towering white oaks, elms and maples under which the Potawattomi often pitched their tents. This home, substantially modified in the ensuing 140 years, still stands. Other structures in the compound included a tavern for stage coach passengers on the Chicago-Detroit run which ran close by the home, a saw mill operated by a son-in-law, a blacksmith shop, a chapel, a storage house and a brick smoke house.

Bailly was a cultured man and a devout Catholic. His home was a mission of his church and the Potawattomi, related to his wife, often received instruction and attended services in the homestead. But his death in 1835 and the financial panic of 1837 ended all plans for Baillytown. His widow, children and grandchildren continued to occupy the home until the death of his granddaughter Frances Bailly Howe in 1917.

· The Park Service plans to restore the Bailly Homestead to represent the period from 1822 to 1917. Both taped narrations and guided tours will be provided. While this work is in progress, tours are offered from the Visitor Center to the homestead site.

A half mile north of the homestead on a high bluff overlooking Rt. 12 is the Bailly Family Cemetery. The cemetery has been badly vandalized and the Park Service is planning to restore it. The Bailly Homestead tour includes a visit to the cemetery.

5. The Chellberg Farm is located on Mineral Springs Road north of Rt. 20. Enter via the first driveway on the west side of the road. This farm property, which was tilled for nearly three-quarters of a century, includes a prairie section where grain was grown, a forested section which shows the beginnings of a beech-maple climax forest, and an old barn. The Park Service plans to restore and operate the farm including the making of maple syrup so that city visitors can experience what life was like on an Indiana farm at the turn of the century. Tours to the Bailly Homestead include a visit to the Chellberg Farm.

6. Tremont-Furnessville area. This section includes the Indiana Dunes State Park and tracts of land which are located from Rt. 12 to Rt. 20 extending from Tremont through Furnessville to the boundaries of Beverly Shores. The Park Service plans to provide hiking, bicycling, and horseback riding trails in this area. Check the Visitor Center for the latest information on the availability of trails. Guided tours to this area originate at the Visitor Center.

The Visitor Center is in this area. Next to the Center is a hiking trail for the handicapped. This trail provides any visitor with a simple introduction to the dunes. It is an easy walk and includes a visit to a stabilized dunes ridge and interprets the flora of an oak woodland.

From the Center, a self-guided loop tour has been developed which extends north to Lake Michigan and south to Rt. 20. On this tour you can see marshes, and a large variety of flora and a succession of dunes. It takes the visitor across the three ancient shorelines of Lake Michigan.

7. Beverly Shores area. This section also contains a fine swimming beach, but there are no life guards on duty and swimming is at the visitor's own risk. The sand bar at this beach drops off sharply and Lake Michigan

A winter dunescape

waters can be treacherous. Keep a careful watch while children are swimming.

Parking is provided on the eastern side of State Park Road (a continuation of Kemil Road north of Rt. 12) about 500 feet from the beach. Parking is also available on Central Avenue. To reach this parking lot, turn left (east) from State Park Road on Beverly Drive. Continue 4 miles to Central. Turn left (north) and proceed .3 miles to parking lot on right hand side of the road.

The Lakeshore does not include all of the town of Beverly Shores. So visitors are advised to be sure to park in Lakeshore parking areas only. It is also important that visitors do not attempt to cross over into the Indiana Dunes State Park which adjoins the Lakeshore on the western side of the State Park Road. The State of Indiana views all access to its park except through the entrance on Rt. 49 as trespassing.

Hikers will find the five mile walk along Beverly Drive a splendid way to see marshland, high forested dunes and stretches of wilderness with not a house in sight.

8. Moon Dune (Mt. Baldy). Located on Rice Street, just east of Beverly Shores. Turn north on Rice from Rt. 12 just before the Michigan City western limits. This section is located within the Lakeshore boundaries but some of the area is presently owned by Michigan City. One of the few remaining high moving dunes, Moon Dune offers the visitor an opportunity to see trees buried in the sand and trees almost buried. Tours are provided from the Visitor Center. If you go on your own, use the Lakeshore parking lot on Rice Street.

9. Pinhook Bog. Located 5 miles south of Michigan City on Wozniak Road near the Indiana Toll Road, this section is an inaccessible area for the general public. The bog, a National Scientific Landmark, contains many varieties of wetland plants and insects. In addition, flowers, trees and insects usually found in the northern lake states and in Canada flourish here. It is considered one of the finest quaking bogs in the Great Lakes area. Because of its fragile nature, the public is not admitted.

History

Man's oldest imprint in the Indiana Dunes is the Indian mounds scattered throughout the area. These mounds are thought to be the burial sites of tribes who lived 2,000 years ago.

Centuries later the great Algonquin nation, primarily centered in the eastern United States, had tribes living along the Great Lakes. First the Miami and then the Potawattomi inhabited the southern and southwestern shores of Lake Michigan and the interior valleys. These Indians were mostly nomadic, living off the bounty of the land, its berries, fruits, animals and fish. The Potawattomi had moved from the forests of northern Wisconsin to northern Indiana which became their great hunting and camping grounds. By 1800 they had established fifty villages throughout the area.

They also developed a major interstate trail system 250 years ago which modern man uses today as the route for his roads. The Great Sauk Trail connected Detroit with the west and passed through the dunes area. The Trail began at Rock River, Illinois on the Mississippi River, crossed Illinois and entered Indiana at Dyer, on what is now Rt. 30. It passed through the present communities of Merrillville and Valparaiso and ran north and east along what is now Rt. 2 to Westville and then to LaPorte and New Carlisle. Crossing the St. Joseph River at Parc aux Vach it continued northeast across southern Michigan from Bertrand and Niles following what is now Rt. 12 through White Pigeon, Sturgis, Coldwater, Jonesville, Clinton and Ypsilanti to Detroit.

A northern branch of the Sauk Trail split off at Merrillville. This trail passed through Chesterton, Porter, Baillytown and the Indiana Dunes State Park to Lake Michigan and along the beach to Chicago. Indians coming from Chicago often used the old Potawattomi Trail which led through Miller, along Lake Michigan and through the dunes to Michigan City. From here it went straight west and converged with the Great Sauk Trail at New Carlisle.

The first explorers to enter the dunes were the French who began in the early 18th century to explore the area. Though they built forts (one in the present Indiana Dunes State Park) and were accompanied by missionaries, the main thrust of the French presence was commercial, largely fur trading with the Indians.

Defeated by the British in the French and Indian Wars, in 1763, France lost all rights to their dune lands. The British assumed control and won the allegiance of the Indians. The dunes area, however, remained Indian territory until almost forty years after the Revolutionary War had ended British rule. Indiana was part of the Northwest Territory and the United States government signed repeated treaties with the Potawattomi, recognizing their ownership of the dunes. But the determination of President Andrew Jackson to force all Indians west of the Mississippi meant the end of Potawattomi occupation. They were forcibly deported in 1838 and sent to a Kansas reservation on a march called the "Trail of Tears". The dunelands were then officially opened to Yankee settlement, though pioneer farmers had begun homesteading during the previous decade.

But most of the first farmers by-passed the present Lakeshore area. It was marshy, boggy, full of mosquitoes, and far removed from a passable transportation route. Few saleable products would grow here whereas just to the south there was good, accessible and cheap farmland available. These dune lands were generally purchased by speculators who secured large holdings. Even with the advent of the South Shore Railroad in 1908 the area remained largely uninhabited, as too far, too wet and too useless for development.

About the turn of the century, nature lovers and scientists began to explore the dunes on a systematic basis. They organized a citizens' movement, led by the Prairie Club of Chicago, to work for the preservation of this wilderness. Stephen Mather, the first director of the National Park Service, endorsed a plan for a national park in the dunes, which was doomed by World War I.

However this first dunes conservation movement did bear fruit in 1923. Then the State of Indiana established the present Indiana Dunes State Park spurred on by contributions from Judge Elbert Gary, president of the United States Steel Company, and Julius Rosenwald, the Chicago philanthropist.

The dunes remained throughout the 20's and 30's largely unpopulated, largely unvisited, and largely unspoiled. Though some sand mining began in the 1870's and continued intermittently, after World War I large scale dune leveling occurred.

In the late 1940's, rumors began circulating among area conservationists that the "best" dune formations had been sold for the construction of new steel mills. It was in 1952 that a group of local housewives under the leadership of Mrs. Dorothy Buell began a new campaign for a national park. At the same time, political leaders in Indiana, industrialists and others began a parallel movement to create an Indiana deep water port on Lake Michigan. The conservationists formed the Save the Dunes Council and, unable to persuade Indiana representatives or senators to their cause, enlisted Senator Paul Douglas of Illinois, a long time dune lover, as their spokesman. After years of Congressional consideration both projects, the Indiana Dunes National Lakeshore and the Port of Indiana were approved as a package by Congress in 1966.

The 1966 legislation provided for the establishment of the Lakeshore and authorized the National Park Service to purchase the land within the Lakeshore boundaries, except land owned by state or municipal bodies (which must be donated) and to demolish all unneeded structures.

Legislation is now pending in Congress to enlarge the Lakeshore with protective buffers and land along the Little Calumet River. This additional acreage would provide visitors with opportunities for canoeing and for hiking along a river area which is rich in beech and maple forests.

Magnified sand particles. Above, the coarser granules of
a dune beach. Below, the windblown particles of the foredune

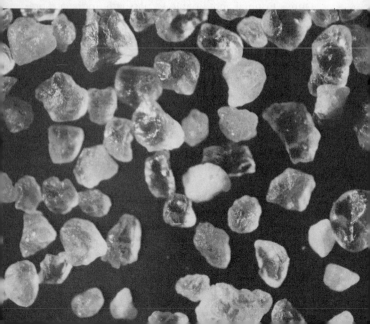

Geology of the Dunes

Scientists estimate that the earth is 4.5 billion years old. Put in this perspective, the story of the Indiana dunes is a modern drama for these great sand hills began to be formed about 15,000 years ago. Their beginnings go back to a time when northern Indiana was an undulating and hilly area like southern Indiana's terrain today. The climate, though, was similar to northern Canada and the hills were covered with forests of spruce and fir. Neither Lake Michigan nor any of the other Great Lakes existed. Instead there was a large north-flowing river system which cut through a wide valley.

During a preceding ice age, more than a million years ago, four glaciers moved south from Canada, advanced over the upper midwest, melted and receded northward as the temperature climbed. These glaciers were probably a mile or more thick, similar to the glacier in Greenland today. (Regardless of the area covered, a glacier is formed by the compression of snow under the weight of its own great thickness. Its strength depends on how much precipitation becomes snow and on the compaction which results from the pressure of layer upon layer of snow. Under the force of gravity, the glacier begins to move. Whenever a glacier pauses in its retreat, it forms a hill of deposited earth materials, sands, gravels and boulders, called a moraine.)

The last major ice advance, called the Wisconsonian, began 75,000 years ago and the recession of this glacier played a critical role in the evolution of the Indiana Dunes. In its waning phase, it stopped not very far south of what were to become the southern shores of present day Lake Michigan and formed a curved belt of hilly land known as the Valparaiso Moraine.

As the Wisconsonian glacier retreated over many millenia, its melting waters were trapped between the highlands of the Valparaiso Moraine to the south, east and west and an ice barrier formed by the receding glacier itself to the north. These waters formed ancient Lake Chicago, the precursor of modern day Lake Michigan. By

*The beginning of the pine forest with the Lake
in the far distance*

10,000 B.C. Lake Chicago was sixty feet higher than Lake
Michigan's level today and its shoreline followed the
eastern slope of the Valparaiso Moraine covering present day Chicago, Gary, and Chesterton and northward
into what is now the shoreland areas of southern Michigan and Wisconsin.

During the next 9,000 years the water level of Lake
Chicago dropped several times before establishing the
modern level of the Lake. Geologists studying the history of Lake Chicago have identified several of its old
shorelines. The Glenwood Stage shoreline, which existed when Lake Chicago was at its highest level, can be
seen where Routes 41 and 30 cross at Schererville. At the
Calumet Stage, Lake Chicago's level had declined
twenty feet and its shoreline was located along what is
now Ridge Road in Lake County and Route 20 in Porter
County. During the Tolleston Stage, another twenty foot

A small blowout surrounded by marram grass on a foredune

drop in Lake Chicago occurred and Route 12 in Lake and Porter Counties follows its shoreline. About 1,000 B.C., the present level was reached and Lake Michigan as we know it today was created. Large sand dune complexes formed as each of these shorelines evolved.

Dune Formation and Succession

Wind and wave combine to form the Indiana Dunes. For thousands of years storm winds across Lake Michigan have whipped up the waves which eat away at the bluffs north of Evanston and the cliffs along the Wisconsin shoreline. These storm waves act as giant grinders disintegrating and rounding the quartz stone. Lake Michigan's prevailing northwesterly winds control the Lake currents and the character of the waves with resulting along shore drift. This drift carries the quartz particles (sand) to the south and east shores of the Lake.

Day in and day out the waves bring this sand onto the beaches to form new sand bars. Notice that the Indiana dune beaches have almost no shells or pebbles.

Next the wind takes over to screen the sand. Heavier particles of sand remain on the beach. The lighter sand granules are swirled inland. Whenever this flying sand is checked by some type of obstruction, a tiny dune forms. This low pile of sand must be held together by some form of vegetation or the wind will surely come along to blow it away. With wind spray providing the moisture, the seed of some sand binder, typically marram grass or sand cherry, takes root. Thus a foredune is formed, like all Indiana sand ridges growing at right angles to the predominant wind direction. The cottonwood is the major tree of the foredune. It can withstand constant blowing sand, shooting out new root systems as more and more of its trunk is covered.

The foredune provides protection from the wind for an older dune growing behind it. This protection allows plant decay to occur and soil to accumulate. Seedlings of the jack pine which reaches its southern limit in the dunes along with the white pine and juniper of the northern woods grow here. In time a pine dune forms with its characteristic cool and scented air.

In turn this dune provides protection for a still older oak dune to its rear. Here black oaks, white oaks, basswoods, elms and sassafrass flourish in its richer soil and dense vegetation.

Still further inland, about a mile and a half from the beach, is the beech-maple dune, the climax forest of the Indiana Dunes, which has been ten thousand years forming. Its shade is so dense that oaks and pines cannot survive in this habitat. Tulip trees and ferns are abundant.

Between the dune ridges, water is often impounded and small lakes or ponds or bogs have formed.

The cottonwood, shooting out new roots despite
the build-up of sand

The dunes landscape is constantly in motion for the dunes move under the pressure of the winds blowing down the Lake. From one decade to the next, the dune-scape is never quite the same.

Plant Life in the Dunes

Any visitor to the Indiana Dunes will likely find at least one old friend among its flora regardless of the part of the country from which he comes, and even visitors from foreign lands may find close relatives of plants they have known at home.

In May a Southerner will find flowering dogwood in bloom in some of the forested areas. In late June and early July a Mexican will spot familiar prickly pear cactus, a plant normally associated with southwestern deserts. The plant lover will find mosses, lichens, and bearberry

A sun-flecked patch of fern in the middle of Cowles Bog

of the tundra; jack pine, white cedar and paper birch of the not so far north; and the beech, maple and white pine of the east. A visitor who has hiked in Vermont's Green Mountains will recognize the common bunchberry. While a visitor from the Alps coming upon the comparatively rare downy gentian in a dry dune prairie in late September will probably notice it faster than a native Hoosier.

Desert, bog, hill and dale, dry prairie and wet, mesophytic forest, river flood plain, and other habitats are all represented in Dune Country. Because of this rich variety of habitats and the area's close proximity to metropolitan Chicago and its centers of learning, it is not surprising that the natural history of the Dunes has been studied extensively.

The Indiana Dune Country is the birthplace of ecology in North America. Here Dr. Henry Cowles and his stu-

Cattails, rushes and sedge in a dune marshland

The Arctic bearberry, vestige of the glacial period, flourishes in the Dune Country

dents developed the concept of ecological plant succession at the turn of the century (1896-1901). The story goes that Cowles, travelling from the east to a meeting in Chicago, looked out of his train window while passing through what is now Dune Acres. He noticed an unusual mixture of plants growing together. Excited, he got off the train in Gary, hired a horse and buggy and returned to study the area. Already an eminent botanist, Cowles became so interested in the variety of plants growing in the Dune Acres bog that he severed his Eastern connections, joined the staff of the University of Chicago, and spent the rest of his life researching the area.

Since the concept of ecological succession (an orderly, progressive sequence of replacement of biotic communities over a given area) is of such historic and scientific importance in the Dune Country, it is appropriate to examine Dune flora from the succession viewpoint.

The prickly pear, native to the southwestern desert, grows in the Dune sands

Succession simply stated is the adaptation of living things, (plants and animals) over the course of time to difference conditions of light, water, temperature, air movement, soil texture and nutrients. That the hot, dry, loose sterile sand of the Dunes supports such a large variety of plants is due in part to succession. Biotic populations tend to modify the physical environment, creating conditions favorable to other plants and animals until a balance between the living organisms and their physical surroundings is achieved. In the process the plant may change its surroundings to such an extent that it is no longer able to survive.

Starting at the beach and hiking inland toward the oak forest the visitor will encounter sooner or later many of the plants that are characteristic of the various dune habitats.

Beneath the surface of the sand at the water's edge is a

An interdunal pond in the West Beach area showing a patch
of pine forest (right) and marram grass in the foreground

A tree graveyard with trunks centuries old

microscopic world of plants and animals that is still not very well known. Passing quickly across the dry loose sand of the beach, one comes to the strip littered with driftwood and other debris left by storm waves. Here rotting fish and other dead animals and plants fertilize the quartz sand and the debris provides protection for the germinating seeds of the searocket plant, a pioneer annual. The stunted Kansas sunflower or cocklebur may also be found growing here. The thick fleshy leaves and stems of the searocket, their waxy covering, long roots, and the shape of this plant are all adaptations to the dry, hot windy habitat in which it lives. All these plants begin to hold the sand, add organic matter to the soil, reduce wind speed, increase humidity, provide shade and reduce soil temperature. In so doing they change the environment slightly. But this is only a temporary zone; winter storms will, most likely, wipe it out and the process will be repeated next season. The first perennial plants occur in the next zone, the foredune.

The visitor's view of the foredune covered with marram grass will depend on whether the level of Lake Michigan has been dropping or rising. If it has been dropping, the beach will rise gradually away from the Lake and the visitor will see a low ridge or two covered with yellow-green marram grass. If, however, the Lake has been rising and the foredune has been eroded by storm waves the visitor may be facing a cliffed dune up to ten feet high with many roots exposed. The cliffed dune provides an opportunity to see how the marram grass has survived burial each winter and has been able to push through its sand covering each new growing season. The sand of the foredune is reinforced with the stolons, roots and shoots of the marram grass as concrete is reinforced with steel. Anyone who has gone barefooted in the foredune early in the season when the shoots emerge from the packed sand knows how well the plant has adapted with its sharp pointed shoots to this environment.

Once at the top of a foredune, the visitor should be aware of a row of cottonwoods growing in marram grass in a straight line that marks a previous "high water mark" when waves washed a former dune away. A prominent woody shrub in this habitat is the sand cherry, its branches slender and dark against the snow in winter; its flowers a mass of white in the spring; its leaves flashing green with purple-grey undersides in the summer sun, with black fruits; and its leaves beautifully red in autumn.

Sand stabilized by marram grass provides an area suitable for the germination of the cherry pits. Studies show that the roots of sand cherry seedlings tend to follow organic matter left by burial of the dune building grasses.

Behind the foredune the yellow-green marram grass is replaced by a blue-green grass, the little bluestem. It lacks the creeping stolons characteristic of the marram grass since it does not have to contend with extensive burial by sand. Reproduction is chiefly by seed.

The marram grass has created the conditions—stabilized sand, reduced wind velocity and shade—suitable for the little bluestem seeds to germinate and the plants to grow. The little bluestem grassland in turn will be succeeded by the jack pine forest, and the jack pine forest will be succeeded by the oak forest in much of the Dune Country. Classically the oak forest will be succeeded by the beech-sugar maple forest, but most of the Indiana Dunes in the National Lakeshore are too young or conditions are not quite right for this climax forest.

From the top of a foredune, a visitor can probably also see a pond at the base of a blowout, and the front of a moving dune burying a pine forest. Note the vigor of the cottonwoods that have been partially buried in the moving dune and compare it with that of the cottonwoods growing in the bluestem grassland. Note also that marram grass is growing on the moving dune where the conditions are similar to those of a foredune. The cottonwood is able to send out adventitious roots from its trunk and branches and thereby survive partial burial; the pine is not. Note seedling pines near the edge of the pond in the bluestem grassland, the beginning of a pine forest.

Around some of the cottonwood trees which grow at the back of the foredunes is a variety of plants. The plants are islands of vegetation seeded chiefly by birds roosting in the trees. They include wild grape, bittersweet, poison ivy, false Solomon's seal and a variety of other plants depending on location and the degree to which humus has built up beneath the trees. The humus is composed of wind blown leaves and stems caught first by the trunk of the cottonwood tree and then by the plants growing up around its base.

Near the pines the visitor will find rather dense mats of bearberry creeping between bunches of bluegrass and shading the soil to prevent germination of many seeds, but creating conditions that seem to favor germination of the pine seeds. There will be little pink flowers on the plant in the spring that will be followed by berries, green at first, changing to orange, and, later, red as the season progresses. Old berries may appear almost black. We may even find cactus growing in the bearberry mats.

Under the pines one finds an accumulation of pine needles, and the older the trees, the greater the accumulation. This is the beginning of the organically rich forest floor. Soon the oaks will invade and the pine forest will be succeeded by the oak forest.

The visitor who inspects the interdunal ponds will observe a rapidly changing and disappearing habitat. Some of these ponds were left as the Lake receded, but others were formed at the base of blowouts by wind excavation during dry spells when the wind could move the dry sand all the way down to the lowered water table. With the return of a higher water table, the depression filled and new ponds were formed. Succession also occurs with ponds. As they fill with decaying vegetation they become wet meadows and the meadows eventually become forests, if conditions are suitable.

Each interdunal pond seems to have its own characteristics. One young pond may be inhabited almost exclusively by Chara, a green algae, that requires pure water containing calcium. Fringed gentian may grow at the edge of another pond. Slightly less fussy is the rose gentian. Kalm's lobelia can usually be found near any of the ponds. Other flowering plants common to the edges of dune ponds are the yellow flowered shrubby St. John's-swort, the foxglove-like purple gerardia and the flat topped aster. The yellow, horned bladderwort may be found blooming in or near the water's edge in late summer. (Most of the plants just mentioned are at their peak then.) A plant of special interest is the ladies tresses orchid which may be found blooming in a grassy meadow portion of a dune pond during September.

There are grasses and sedges, rushes, willows and many other plants to be seen near the Dune ponds, and in the rest of the dunes. The orange flowers growing almost everywhere are the hairy puccoon. Dune visitors will likely see the blue spiderwort, the orange milkweed, the lavender lupines, the red columbines, the tulip trees and the sassafras, that grows only on the south and east shores of Lake Michigan. There are also the rare plants—the white, yellow and pink ladyslipper orchids and the carnivorous sundew and pitcher plants. But their locations are carefully guarded so that future generations can enjoy their beauty.

Birds of the Dunes

The Dunes are a bird paradise. Protected from hunters, relatively undisturbed by human contact, and amply supplied with wild fruits, berries, and nuts as well as insects and fish, birds rest, nest or winter within the Lakeshore. Some birds such as plovers and warblers fly up from as far away as South America and others like the

Duck migration on Long Lake

snow goose fly down from as far north as the Arctic Circle. Because the dunes are in the path of the great Mississippi Flyway, thousands of migrants can be seen overhead in the spring and fall. Well over two hundred varieties have been observed in the Lakeshore.

But the dunes are more than a bird refuge. A number of birds here reach either the northern or southern limits of their range. Northern birds who regularly migrate south as far as the dunes include scoters, oldsqaws, northern shrikes, crossbills, redpolls, evening grosbeaks, and snow buntings. Among the southern birds who come as far north as the dunes are the little blue heron (who breeds along the Little Calumet River in an area proposed for inclusion in the Lakeshore), yellow crowned night herons, red bellied woodpeckers, Acadian flycatchers, tufted titmice, Carolina wrens, mockingbirds, white eyed vireos, blue winged warblers,

Sandpipers feeding on the storm beach

prairie warblers, Louisiana waterthrushes, Kentucky warblers, hooded warblers and yellow breasted chats.

There are five distinct bird habitats within the Lakeshore. They are:

1. Lake Michigan. Its waters and beaches attract such birds as the loons, grebes, bay ducks, sea ducks, mergansers, gulls, terns and numerous shore birds. You can watch terns swoop down to catch fish or sandpipers comb the sands in search of tiny morsels of food. In the spring and fall look for the migrating shorebirds and in the winter watch for flocks of herring gulls and sea ducks. Good vantage points are the Indiana Dunes State Park beach and the West Beach.

A rare sight on a cold day is the great horned owl. If you walk the beaches early in the morning and keep a sharp eye out you might spot this nearly two foot tall, white throated bird with his conspicuous ear tufts. From far away he resembles a clump of ice.

2. The foredunes. Prairie warblers and chipping and field sparrows nest in the sand reeds and marram grasses on the low dunes just behind the beach. You can see the nests of the bank swallows who burrow into the steep banks above the beach at either Beverly Shores or Dune Acres. If you approach a kildeer's nest, he'll sound his distress cry and perform his broken wing act for you. During the winter you might find tree sparrows, redpolls and once in a while snowy owls in these dunes.

3. The permanent dunes. Bird life is most abundant here of any area within the Lakeshore. Where the red and black oaks and the red cedar have taken root and woods have covered the sand base, warblers, thrushes, vireos, kinglets, chickadees, titmice, flycatchers, woodpeckers, cuckoos, wrens, orioles, grosbeaks, nuthatches and owls can be seen.

Along the edges of these woods, the most common of all dunes birds, the black throated, white cheeked house sparrow resides all year long. His companions include the rufous sided towhees; Indiana's state bird, the brilliant red cardinal (who is especially fond of sunflower seeds), lovely blue indigo buntings, brown thrashers, catbirds, and house wrens. In the spring you may recognize the noisy oven bird calling "teacher, teacher, teacher", but finding his dome shaped nest is another matter. Trail 9 and the south side of the Trail 10 loop in the Indiana Dunes State Park cross wooded dunes. Other good locations for sighting these birds are the woods west of the Visitor Center and those north of Cowles Bog.

4. Wetlands. South of the permanent dunes in the bogs, marshes and ponds, you can find herons, dabbling ducks, rails, shorebirds, black terns, marsh wrens, kingfishers, swallows and swamp and song sparrows. Here the yellow throated warbler calls "witchety, witchety, witchety" in the spring and summer. To observe these birds, visit Cowles Bog, the marsh and pond in the West Beach area or Trail 2 in the Indiana Dunes State Park which traverses a wooded swamp.

5. Fields. Bobolinks, pheasants, sparrows, kingbirds, bluebirds, barn swallows and phoebes are common in this habitat. Watch for the meadowlark, whose yellow breast trimmed with a black v makes him easy to recognize sitting on a fence. These birds frequent the Chellburg Farm and power line right of way bordering Route 12 from Beverly Shores to Dune Acres.

Small stands of conifers scattered throughout the Lakeshore attract red breasted nuthatches, long eared owls and winter finches.

Dunes dwellers especially enjoy the ruby throated humming birds who visit their feeders. These smallest of all birds dart with amazing speed to suck colored sugarwater. From spring to fall, at dusk they can also be seen sipping nectar with their long needle-like beaks from flowers.

The most majestic of all large birds nesting in the dunes to watch in flight is the great blue heron. This shy, blue-gray, four foot tall bird is the second largest in North America. Only the great white eagle is bigger. This heron can sometimes be found in very secluded marsh areas near the Lake. He can be recognized by his folded neck, six foot wingspan, slow wing beat and long trailing legs. Turkey vultures are another sight to see. Look for them aloft from the foredunes south to the fields. They are soarers, riding the currents off the dunes with their five foot wingspread. Though charming and graceful in flight, they're down right ugly on the ground with their bare, red heads.

Other familiar guests in the dunes during the spring, summer and fall are the grackles, song sparrows, American redstarts, yellow throated starlings, wood thrushes, long billed marsh wrens, downy woodpeckers and above all the blue jays. Easy to spot with their bright blue coats, these greedy birds can gulp down 15 or 16 seeds at a time and come back for more within a second.

The cacophony of the birds is everywhere in the dunes. Bird buffs get up before dawn in the late winter and early spring to catch the hooting of the great horned and barred owl. For sheer noise volume it's hard to beat the ceaseless racket of the wrens. Lucky birders sometimes hear the marvellous laugh of the loons down on the beach. Easier to recognize are the white breasted nuthatches who dash back and forth crying "ma-ma, ma-ma, ma-ma" or the seemingly compulsive chant of the whip-poor-wills early in the morning or at dusk in the late spring or early summer.

TRY NOT TO MISS:

• The semi-annual visit of the blackbirds to the marsh at the corner of Beverly Drive and State Park Road in Beverly Shores. Rusty (only in the fall) blackbirds, red winged blackbirds with shiny epaulets and grackles cover the reeds and cattails in this swamp. Their din can be heard for miles.

• The gold finches who come to Furnessville every spring. These brightly colored birds are easy to spot against the new soft green foliage.

• The almost tame, strutting pheasants who abound in the Lakeshore and often dart across roads. Grouse and quail are other common game birds you can observe.

• The red tailed sparrow hawks sitting on a telephone

The Hog-nosed snake (above) is a common dune reptile. The Massassauga rattler is the only poisonous dune snake.

pole waiting to attack some small animal. Other predators in the dunes include shrikes, scavenger crows and some owls.

A checklist of birds of the Indiana Dunes has been compiled by the Chicago Audubon Society and is available at the Lakeshore Visitor Center. If you want to know more about bird life in the dunes either attend one of the illustrated bird programs given evenings at the Visitor Center or take part in an Audubon bird count. They're held twice yearly and you can sign up at the Visitor Center.

Animals of the Dunes

Don't stretch out on a sandy dune in the belief that you are alone. The area abounds in insect and animal life and each dune zone supports its own species. The storm beach, now being formed by wind and wave action, provides a feast of drowned insects for birds and predator insects like the fiery searcher. The foredune, which becomes a veritable furnace in midsummer, is far too hot for most living creatures. The digger wasp, however, copes by living here and tunneling down to the core of cool sand below. So does the night prowling wolf spider.

Behind the foredune is the pine dune with an abundance of wood and tiger beetles, ants and termites. And back of it comes the oak dune, with far richer soil, and here one finds the doodle bug. In the climax forest of beech and maple the variety of insect and animal life is greatest.

Among the interesting inhabitants of this woods is the Massasauga rattler, the only poisonous snake in the area. The Massasauga is becoming rare now. Always sluggish and slow to rattle, its bite can be deadly. The Massasauga in maturity is about thirty-two inches long. His snout is rounded, his eyes are small, his body stout, and his color ranges from grey to black, always with white markings.

Two hundred years ago had you visited the dunes you might have come upon a black bear, a timber wolf, or a marten. Or conversely, a lynx, cougar, bobcat, elk or a bison might have come upon you. All these mammals, once so plentiful in the area, are hunted out. If you are lucky you may spot an otter, a coyote or a fox, though they too are becoming rare.

Zoologically the Indiana dune country is important because here many species reach their geographic limits. For instance, the Bonaparte weasel, grey squirrel, white tailed deer and rufescent woodchuck travel no farther south than the dunes. The opossum, pipistrelle bat, southern woodchuck and Rafinesque's bat go no farther north. The dunes country is the eastern boundary for the western raccoon, Illinois skunk, Mississippi Valley mink and the Franklin ground squirrel. The chipmunk, bachman's shrew and pocket gopher go no farther north or west.

The following are mammals you may spot:

1. Opossum. Two or three feet long, four to twelve pounds heavy, the opossum has a silly grin, a pointed chin, and a ratlike tail which he uses like a hand. He also hangs by the tail and plays dead to avoid a fight. The female opossum, like the kangaroo, carries her young in a pouch. Called marsupials, the species has survived since the time of the dinosaurs.

2. Eastern chipmunk. This tiny animal with big cheeks has been known to gather four quarts of hickory nuts and corn in a day. Chipmunks feast on berries, seeds, nuts, fruit, and of course, garden bulbs. They hate heat and tend to aestivate (hibernate in summer). They are community-minded and live in groups rather than jealously guarding private territory.

3. Red squirrel. This fellow with the rusty coat is sometimes called pine or red robber or red jig or woodland squirrel. He alternately chatters, barks, sputters and stamps. Smallest of the tree squirrels, he is the clown of the pine woods. He flips from branch to branch, and tree to tree, and also can retreat through a labyrinth under and through the pine woods. He is a born conservationist, for he buries hundreds of seeds and cones, many of which are never recovered. These sprout and in time become aerial highways for his descendants. The red squirrel is also one of the true sentinels of the forest. When he calls an alarm, the woodland listens.

4. Fox squirrel. This is the largest of North American squirrels. Bushy tailed, the fox can be reddish, grey or black. His is a diminishing breed, already gone from New England. The fox squirrel often takes over a tree cavity left by a red headed woodpecker, enlarging it with his teeth. In hot weather he may build a dozen leaf nests, ranging over a territory of forty acres. When chased the fox squirrel prefers a ground escape route, because he is clumsy and frequently falls when attempting an aerial leap. He likes midday activity, enjoys the sun, and is a great hoarder of nuts, corn, mushrooms and insects.

5. Thirteen lined ground squirrel. Some people call

him the "Federation Squirrel" because he sports thirteen whitish stripes, interrupted by rows of spots or stars. He measures less than a foot, has a long head, a bushy tail, and big eyes. He chatters "seek-seek" as he guards his twenty foot long prairie burrow. He loves the sun and prefers to stay home—and inside—when it's gray.

6. Woodchuck. Largest of the squirrel family, the woodchuck is also called ground hog, marmot, or monax (Indian for digger). Chunky, dark brown, bushy of tail, the woodchuck is the size of a cat. He lumbers along on short legs, has buck teeth which give him a foolish look and help him greatly in gnawing. The latter he does in burrowing and eating.

The woodchuck is a great aerator of soil, digging down as much as five feet a day as he burrows and turns over the subsoil. He is a true hibernator. Late in October he curls up in the woods for the cold weather, but he prepares for this time by fattening up all summer on clover and alfalfa, buttercup and daisies. Unlike the nocturnal raccoon and opossum, the woodchuck is a lover of light and does his work and travelling by day.

7. White tailed deer. The white tail is the only deer found in the dunes. A vegetarian, he also enjoys ice cream and oranges when offered. He has keen eyesight, hearing and sense of smell. In times of danger, his raised white tail is a warning flag. He also has glands in his feet which leave a scent so other animals know when he's running from danger. His fallen antlers provide a source of calcium for many forest animals. The white tail has a repertoire of sounds: shrieks, bugles (for battle), bleats (for pain), snorts (for rage). During winter the gregarious deer prefer to stay in herds.

8. Raccoon. The dune area abounds in raccoons, their fanciers and feeders. There are families who have been playing host to raccoons for decades, and there are raccoons who have brought their babies visiting for generations. So, although the raccoon is by nature a nocturnal animal sometimes his clock gets turned round when the feeding is good.

The furry raccoon is one of nature's most adaptable creatures. He can climb, swim, fish, and use his hands with unbelievable skill. He washes his food before eating, not because he's clean, but because he lacks salivary glands. Raccoon intelligence is great. So is his capacity for concentration. Families have spotted raccoons at living room windows, busily watching all the motions on the TV screen.

9. Red fox. The chances are slim that you will spot a red fox, but they do live in the dunes. The animal is beautiful and bright, has a rust colored coat, black legs, black ears, black nose, and a white tip on his tail.

Dune Poisons and Dune Edibles

Euell Gibbon may be an expert at foraging through wood and field and coming up with a five course dinner of grass and seed, nut and weed. Don't attempt it until you have his expertise. It's a wise axiom also to keep your children from nibbling on anything out in the wild. In the dunes area avoid the following in particular:

Jack-in-the pulpit. All parts of this plant cause intense irritation of the tongue and mouth.

Mayapple contains more than a dozen toxic substances.

Water Hemlock. All parts of this swamp plant cause violent convulsions, often death.

Buttercups are seriously damaging to the digestive system.

Nightshade, which has purple berries, is generally fatal.

Mushrooms. Avoid them all unless you are sure. Dune natives adore morrels in early spring. They are harmless—if you are sure you can identify them.

Unfortunately the dune area abounds in poison ivy, which is three-leafed, shiny and low lying. There are blackberries, blueberries, even some red raspberries growing wild, but when you reach for them, make sure you aren't stepping into ivy.

If you must eat au naturel, make sure you can identify the following which grow in the dunes and are edible:

Wild asparagus, wild blackberry, wild blueberry, choke cherry, chicory, yellow clover, wild grape, day lily (seed pods and flowers), water lily seeds, wild mustard, wild onion, sassafras, wood sorrel, wild strawberry, sunflower seeds.

Perhaps the most versatile of all the dunes flora is the omnipresent cattail. You can eat its root, shoot, stem, pollen. You can take the cotton from its head and stuff a cushion. You can use its leaves to rush a chair. You can make dried floral arrangements with the whole plant or any of its parts.

DUNE BIRD & FLORA CALENDAR

BIRDS	FLORA
January	
Ducks and gulls winter on Lake Michigan. Purple finches, redpolls, evening grosbeaks, pine siskins, and crossbills frequent evergreen woods.	This is an ideal time to identify trees by their individual shape, bark, leaf scars and buds. Tips of the skunk cabbage often appear.
February	
Early courting of titmice and chickadees occurs in the State Park. Owls mate.	Skunk cabbage matures throughout the swampy areas late in the month.
March	
The early migrants arrive: robins, grackles, kinglets, geese and ducks.	Pussy willows blossom. A few early blooming hepaticas push up through the fallen leaves on Trail 2 in the State Park.

BIRDS	FLORA

April

Sandhill cranes pass through early to mid-month. The last of the wintering birds, juncos and tree sparrows, head north while the early warblers arrive. Other sparrows begin to nest. The mating call and spiraling flight of the woodcock over a swale is an unforgetable experience.

Marsh marigolds bloom in swamps. Lyre leaf rock cress grows in open sandy locations. Red and yellow columbine flower among the black oaks. Trailing arbutus blossoms on northern dune slopes.

May

Peak warbler migration occurs early this month. Black bellied plovers and other shorebirds are on the beaches. Ducks, teals, and coots are seen in small ponds. Marsh wrens and rails are in song. The cry of whippoorwills fills the evenings.

Trail 2 in the State Park is the best place to see spring flowers: masses of white trillium, spring beauty, bellwort, toothwort, douglas cress, red trillium, yellow violets, blue cohosh. Throughout the Dunes, one finds the lovely birdsfoot violet. In open areas late in the month lupine is profuse and blue phlox abounds in wet areas around the State Park.

June

The great blue heron, mallards, turkey vultures, and teals are nesting. Male birds sing in their territories. Most migrants have gone on to their breeding grounds. The evening air is full of the newly arrived nighthawks feeding on insects.

Lance leaf coreopsis and puccoon bloom profusely. The loveliest June flowers are the prickly pear cactus and the Philadelphia or wood lily which bloom the last two weeks of the month.

July

The woods are full of the chirping of baby birds. The mourning doves, ruby-throated humming birds, red-headed woodpeckers and house wrens are raising a second brood. Male tree ducks molt their flight feathers to get ready for their long journey south in the fall.

The Turk's cap lily is found in damp soil, arrowhead in ditches, prairie coreopsis on low open dunes, and showy false indigo in meadows. The greatest variety of fern can be seen on Trail 2 in the State Park.

BIRDS

FLORA

August

Sanderlings, yellowlegs, and pectoral sandpipers are among the shorebirds southward bound. Gold finches and warblers begin to change to winter plumage while ducks regain their bright colors.

Many of the swales and meadows are bright with blazing star. There are clumps of cardinal flower in wet areas. Goldenrod, Joe Pye weed, false foxglove, ironweed, sunflower and boneset are everywhere.

September

The peak migration of land birds is taking place. Ducks, geese, turnstones, willets and other water birds begin moving south. On a clear day with a north wind, watch the hawks start southward.

Asters abound. In damp areas fringe and soapwort gentians flower. The sour gum tree leaves are a shiny brilliant red.

October

Lake Michigan and dune ponds are stopping points for waterfowl migrants. Winter residents, the roughlegged hawks, redbreasted nuthatches, tree sparrows and juncos arrive in woods and field.

The leaves of the sumacs, white oaks, sassafras, white ash and red maples set the dunes afire.

November and December

The last of the migrants, red shouldered hawks, red winged blackbirds and grackles depart. Blue jays, cardinals, tufted titmice, chickadees, white breasted nuthatches, purple and gold finches, tree sparrows, juncos and woodpeckers remain in woods and fields. A few mallards stay on the ponds. Mergansers, herrings, ring bill gulls, frequent the beaches, harbors and Lake. Often old squaws and buffleheads are seen off the shore.

When the leaves are gone, witch hazel flowers. The striking red clusters of berries may still persist on winterberry bushes in wet areas.

Community Guide

This chapter provides a detailed account of available sights and activities in the five counties within an hour's driving distance of the National Lakeshore. Porter County is covered first because it's the home of the Park. Lake, LaPorte, St. Joseph and Berrien Counties follow. (The latter is the only Michigan territory included). The final section, the Kankakee area, cuts across five counties because of the route of the Kankakee River and describes the little river towns which have a flair and a flavor all their own. There's a map covering the entire area so you can see how the parts fit into the whole. In addition you'll find a map for each county, one for the Kankakee area and a Blossom Trail map to aid you in driving through southwestern Michigan in spring time.

The communities within a county are listed alphabetically. Each community has a bit of history, and an alphabetical listing of things To See and Do. Each county map gives the major road systems to help you get where you're going. If your day's destination seems to be in the middle of nowhere, don't despair. You'll find it, if you start by identifying the county, then the nearest town and lastly the major road system. In case you have trouble, knock on any farm door. Most farmers have phones and cordial, knowledgeable wives. If you have chosen to visit an old cemetery, chances are the farmer's wife explored the grave sites as a child.

A final word, more to increase your efficiency than our sales; carry an extra copy of this guidebook in your car's glove compartment. It's always available that way. We have one friend who says she might have saved her marriage if, on every family outing, she really had known exactly what the directions were. Most husbands dislike guessing where they are going. The lovely old tree you remember from "last time" has probably fallen victim to the subdivider's bulldozer. So "go with God" . . . and directions . . . and us.

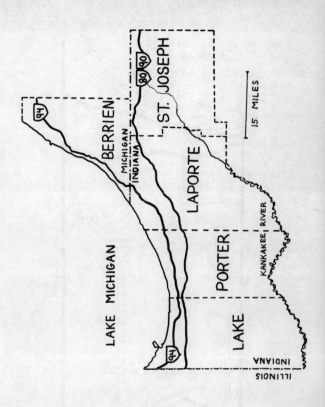

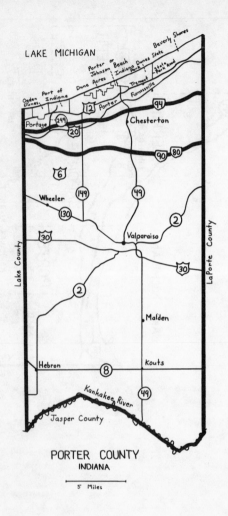

LAKE MICHIGAN

Beverly Shores

Porter or Beach
Johnson Indiana Dunes State
Dune Acres Tremont State Park Road
Furnessville

Ogden Port of
Dunes Indiana
12 Porter 94
Portage 249 Chesterton
20

90 80

6

149 49
Wheeler
130 2

30 Valparaiso

30 LaPorte County

Lake County

2

Malden

Hebron 8 Kouts

Kankakee River 49

Jasper County

PORTER COUNTY
INDIANA

5' Miles

PORTER COUNTY
(87,114 population)

Porter County's 425 square miles extend from the shores of Lake Michigan south to the Kankakee River and from LaPorte County on the east to Lake County on the west.

For its first century, Porter County was a quiet, predominantly farming area, celebrated only for its wild, sparsely populated dunelands. This northern section of the county bordering on the Lake with its high sand hills, beautiful beaches, and unique flora has attracted artists and nature lovers for generations.

The remainder of the county is rich farmland used to grow corn, soybeans, and dairy herds. In the late 1950's, with the construction of new steel plants, Porter became the fastest growing county in Indiana. Porter County claims to have the most solid Republican voting record in the nation.

There are also some who believe that the nickname Hoosier originated in Porter County. There was an old stagecoach stop three miles west of Valparaiso called the Hoosier Inn, supposedly a contraction of "who's there" called out by an inarticulate or inebriated innkeeper.

BEVERLY SHORES (946 population)

In the late 1920's this town was the site of a giant land speculation. A well-known Chicago real estate developer, Frederick Bartlett, acquired more than 8,000 acres and built eighty-five miles of winding roads along Lake Michigan, around dunes and through marsh land. Special South Shore excursion trains brought thousands of Chicagoans to the area where they were met by fast talking salesmen who wined and dined them and gave them the grand tour. Sure that fortunes were to be made through this real estate gamble, many invested their savings—only to lose them in the Great Depression. Today three-quarters of the town has become part of the

National Lakeshore and the remainder is included in a proposed park expansion.

Prior to the Bartlett era, Beverly Shores land was used for large scale cranberry and blueberry farming. After World War II it became a small summer colony for Chicagoans, so that today there are about 300 full time and 700 summertime families. About one-half the property owners are of Lithuanian descent, drawn to the area because of its similarity to the Baltic dunes.

Riding along the town's meandering back roads will give you a good feel for dune country, with lovely views of the Lake and miles of marshland covered with wild vegetation, particularly beautiful in spring and fall. Bird and flower lovers can hike for miles in solitude, and in the wintertime, see spectacular ice formations along the shore.

To See and Do

ARCHITECTURE. World's Fair Houses. Mr. Bartlett brought ten buildings from the 1933 Chicago Century of Progress across Lake Michigan by barge as part of his promotional campaign. Four are still standing and worth seeing:

House of Tomorrow. Lake Front Drive west of Broadway.

Old North Church (minus its steeple). Beverly Drive west of Broadway.

Paul Revere and Ben Franklin Houses. Both on Pearson Street.

ENVIRONMENTAL CENTER. Save the Dunes Council. Rt. 12, in the Beverly Shores Post Office building (879-3937). Wednesday–Saturday, 10–4. Provides information about the Indiana Dunes National Lakeshore. Dunes books and paintings for sale.

RESTAURANT. The Red Lantern. Lake Front Drive (874-6201). Dinner only. Monday-Saturday, 4-10:30; Sunday, noon-8. Bar.

BURNS HARBOR (no residential population)

Burns Harbor was incorporated as a town in 1967 and is the newest community in Porter County.

Most of Bethlehem Steel's Burns Harbor plant is within its borders. The Bethlehem plant, which began operating in 1964, is among the newest and most modern steel making facilities in the country. Every step in the manufacture of steel is carried on within its confines. Huge boats deliver iron ore to the company docks on the eastern side of the Port of Indiana. The largest blast furnace in the Western Hemisphere produces molten iron which is then converted into steel slabs. Various steel products are fabricated from the slabs. Bethlehem, the largest employer in Porter County, has a work force of over 6,000.

To See and Do

SHOP. Jack's Gun Shop, Rt. 20, one mile north of Rt. 149 (787-8311).

TOUR. Bethlehem Steel Company, Rt. 12 (787-3241). Only specialized large group tours. Must provide own bus. Write well in advance to make arrangements.

CHESTERTON (6,177 population)

In the beginning Chesterton, alias Calumet, alias Coffee Creek, was to have rivalled Chicago. One hundred and twenty years later this "Gateway to the Dunes" has the charm of another century.

Because some original settlers had the great good sense to plant hundreds of maple trees, the Chesterton autumn is as spectacular as that of any Vermont village.

Chesterton was a stop on the underground railroad during the Civil War. It was also the scene of several shoot-outs when the dunes area became a haven for Chicago gangsters.

For years the big industry in town was the Hillstrom Organ Company which shipped instruments as far as West Africa. There, little girls in an embroidery class run by the missionaries copied the designs painted on the organ and stitched them on their skirts. More than one little Nigerian flounced about with "Hillstrom Organ, Chesterton, Indiana" stitched on her bottom. The Bethlehem Lutheran Church, 135 Lincoln, still has a Hillstrom organ in its archives, available to any visiting organist.

Railroad Park, now Thomas Centennial Park, in Chesterton celebrates the town's early heyday as a rail center. The Michigan Central alone ran twenty-four trains through town each day. Farmers in the area, eager to have transportation for their crops, trundled cords of wood into town and loaded the park four feet high so that the engines could be stoked. Chesterton's rail supremacy lasted long enough to snuff out half a dozen rival settlements in the area. But today the only trains that come through are freights which tie up traffic at frequent and unpredictable hours.

Chesterton is populated by old Scandinavian and German farm families, by Irishmen who came to work the rails, by steel workers who are employed in the nearby mills, and by a smattering of artists and professionals who just liked the place and settled down.

To See and Do

AMUSEMENT PARK. Enchanted Forest. Rt. 20 west of Rt. 49 (926-1614). Memorial Day–Labor Day, daily, noon–9:30. Rides, small zoo, picnic area.

ANTIQUES. Antique Shop. Porter Avenue and Calumet (Dreswell Building) (926-1400). Daily, 10–8; Sunday, 12–6. Run by four businesswomen. A little bit of everything; expensive.

ARCHITECTURE. Holmes-Brown Mansion. 700 West Porter. Now the administration center for Duneland school system, this red brick Victorian mansion was once owned by farmer Brown who supplied most of the wood for the Porter brick factory kilns. His home reflected his affluence with its high peaked roofs, stained glass fan light over the front door and a ballroom on the third floor.

Friday Farm. Friday Road. A beautiful old red brick farm house with handsome barn.

Mansion at Camp Farr. 1050N and 350W. This typical Hoosier dwelling of the Civil War era has a gabled roof, two stories with wing and a bull's eye window under its roof peak.

Triple-sized Barn. East of Rt. 49, 1100N and 150E. This interesting and weatherstained barn and house is owned by the Rhoda family.

ART AND ARTISTS. Gilbert Gallery. 115 4th, Tuesdays and Sundays, 2–5 (no phone). Run by the Porter County Association of Artists and Craftsmen. Rotating shows and craft demonstrations with some items for sale.

GARDEN. Mr. and Mrs. Sylven Cook (926-4029). Call for appointment. This is a small but choice rose garden with many prize varieties. The Cooks are consulting rosarians of the American Rose Society.

RECREATION.

BOWLING. Gateway Lanes. 535 West Broadway (926-9036).

Westchester Lanes. North 8th Street (926-2523).

CAMPING. Camp Farr. 1050N, 350W (926-4900). Swimming pool.

HAY RIDES. Ted Groszek. 1400N west of Brown Road (926-1051). Tractor-drawn hay rides.

Keith Simms. Burdick Road (926-4883). Clydesdale-drawn hayrides in spring and summer; tractor-drawn sleigh rides in winter.

HORSEBACK RIDING. Camp Farr. 1050N and 350W (926-4900). Good trails on an old estate.

ROLLER SKATING. Skateland Arena. 878 West Indiana (926-1791 or 932-2370). Wednesday–Sunday, 7–10; Friday and Saturday, 7:30–10:30 p.m.; Saturday and Sunday, 2–5. Call first.

SHOPS. Casa Morena. 216 Grant (926-6916). Tuesday–Sunday, 11–6. A tiny but attractive shop with imported folk art, Navajo and Aztec jewelry, East Indian clothing and some Indiana crafts.

Chesterton Feed and Garden Center. 400 Locust (926-2790). The owner turned her interest in gardening into a second career and offers items ranging from hamsters to horse feed to finest Holland bulbs.

Chesterton Sporting Goods. 104 North Calumet (926-5526).

W. Merle Fisher. Hadenfeldt Road, one-half mile
north of Rt. 20 (926-2555). Monday-Saturday, 9–5. Fine
jewelry in this shop at home, with custom designed
pieces available. Also see his pet cemetery.

SPECIAL EVENT. Chesterton Art Fair.* This gala event, held
on the St. Patrick's School grounds, draws more than 100
artists from six states for two days in early August. Every
craft and art form imaginable is on display, and there is
supervised painting for kids. Proceeds go to the Association of Artists and Craftsmen of Porter County. Call the
Chamber of Commerce (926-5513) for schedule.

SPECIAL FACILITY. Westchester Chamber of Commerce.
209 South Calumet (926-5513).

DUNE ACRES (301 population)

Squeezed between the new steel mills and Porter Beach
is the select little community of Dune Acres, with elegant homes nestled on and around high dunes. A private
guard keeps the general public out. The community, a
mixture of commuters and week-enders, has its own
club house and a high regard for aesthetics and good
planning. It preferred to remain outside the National
Lakeshore.

The Richardson Wildlife Foundation is headquartered
here. The Foundation, beneficiary of the magnificent
dune slides and movies taken by the late Dr. Henry
Richardson, makes the collection available to educational and conservation groups around the country
upon written request. Cowles Bog is also here and can
be viewed only by pre-arrangement with the National
Park Service.

FURNESSVILLE (part of Chesterton)

Sandwiched between Tremont and Beverly Shores is this
tiny community which was settled by the Furness family
in 1840. The family influence is evident in Furnessville
Road; the Furnessville blow-out (a magnificient dune
formation in the Indiana Dunes State Park); the charming little Furnessville Cemetery (where one can visit ear-

lier generations of Furnesses as well as the Ways and the Teals of Edwin Way Teal literary fame); and the rambling white Furness mansion on Rt. 20 just west of Kemel Road.

To See and Do

ANTIQUES. Tree House Antique Shop. Basement of the Schoolhouse Shop, Furnessville Road (no phone). Wednesday–Sunday, 1–4:30. A collection resulting from years of prowling in New England.

ART AND ARTISTS. Hannell Pottery. Furnessville Road (926-4568). A long drive through lovely woods leads to Hazel Hannell's good-sized pottery—open daily and supplied with a blackboard for messages when the owner is out.

SHOP. The Schoolhouse Shop. Furnessville Road (926-1875). Tuesday–Saturday, 9–5; Sunday, noon–5. A gift shop par excellence which was started in an old red brick schoolhouse by two self-exiled Chicagoans. Over the years it has remained extensive, expensive and tasteful. People sometimes try to elicit the formula for the store's marvelous odor, but the owners don't know—sachets, candy sticks, elegant soaps, dried herbs, no smoking. They carry a line ranging from lemon drops to evening skirts, from butter molds to wrapping papers.

INDIANA DUNES STATE PARK*

The entrance to the park is at the northern terminus of Rt. 49 (926-1215). Memorial Day–Labor Day, 7–11; fall, 8–6; winter, 8–4:30 (no admission charge in winter). Large parking area, extensive camping facilities, beach houses, concessions. This 2,182 acre park is Indiana's most profitable and supports all others in the state. Seven hiking trails of various difficulty lead along ravines, over great dunes, into blow-outs, alongside 300 year old tree graveyards, parallel to marshes, into pine woods, and down to three and a half miles of unbroken and glorious beach. A joy for ornithologists, botanists, hikers, swimmers. Part of the park is now set aside as a wilderness area. Warning: enter at proper gate and pay admission charge or risk being arrested and fined.

JOHNSON BEACH or PORTER BEACH or
WAVERLY BEACH (part of Porter)

Johnson Beach, north of Rt. 12 off Waverly Road is an area of splendid high dunes, blow-outs, and clusters of houses, some year round, some very simple and summery. The eastern part of the area is included in the National Lakeshore. The western section, like Dune Acres which it abuts, remains out of the park.

Johnson Beach was named for a commercial fishing family who once had a thriving fishery in what is now the Indiana Dunes State Park. When the park was officially opened in 1923, the Johnson brothers moved westward on the beach and opened an inn, a restaurant, and a fishery. The Johnson boats went out daily and brought back perch, herring and salmon. In the late '50's the Johnsons sold out their interests and the fishery is now closed. The inn is open summers, with a "barefoot bar", and for the price of parking permits guests to use the beach. No facilities offered, and in recent years the beach has been eroding at a frightening speed.

OGDEN DUNES (1,321 population)

Since its founding in 1925, this has been a lakefront residential community, and no commercial enterprises have ever been permitted here. Named after Francis Ogden, the owner of the whole property, the town was developed by Gary realtors, who foresaw the attraction of a suburban community in the dunes. Visitors can travel the Stagecoach Road, which begins on the south side of Rt. 12, just east of the town's entrance and meanders to Gary following the route which was used more than a century ago.

Before Ogden Dunes was established, these isolated sand hills were the home of Diana of the Dunes, a famous female hermit also known as "Dunehilda." Though spotted occasionally by fishing crews, Diana, reputedly the daughter of a physician, came back to civilization only occasionally—to peddle a wine she had brewed from the berries which covered the dunes.

The town was also the site of an olympic-size ski jump built in 1927. Only remnants of the jump remain. Ogden Dunes boasts a Frank Lloyd Wright house, the first home on Cedar Trail north of Ogden Road. The garage has been added recently.

To See and Do

FARMS AND FARM PRODUCE. Leroy Ewen. Stagecoach Road (762-2339). For home-grown vegetables.

SPECIAL EVENT. Every year in late April, the town Fire Department sponsors a giant rummage sale, which attracts buyers from all over Lake and Porter Counties. Furniture and appliances and thousands of clothing items. Call (762-9995) for date and hours.

PORTAGE (19,127 population)

Spanning three miles of Lake Michigan shoreline between Dune Acres and Ogden Dunes is a large industrial and shipping complex which includes the Bethlehem Steel Company plant, the Port of Indiana, the Midwest Steel Company plant and Burns Ditch.

For years controversy raged over whether this portion of the Indiana Dunes should be preserved unspoiled or transformed to its present use. The issue was resolved in 1966 with the passage of the bill authorizing the Indiana National Lakeshore. Congress simultaneously approved legislation providing federal funding for the construction of the Port of Indiana, a facility needed by the steel plants for iron ore ships. The Port is the State's only public deep water harbor on the Lake. It connects Indiana to world shipping via the Great Lakes-St. Lawrence Seaway route and to the inland water barge routes via the Grand Calumet River.

The town of Portage was incorporated in 1958 and became a city in 1969. It includes within its boundaries the Port of Indiana, Midwest Steel, Burns Ditch and part of Bethlehem. Previously the area had been farm land dotted with a few subdivisions. Midwest began operations in 1957. Its plant has 2.3 million feet under roof, and produces a variety of cold steel rolled products. Today Portage continues to grow as a residential and commercial center. A number of boat launching facilities are located where the Little Calumet and Illinois Rivers empty into the Lake.

To See and Do

ANTIQUES. Mrs. Charlotte Curtiss. 6574 Sand (762-7441).

ARCHITECTURE. Wolf Homestead, 450N and East Cleveland. A big red brick farm house built in 1885 by Josephus Wolf, then owner of the largest farm in Porter County.

MOVIE. Jerry Lewis Theater. 6224 Central (762-7979).

RECREATION.

   BOATS-MARINAS. Burns Harbor Marine. 1700 Marine (762-2304).

      Doyne's. Burns Ditch off Rt. 249 (938-3551).

      Lefty's Coho Landing. Rt. 12 (762-1711).

   FISHING. Public fishing is permitted at the Port of Indiana docks. Call (787-6816) for specific location, dates and hours.

   GO-KART RACING. K & R Raceway.* One-quarter mile north of Rt. 6 on McCool Road (762-3422). Noon–sundown on Sundays.

   PARK. Woodland Park. 2100 Willow Creek (762-1675). Sixty acres, picnicking, swimming, ice skating, tennis and nature area.

SHOPS. Brandt's Sports. 5700 Central Avenue (762-3421).

      Coast-to-Coast Sports. 2565 Portage Mall (762-7717).

      Sport-Port. 2548 Portage Mall (962-3387).

SPECIAL FACILITY. Chamber of Commerce. Portage Mall (762-3300). Monday–Friday, 9–5; Saturday, 9–noon.

PORTER (3,058 population)

Porter is a quiet little town which once had a thriving brickyard, a booming rail traffic, and big dreams for its future. The brickyard has gone. The trains have all but disappeared. What remains are some fine old brick houses, remnants of better days, and a feudin' spirit with neighboring Chesterton.

To See and Do

ARCHITECTURE. Augsburg Svenska Skola (1880). North side of Oakhill Road, two miles east of Mineral Springs Road. This charming white shingled church seats only seven. The cemetery behind the building is believed to cover an Indian mound. View from road only. Private property.

AUCTION. Frye Barn. Old Porter Road (926-2501). Mondays and Wednesdays, 7:30.

RESTAURANTS. Meltz's Inn. 112 Lincoln (926-9967). Monday–Friday, lunch, 11–2; dinner, 5–midnight; Saturday, 11–midnight. Old-fashioned tavern with food. Occasional dancing.

The Spa. Mineral Springs Road south of Rt. 20 (926-1654). Monday–Saturday, 9 a.m.–2 a.m. Bar. This restaurant, on the site of mineral springs which fleetingly held promise for a posh resort, race track, baths. Now it offers dining in a beautiful setting in the woods, and fun watching birds and raccoons at feeders.

SHOPS. Gem Tree Rock Shop. Rt. 12, east of Mineral Springs Road (926-1919). Open daily in summer except Tuesday and Wednesday. Call for an appointment the rest of year. The owner is a lapidarist and caters to rock hounds. Gem stones, fossils, crystals, minerals, settings, polished stones—everything to do with rocks collected all over the world.

Sander Wood Engraving Company. 212 Lincoln (926-4929). By appointment only. This illustrious wood engraving house, last of a kind, moved out from Chicago. This is a great chance to see modern craftsmen at work on a printing process which was once the method of illustrating all books, magazines, newspapers and catalogs. (Wood blocks and tools are also for sale.)

SPECIAL EVENTS. Fourth of July fireworks. Porter Park, 1.5 miles south of Rt. 20 on Waverly Road, at dusk. Bring your own chairs.

TREMONT (part of Chesterton-150 population)

Today this tiny settlement which fronts on the Indiana Dunes State Park is mainly a flag stop on the South Shore Railroad. It has had more illustrious days. Father Marquette slept here on a sandy beach on his last trip. From 1845-1875 Tremont was called New City West and was the center of social life for the region. Pioneers on their way to the Gold Rush and Pikes Peak stopped at its hotels. Tremont was also a leading station on the underground railroad during the Civil War. The name Tremont comes from the three sand hills to the north in the State park, Mt. Tom, Mt. Holden and Mt. Green.

To See and Do

ART AND ARTISTS. Loretta Cohn (926-4358). Hand crafted wheel and coil pottery.

SPECIAL FACILITY. Dunes Lakeshore Hostel. Rt. 12 (926-1414). This is the only hostel in Indiana. Capacity forty-eight. Closed in winter. Cooking facilities. $1.50 per night to American Youth Hostel members. No age limit. Bicycle rentals. Single speeds, tandems.

VALPARAISO (20,020 population)

Valparaiso is the seat of Porter County. The town perches on the Valparaiso moraine which was dumped by an ancient glacier as it began to melt and retreat north. As a result the land rolls, is studded with glacial lakes and has fine deep ravines. The town itself boasts fine white houses, many more than 100 years old.

Early settlers of Valparaiso were German Lutheran and that is still the predominant stock judging by the many Lutheran churches. But the name of the town is Spanish (Valley of Paradise) and honors a local hero, Commodore David Porter, who did battle in Chile during the War of 1812.

"Valpo" is surrounded by rich farm lands (some of which produce the nation's largest crop of hybrid popcorn). It is dotted with industrial plants (some of which produce roller bearings and eighty per cent of the country's magnets). Among its firsts, the town once had the only School of Piano Tuning in America. It now boasts both Valparaiso University and the Valparaiso Technical Institute.

To See and Do

ANTIQUES. Corner House Antiques. Franklin at Monroe (462-3538). Tuesdays–Saturday, 10–5.

Marc Nielsen Country Shop. Old Suman Road (462-9812). June 14–December 14, Tuesday–Friday, 10–4. The trip to the shop takes one through the beautiful Suman Valley which is named for Civil War General Isaac Suman. The Nielsen's Tudor-style farm is like a medieval village with craft shops for upholstery work, cabinet-making, furniture building. Call for appointment to tour craft shops. The shop itself handles choice English and continental antiques.

Uphaus Antiques. 300W east of Rt. 2 (462-2810). Daily, 9–5, except Sunday. Country collection on a charming farm.

ARCHITECTURE. William Barnard Home (1835). One-quarter mile north of Rt. 6 on 825E. Old white frame house of early Quaker settler.

Joseph Robbins Home (1897). 800N and 800W. Built of Joliet stone and designed by a Tennessee architect which accounts for its southern style.

Rose-Kuehl Home. 156 South Garfield, across from Porter Memorial Hospital. An octagonal white frame house with interesting gingerbread woodwork.

Tratebas Mill (1856). Tratebas Road, east of Rt. 49. This former grist mill, with its pond and dam, has been restored by the Hopkins family as a home retaining much of its 19th century feeling.

ART AND ARTISTS. William and Pamela Reddick (464-2757). Painters.

Nancy Searles (462-7405). Weaver, dyer, spinner.

Harriet Rex Smith (462-4567). Painter.

CEMETERY. Quakerdom Cemetery. North side of Rt. 6, east of Jackson Center. Quaint old cemetery marking movement of the Quakers from Richmond, Indiana, into

Illinois. Arriving here and learning of a battle between Indians and soldiers near Chicago, the Quakers settled down, built a school, a church and eventually this graveyard. Abolitionist Charles Osborne is buried here.

AUCTION. Community Sales. Rt. 13 off Rt. 49 (462-4570). Every Thursday except Thanksgiving, 7 a.m.–9 p.m.; auction, 12:30. A miniature stockyards with pigs, sheep, cattle and ponies for sale. Great fun for kids.

FARMS AND FARM PRODUCE. Anderson Orchards. Rt. 6, east of Rt. 49 (462-8568). Pick-yourself apples, pears, grapes. Also a lovely produce stand.

Esserman. One-half mile north of Rt. 6 on 75W (926-2749). Walter Esserman's strawberry patch is big, organically nourished and very popular. Do-it-yourself pickers arrive at dawn.

GARDEN. Mrs. Edith Podresky (462-3531). Call for an appointment. If Mrs. Podresky's garden is not in proper bloom, she will steer visitors on to gardens which are. Mrs. Podresky is a consulting rosarian of the American Rose Society.

MOVIES. 49'er Drive-in Theater. Rt. 49 (462-3609).

Premier Theater. 69 Lincolnway (462-3012).

MUSEUM. Porter County Historical Society Museum (462-2233). For group tours call ahead. Open Tuesday, Wednesday, Friday, 9–4; closed 12 to 1. Currently housed on the fourth floor of the County Building, the museum is scheduled to move to the old jail building when the new jail is completed. An eclectic collection: mastodon bones, dresses from the Lincoln inaugural ball, guns, and many items from the Bailly Homestead.

RECREATION.

BICYCLE RENTAL. United Rent-All. 906 Calumet (464-3594). Tandems, single speeds.

BOWLING. Inman's Bowling Lanes. 711 Calumet (462-9250).

Wellman's. Rt. 30 (462-5681).

DANCING. Stone Balloon Tavern.* 1409 Lincolnway (462-9363).

GOLF. Forest Park Golf Course. West Harrison at Yellowstone (462-4411). April 1–October 31. 9 holes.

Mink Lake. Rt. 49 south of Rt. 6 (462-2585). March 15–November 21. 9 holes.

LAKES. Lake Eliza.* Five miles west and three miles south of Valparaiso on Rt. 30 (462-1953). April–December. Camping, swimming, fishing, boat rental.

Flint Lake.* Three miles north of town off Rt. 49 (464-1441). Swimming, public fishing, picnicking area, and boat ramp.

Long Lake.* West on Edgewater Beach Road from Rt. 49. Boat rental.

Loomis Lake.* Two and a half miles north on Burlington Beach Road off Rt. 49 in Harold Rogers-Lakewood Park (462-5144). Swimming, fishing, picnicking, boat rental, launching ramp.

Mink Lake.* Rt. 49 south of Rt. 6 (462-2585). Hiking, picnicking, boat rental, camping, fishing, sledding, toboganning.

Wahob Lake.* 700N, five miles north of town off Rt. 49. Public fishing, swimming, picnicking, boat ramp.

PARKS. Harold L. Rogers-Lakewood Park.* One mile north of town on Campbell Road east of Rt. 49 (462-5144). Open year round for campers. Soapbox derby course.

Womar Woods. East of Rt. 49 and south of Rt. 6 on County Road 750N. Acreage given by John Womar family to the Indiana Department of Natural Resources. Open by special arrangement only.

SKIING. Pines Ski Area. Meridian Road south of Rt. 6 (462-1465). December 1–March 15. Weekdays noon–10; Saturday, 10–10; Sunday, 10–5. Poma lift, four rope tows, seven slopes, lighted night skiing, refreshments, ski shop rental.

RELIGIOUS SITE. Seven Dolors Shrine (Our Lady of the Seven Sorrows). South on 700N from Rt. 149 (759-2521). Daily until dusk. Sunday mass at 9 and 11. 100 acre site includes rock formations, gardens, outdoor grotto, stations of cross, three-story monastery. Established in 1931 under the auspices of an American-Czech branch of Orders of Friars Minor and is now operated by the Franciscans. Gift shop, picnicking facilities.

RESTAURANTS. Hotel Lembke. 15 Lafayette (462-1141). 11-11. Bar.

Old Style Inn. 5 Lincolnway (462-9196). Across from Courthouse. Daily, 11-11. Busy at lunch. Need reservations Saturday night when roast prime ribs are featured. Bar.

Strongbow Turkey Inn. Rt. 30 east of town (462-3311). Daily, 11-9. Special buffet on Sunday. Any part of the gobbler cooked in every fashion: soup, salad, pies, sandwiches.

The Fishery. 714 Calumet (462-0436). Excellent Danish fish store. Carry-outs and a few tables for lunch.

Wellman's. Rt. 30 west of town (462-6141). Daily, 6 a.m.-2 a.m. Breakfast, lunch, dinner.

SHOPS. Artists' Den. 203 Jefferson (462-3883). Art supplies, framing, paintings.

Fetla's. Rt. 2 near town (462-5221). 6:30 a.m.-9 p.m. Huge discount house. Attraction: caged bear.

Hans and Fritz Antique Clocks. 9 Lincolnway (464-2010). Tuesday, Wednesday, Thursday, Saturday, 9-5; Monday and Friday, 9-9. Fine collection of antique clocks purchased on four annual trips to Europe. Prices range from $75-$1,500. Repair work available.

Johnston's Sports. 119 Lincolnway (462-2671).

McMahan Seed Company. 6 North Michigan (462-1411). Complete line of garden supplies. Seed from drawers by ounce, pound or envelope.

Triangle Sporting Goods. 2608 Calumet (462-5041).

Wooden Shoe Crafts. 504 East Lincolnway (462-7455). In old Valpo house. Paints macrame supplies, tole ware, kits of all kinds. Craft lessons.

SPECIAL EVENTS. Porter County Fair. The fairgrounds are at Evans Street and Indiana Avenue adjoining Rt. 49, north of the business district. First week in August, Monday-Saturday. Admission free. If not the greatest show on earth, it does very well on rides, exhibits, prize lambs, hams, jams. "Bronco John" of vaudeville fame left his stagecoach here, where it has become a permanent feature. Call Chamber of Commerce for details (462-1105).

Valparaiso Arts Festival. Courthouse Plaza. Third weekend in June. Seventy-five artists and craftsmen, working demonstrations, childrens plays, musical events. Refreshments.

THEATER. Opera House. South Franklin (462-3704). Home of Community Theater Guild. This building was the community's memorial to its Civil War dead, and is now used for the liveliest of the arts. Phone for schedule.

Wellman's Bridge-Vu Theater. Rt. 30 (462-0563). Monday–Thursday, 9 p.m.; Friday–8 p.m.; Saturday, 9 and 11:30 p.m. An occasional play, but generally radio and television talent. Revivals, jazz bands, comedians.

TOUR. Strongbow Turkey Farm. Rt. 30 (462-3311). October 23–November 10. Monday, Wednesday, Friday, 9:30–2:30. Call for arrangements.

UNIVERSITY CAMPUS. Valparaiso University, 651 College (462-5111). The University has graduate schools of nursing and law as well as an undergraduate college. It has an interesting history which began in 1859 under Methodist auspices. The school was bought in the 1870's by nonsectarians and became known as the "Poor Man's Harvard," was almost bought by the Ku Klux Klan in 1914, but fortunately passed into the hands of the Lutheran Church in 1925. Of particular interest on this campus is the world's largest college church, the Chapel of the Resurrection, which is handsome, ultra-modern and enhanced by stunning mosaics and stained glass. There is also an accoustical system sensitive enough to carry whispers from the altar to the rear.

The University has good musical events, and the Sloan Art Gallery is located in its library basement.

SPECIAL FACILITIES. Chamber of Commerce. 106 North Franklin (462-1105). Monday–Friday, 8:30–5 (except noon until 1).

Porter County Municipal Airport. East of Rt. 30 on 100N (462-6508). Daily scheduled flights to O'Hare and

Meigs Fields via Joe Phillips Air Line. Charter flights.
Porter Memorial Hospital. Monroe Street (462-1121).

WHEELER (400 population)

This small town is a principal shipping point for grain
and livestock farmers. The town was platted in 1858 and
was first called Twenty Mile Prairie because it was that
distance from Michigan City.

To See and Do

FARMS AND FARM PRODUCE. Robert Cochran Black Rasp-
berry Farm. Five miles west of town on Rt. 30. Turn north
on 475W for three-quarter miles. Or, take Rt. 130 east of
town until you get to the most precarious looking railroad bridge in the county. Cross and go two-and-a-half
miles south (759-2980). Eight acres of beautiful pick-it-
yourself black raspberries. Opens around July 1 for two
weeks.

LAKE COUNTY
(546,253 population)

Lake County's northern tier, the Calumet Region, is America's Ruhr Valley. One of the great industrial centers of the world, its plants produce vast quantities of steel, oil, petro-chemicals, cement, soap and thousands of related products in a narrow strip along Lake Michigan from the Illinois border to Gary. Suburban bedroom communities—Highland, Munster, Griffith, Merrillville and Schererville—ring the Calumet Region. They are home for the hundreds of thousands of Calumet workers.

Southward is a rolling farm belt, much of its land reclaimed from the Kankakee marshes. The Kankakee River itself is the county's southern border. Small lake and river resorts are the remaining traces of the days when the river area was a fisherman's and hunter's paradise.

The county's present population and industrial might are a twentieth century development; the French voyagers in the 1600's saw only a great marshland. They named the two rivers flowing through the county the Little and Grand Calumet after the tiny marsh reed which the Indians used as the stem of their peace pipes. The Indians roamed the whole terrain, using the Kankakee as their river highway to the Mississippi and hunting and berrying in the Dyer-Merriville-Hobart area. Many of their villages were located on the high ground between the Kankakee and Calumet marshes.

But to the pioneer settlers who founded Lake County in 1837 as the last of the northern Indiana counties, most of its 513 square miles were not suitable for farming. The dunes along Lake Michigan made travel southward difficult and the marshes themselves were impassable most of the year. It took travellers braving the Lake's icy winter blasts and the rough sand trails six days to reach Chicago from Michigan City—a distance of sixty miles.

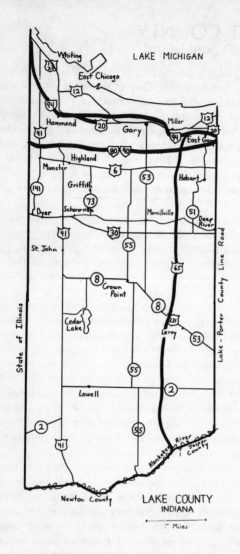

LAKE MICHIGAN

Whiting

East Chicago

Hammond

Gary

Miller

East Gary

Munster

Highland

Griffith

Hobart

Dyer

Schererville

Merrillville

Deep River

St. John

Crown Point

Cedar Lake

Leroy

State of Illinois

Lake - Porter County Line Road

Lowell

Kankakee River

Jasper County

Newton County

LAKE COUNTY
INDIANA

5 Miles

Yet Lake County's proximity to the expanding industrialization of South Chicago made growth inevitable. There was cheap available land; the tracks of a dozen railroads crossed the county en route to Chicago; the water supply of Lake Michigan was available for the taking; and the Lake's shoreline could be dredged for harbors. Beginning with the development of Whiting by Standard Oil in 1899 and followed by United State Steel's creation of Gary in 1903, Lake County quickly was transformed by men and machines.

For the past forty years a staunch Democratic stronghold in a Republican state, Lake County is an anomaly to most Hoosiers. In practically every session of the Indiana legislature, some rural representative suggests a law deeding Lake County to Chicago. Indeed Lake County is more ethnically diverse and more urbanized than its sister counties in northern Illinois.

CEDAR LAKE (10,182 population)

The glamour days of Cedar Lake, once a lively resort town, began when the Monon Railroad carried Chicagoans by the train load out for a day in the country. Hotels began booming in the 1890's and honeymooners, convalescents, hunters, fishermen and even Mrs. Walgreen of the drug store chain fortune (who arrived in her private plane) were among the guests. Cedar Lake hotels were famous for their Sunday chicken dinners.

There was also a booming ice industry. Day and night throughout the winter Chicago skid-rowers with their feet wrapped in gunny sacks cut huge ice cakes from the lake to supply Chicago meat packers.

The glamour days ended with the 1929 depression. Today the summer cottages from this era are perched crazily close to one another around the two mile lake.

Thousands still flock to Cedar Lake on summer weekends to enjoy boating, swimming and fishing. On Saturday evenings during July and August, sacred music concerts* can be heard in the Torrey Auditorium of the Moody Bible Institute on 137th Street. The concerts are given on the site of the old Monon Park.

To See and Do

ARTS AND ARTISTS. Ericson Violin Shop. 13321 Calumet (374-7864). Violin maker.

CEMETERY. Indian Mound Cemetery. Meyer Manor subdivision, Lake Shore Drive to Marquette Street, south on Marquette. Tombstones of early settlers supposedly on site of Indian burial grounds.

RECREATION.

BOATS-LAUNCHING. Public ramp. Cline and Lake Shore Drive.

BOATS-MARINA. Pinecrest Marina. 14415 Lauerman (374-5771). March 1–November 15. Swimming, fishing, picnicking, boat rental, water sports.

BOATS-RENTALS. Chuck's Pier. 13947 Huseman (374-5791). Also fishing.

Ernie's Canoes. West 133rd (663-2809). Make advance reservations.

Shell Harbor. 133rd Court (374-9833).

FISHING. Public fishing site. Corner of Cline and Lake Shore Drive. For perch, blue gill, crappies, and bass.

GOLF. Cedar Lake Golf Club. 9728 129th (374-7750). April 1–October 15. 18 holes.

South Shore Country Club. Lake Avenue (374-6070). April 1–inclement weather. 18 holes.

HORSEBACK RIDING. Willowdale Farm, Rt. 41 (374-9876).

PARK. Lemon Lake County Park. 133rd Avenue and Cedar Lake Road. Open daily until dusk. 286 acres in lovely rolling country with bridle paths, picnicking and hiking. Overnight camping by reservation only. Call or write Lake County Park and Recreation Department, 111½ West Joliet, Crown Point (663-6804).

RELIGIOUS SITE. Franciscan Retreat. Lake Shore Drive to Parrish, north one mile on Parrish (374-5741). Stations of the Cross. A lake with a rosary of stones and flowers built around it. Picnicking permitted.

RESTAURANTS. Hanover House. 133rd and Parrish (374-5232). Daily, 7 a.m.–11 p.m. Bar.

Heritage. 133rd and Wicker (374-6200). Daily, 7 a.m.–1 a.m. Bar.

Tobe's Steak House. 7301 West 138th (374-9605).
Monday–Saturday, 5–10. Bar.

SHOPS. Cedar Lake Flea Market. 9600 West 151st (696-8855). Saturday and Sunday, 10–5. Held in barn during winter; outside in summer. Lots of glass items.

Cedar Lake Sport Shop. 7926 Lake Shore (374-6133).

Kiefer's Sports. Lake Shore Drive (374-9601).

CROWN POINT (10,931 population)

Crown Point is the oldest town in Lake County, the county seat and a bedroom community for the mill towns to the north.

Solon Robinson, its founder, came from New England by oxdrawn cart and pushed on to the Calumet area in 1837 because LaPorte was too crowded for his pleasure. He wrote home to urge all his friends to join him. They came in droves, and to make sure they didn't lose the path, he left signs posted for them all along the way. Eventually he earned the nickname of the "squatter king" because he led a rebellion against speculators who were trying to steal the homesteaders' land.

Crown Point became the county seat despite competition from the older communities of Liverpool, Deep River and Cedar Lake. Later when Hammond suggested the courthouse at Crown Point be converted to a house for the insane, an irate Crown Pointer replied, "When that happens, its first inmate will be the Hammond crank that suggested it."

From 1916 to 1941 Crown Point had a reputation as the Gretna Green of the midwest. Instant marriages were performed here by "Marrying Justices" for Rudolph Valentino, Colleen Moore, Red Grange, Joe DiMaggio. John Dillinger escaped from the Crown Point jail.

Today visitors will find the town a pleasant residential community ringed by rich farmland, with a handsome old courthouse in the town square.

To See and Do

ANTIQUES. Dan's. 8703 East 109th (663-4571). Good selection.

ARCHITECTURE. The Old Homestead. 227 South Court (663-0456 or 663-0590). Call for an appointment. The house is managed by two very agreeable ladies who will bring the key and escort you through this charming, well preserved house built in 1847. Notice the hand wrought hinges, hardwood floors imported from Chicago, and the siding which was an innovation replacing the usual logs.

ART AND ARTISTS. Station Gallery. Goldsboro Street (663-8870). Located in the old station house of the Erie Railroad. Hoosier artists.

The Little Gallery. 321 Rose Ellen (663-1869). Located in the home of Betty McDonald. Appointment necessary to see collection of ceramics and paintings.

CEMETERY. Civil War burial grounds. I-65 to Rt. 8. East on Rt. 8 to Iowa, south on Iowa three miles to large grove of trees.

FARMS AND FARM PRODUCE. Rinkenberger Farm. North side of Rt. 53 (109th Street) (663-5019). Pick your own berries, all varieties.

MOVIE. Crown Theater. 19 North Court (663-1616). Daily, 8 p.m.

RECREATION.

BICYCLE RENTAL. Crown Rental. 113 North Indiana (663-0164).

BOWLING. Fricke's Recreation. 519 North Grant (663-0529).

GOLF. Golden Key Golf Center. 7611 East Lincoln Highway (942-8929).

Oak Knoll Golf Course. Rt. 8, west of Crown Point (663-3349). Open year round.

Pheasant Valley Golf Course. 3834 West 141st (663-5000). March 1–first snow. 18 holes.

HORSEBACK RIDING. Walk Away Stables. 709 East 101st (663-6865).

SQUARE DANCING. Presbyterian Church. 218 South Court (663-2476). Second Sunday, 3 p.m. Advanced and inexperienced.

RELIGIOUS SITE. Capuchin Seminary of St. Mary. 8400 Burr, one-half mile south of Rt. 30. The first Catholic Church in northwest Indiana, built of logs, has been moved to the Seminary grounds. The chapel of the Seminary has beautiful stained glass windows with clear glass insets which permit sunshine to flood the church. The mosaics are made of branches and leaves, and one feels an integral part of the natural world.

RESTAURANT. Lighthouse South Restaurant. 101 South Courthouse Square (663-7141). Monday–Thursday, 11–11; Friday and Saturday, 11–midnight. Bar.

SHOPS. Henderlong Lumber and Sports. 500 Foote (663-0600).

Safford Enterprises. 102 North Main (663-1672).

SPECIAL EVENT. Lake County Fair. Fairgrounds, South Court and West Greenwood (663-0428). Third week in August. This is one of the oldest and best fairs in Indiana with aquatic shows, horse and dog races, farm exhibits, crafts. The fairgrounds surround Fancher Lake which is spanned by the only covered bridge in the county. Apart from the fair, this is a fine recreational area: eighty acres, swimming, fishing, picnicking, camping, skating in season.

SPECIAL FACILITY. Chamber of Commerce. 150 West Joliet (663-1800).

DEEP RIVER (100 population)

Deep River is a tiny cluster of houses and ruins south of Hobart, filled with history and the promise of a big future. Take Rt. 51 (Grand Boulevard) north from Rt. 30 and turn east at the first stop sign on County Road 330 for 1.8 miles.

In 1835, John Wood, from Massachusetts, laid out this town around a typical New England common. A marker in front of the common has been placed by his descendants which proclaims his honesty, morality, temperance and liberal religion.

The Lake County Park and Recreation Department has developed an extensive plan for this site, which includes restoration of Wood's old grist mill, and development of a 280 acre park to the northwest.

Deep River boasts a number of century-old homes, which are well-kept and beautiful. The church at the edge of the community also dates back to pioneer days.

North of the mill a trader's post has been discovered and purchased by the Park Department. Still further north is the site of an Indian mound, which was probably used for a water cure.

Along the Deep River further to the west is the Deep River Nature Center at 3100 Liverpool (962-1579). This 144 acre tract has a forty acre lake, a wilderness area, hiking trails, a library, mess hall and classroom buildings. It is part of the Gary Public School system and is one of two outdoor education centers run by school systems in the United States. Gary school children come to the Center by bus to learn about a world vastly different from their city life. The Center may be visited by appointment only. Call well in advance.

DYER-ST. JOHN AREA (6,663 population)

Dyer is the last town in Indiana at the point where the Sauk Trail crossed the state line. Nearby St. John is named after John Houck, the town's first German settler, who built northwest Indiana's first Catholic church here in 1842. (The log cabin church has been moved to the grounds of the Capuchin Seminary near Crown Point.)

For the past ten years, this area has been horse country. Within a ten mile area, there are fifty or more stables that board, buy, rent, sell, groom or stud. A number have indoor arenas. In the Dyer-St. John area there are horse shows every weekend during the summer and once a month in winter. The experts say that there are more riding horses in this one area than any place in the country. There are also a number of bridle paths open to all horse owners, and individual stables have their own fields and woods. The countryside is rolling, rustic and lovely to ride or drive through, especially in spring and fall.

Note the marker on Rt. 30, south side of street, one mile out of Dyer, which marks the continental watershed. At this point the water on the south side of the street drains toward the Kankakee, the Mississippi and on to the Gulf. On the north side it drains into the Great Lakes, the St. Lawrence basin and on to the Atlantic.

To See and Do

RECREATION.

FISHING. Bingo Lake.* Rt. 41.

Stan's Fish Lake.* Rt. 41.

GOLF. Lake Hills Golf and Country Club. Two miles north of Rt. 30 on Rt. 41, St. John (365-8601). Open year round. 27 holes.

HORSEBACK RIDING. Trails Bend Ranch. 14620 West 93rd, St. John (365-5789). Trails, rental and lessons by day; hay rides.

HORSEBACK RIDING-BOARDING. Pleasant Hill Farm. 9300 Sheffield, St. John, 3 miles south of Dyer (365-5984). Billed as "Midwest's largest indoor riding arena". Trains; sells English and western tack.

RESTAURANT. Dick's Tap. Rts. 8 and 41 (365-5041). 4—midnight. No reservations taken. Fish on Friday. Bar.

SHOP. Schereville Bait and Sports Shop. Rt. 41, one mile south of Rt. 30, St. John (365-5158).

SPECIAL FACILITY. Our Lady of Mercy Hospital. Lincoln Highway (365-2141).

EAST CHICAGO (46,982 population)

East Chicago is the most industrialized city in the Calumet area. Its eleven square miles contain a maze of railroad tracks, a harbor, a ship canal and the plants of more than sixty companies. The density of its population—a third White, a third Black and a third Spanish-speaking—is the highest of any Indiana community.

East Chicago was developed to accommodate heavy industry and is the most important Indiana terminus for land and water transportation. Inland Steel, Youngstown Tube, DuPont, Blaw-Knox, American Steel Foundries and Union Carbide are East Chicago employers. Within the city many of the country's largest oil companies have terminals for their crude oil pipelines and refineries.

Until the early twentieth century, sand ridges, swamps and sloughs covered the East Chicago area. Then industrialists and speculators crossed the Indiana line and began buying land in this desolate and inaccessible portion of the Calumet region. English bankers and American promoters joined forces as the East Chicago Company to develop the area, choosing the name East Chicago to associate their land with South Chicago, though the city is twenty miles from the Illinois line. They conceived of a grand plan to construct a harbor on Lake Michigan and connect it with the Grand Calumet River which flows through the city. This harbor, called Indiana Harbor is linked to the Grand Calumet by a ship canal. The canal runs for two miles inland to the "forks" where large public wharves are located. The Indiana Harbor Belt Railroad connects all the railroads in the area with the Canal's docking facilities.

To See and Do

ART AND ARTISTS. Fine Art Gallery. St. Joseph's College, 4721 Indianapolis (397-9197).

Municipal Art Center. Chicago and Kennedy (398-4200).

Helen and John Powers (EX7-1365). Irish linen weavers.

RECREATION.

GOLF. MacArthur Golf Course. Todd Park, 142 Henlock (398-4200, extension 264). April 15–October 15. 9 holes.

PARKS. Joerose Park or Lake Front Park. Michigan at Indiana Harbor (398-4200, extension 246). Thirty-seven acres. Beach on Lake Michigan. City-owned marina, public boat ramp, picnicking.

Washington Park. 141st and Grand (398-4200, extension 246). Conservatory, ice-skating, tennis.

RESTAURANTS. Puntillo. 4905 Indianapolis (397-4952). Daily, 8 a.m.–2 a.m. Bar.

SHOPS. A. P. Davis Sports. 4532 Indianapolis (397-0274).

Main Sporting Goods. 3822 Main (EX7-5870).

SPECIAL EVENT. Mexican Independence Day. Early September. Parade, dancing, booths, food. For details call Chamber of Commerce (EX 8-1600).

UNIVERSITY CAMPUS. St. Joseph's College-Calumet Campus. 4721 Indianapolis (397-9197).

SPECIAL FACILITIES. Chamber of Commerce. 20001 East Columbus (EX 8-1600).

St. Catherine Hospital. 4321 Fir (392-1700).

EAST GARY (9,858 population)

Another community spawned by the railroad era, East Gary was once the site of an important terminus of the Potawattomi Trail where the Indians had workshops, dancing floors and burial grounds.

Settlement began in 1851 when the Michigan Central Railroad built roundhouses, shops and a depot called Lake Station. All trains were required to stop so the passengers could eat at the station restaurant. Lake Station was a busy rail and shipping center until its decline after the Civil War. It then remained a small village until the population of Gary began to expand southward. In 1908, the town's name was changed to East Gary. Today it is a small residential and commercial center.

To See and Do

ANTIQUES. The Barn. Difficult to find. Take Rt. 51 five miles north of Alternate Rt. 6 and turn right (east) onto East 33rd Avenue and continue for about a mile (962-9697). Country and imported furniture.

HISTORICAL MARKER. Rt. 51, just south of ramp to I-94. Marks the route to the Potawattomi Trail from old Lake Station southwesterly to the Indian ceremonial grounds at Merrillville.

MOVIE. Dunes Outdoor Theater. Rt. 51 (962-1307).

RECREATION.

BOWLING. Ray's Lanes. 3221 Central (962-1297).

HAY RIDES. William Remus. Rt. 6 (962-2213).

PARK. Riverview Park. Rt. 51, overlooking Deep River.

SPECIAL FACILITY. The Chamber of Commerce. Has no office but gives information by phone (962-1196).

GARY (175,415 population)

Long before the current vogue for new towns, 12,000 acres of sand hills and swamp lands were transformed in thirty-six months into the city of Gary. The United States Steel Company chose this location on the southern shore of Lake Michigan midway between the Minnesota ore fields and the southern coal mines to build what was then the largest integrated steel plant in the world as well as a community to house its workers and service their needs.

Construction began in 1906 and $100,000,000 later, steel was poured. On the south bank of the Grand Calumet River, streets, stores and houses for thousands of workers created the "City of the Century" the largest American community built in the 1900's.

Thousands of immigrants from Poland, Roumania, Serbia, Hungary, Greece, Czechoslovakia and the Ukraine poured into Gary to become mill hands. Today Blacks, Appalachian Whites and Mexicans predominate in the labor force.

For many years Gary was a company town. U. S. Steel plants lined the Lake Michigan shores and steel and steel products were synonomous with the name of Gary. The bitter CIO struggle to organize the steel mills centered in the Gary area, and union contracts signed in the late '30's began a shift toward community control. So did the changing racial complexion of the city. The 1969 election of Richard Hatcher as the first Black mayor of Gary illustrates the dimensions of the change.

Indiana's third largest city today is a fifty-three square mile sprawling complex of heavy industry; a shabby, decaying downtown area undergoing urban renewal; and miles of residential sections ranging from middle class to poverty level.

Major Gary employers are Universal Atlas Cement, the American Bridge Company, American Sheet and Tin

Plate, the Budd Company, which produces auto bodies and the Anderson Company, which makes auto accessories. The Gary plant of U.S. Steel alone turns out 8,000,000 tons of ingots annually.

The Indiana Toll Road (Rt. 80-90) runs along the south side of the Gary mill area and from its elevated roadway, travellers can get a panoramic view of the miles and miles of plants—and their smoke, noise and stench.

To See and Do

ARCHITECTURE. Frank Lloyd Wright house. Northeast corner of 7th and Van Buren. An early work.

Gary-Hobart Water Tower. 7th and Madison. Its modern design won an award from the Waterworks Association of America.

ART. Richard Hatcher Art Gallery. Community Resource Center, 2137 Broadway (885-0591).

CEMETERY. Grant Street at 19th. Graves of pioneer settlers in the Gary area.

HISTORICAL COLLECTION. Indiana Room, Gary Public Library. 220 West 5th (886-2484). A good collection of books about the dunes and the Calumet area.

MOVIES. Dunes Plaza Cinema I and II. Rts. 20 and 51 (938-0700).

Ridge Plaza Cinema I and II. 5900 Ridge (923-9100).

RECREATION.

BOWLING. Tri-City Bowl. 4255 Tri-City Plaza (949-1541).

GOLF. North Gleason Park. 3200 Jefferson (944-0607). April 15–October 15. 9 holes.

South Gleason Park. 3400 Jefferson (944-6417). April 15–October 15. 18 holes.

PARKS. Gateway Park. 4th and Broadway. An old fashioned steam engine is on display and there is a real bowling green.

South Gleason Park. 3400 Jefferson (944-0607). April 15–October 15. 9 holes.

RESTAURANTS. The Lighthouse. 644 West 5th (886-1922). Monday–Saturday, 11–10:30. Bar.

Miner-Dunn. 301 West Ridge (887-5124). Daily, 6 a.m.–10 p.m. For hamburgers. A diner with white curtains at the windows.

Pete's Grecian Cafe. 612 West 5th (886-9491). Monday–Saturday, 6 a.m.–9 p.m.; Sunday, 8 a.m.-9 p.m. Unpretentious. Authentic Greek food. Home-made yogurt. Bar.

SHOPS. Archer's Lodge. 560 West 5th (939-8444).

Mike's and Tom's Sports. 739 East 41st (981-3123).

Oriental Bakery. 28 East Ridge (981-2020). Greek specialties.

Westforth Sport Shop. 4704 Roosevelt (844-8680).

UNIVERSITY CAMPUSES. Indiana University-Northwest Campus. 3400 Broadway (887-0111).

Indiana Vocational and Technical College-Gary. 1440 East 35th (887-9646).

SPECIAL FACILITIES. Chamber of Commerce. 538 Broadway (885-7407).

St. Mary Mercy Hospital. 540 Tyler (882-9411).

Methodist Hospital. 600 Grant (882-9461).

Gary Municipal Airport. Industrial Highway (944-1663). Charter flights.

GRIFFITH (18,168 population)

Griffith owes its existence to the location of nine railroad crossings on Broad Street, and most of its early settlers were German railway workers. The town was originally marshland and the pioneers travelled from Highland to Merrillville by boat.

The land boom which was anticipated to follow the 1893 Columbian Exposition in Chicago never materialized, and Griffith grew slowly until it boomed as a residential suburb of the Gary-Hammond area, following World War II.

To See and Do

MOVIE. Ridge Road Drive-In. Ridge Road (TE 8-1600).

RECREATION.

BOWLING. Bowl Arena. Broad Street (838-4123).

CAR RACING. G and G Model Raceways. Broad Street (838-2686).

FISHING. Wild Lake*. Broad Street.

GOLF. Colonial Golf Course. 1901 North Cline (923-3223). April 1–November 1. 18 holes.

ROLLER SKATING. Twilite Skating Club. 135 West Main (838-9882). Wednesday and Thursday, 6–9; Friday, 8–11; Saturday, 2–5 and 8–11; Sunday, 2–5 and 7–10.

RESTAURANT. San Remo. 112 East Ridge (838-6000). Monday–Saturday, 4:30–midnight; Sunday, noon to 8. Bar.

SHOP. Blythe's Sport Shop. 138 North Broad Street (838-2203).

SPECIAL FACILITY. The Chamber of Commerce. Has no office but gives information by phone (923-2200 or 838-7230).

Griffith Airport. 1701 East Main (838-7110). Charter flights.

HAMMOND (107,790 population)

Hammond is the oldest city in the Calumet Region but until 1850 was an area of sand ridges and swamps. Its first permanent settler was a Prussian tailor, Ernest Hohman, who escaped here from the 1851 cholera epidemic in Chicago and built Hohman Inn. Today the American Steel Foundries plant is located on the site of the Inn.

George Hammond, a Detroit butcher who perfected the method of shipping beef in refrigerated railroad cars, located his slaughterhouse across from the Inn. Few people were around to complain about the stench of the operation. From 1869 on the Hammond plant was an enormous success shipping hundreds of thousands of pounds of meat as far as Europe. It employed more than 1,500 men in the most important industry in the area. In 1901, after a fire gutted the plant, the operation was moved to the Chicago Stockyards. But the city had become and remains a commercial hub for the area, and is today Indiana's sixth largest city.

Hammond was the home of the nation's first professional football team. The first automatic potato digger was invented in the city. Alvah Roebuck was a local jeweler, but left town after a school janitor stole his girl friend. Richard Heine, the janitor, later became a millionaire banker, and the jilted Roebuck became co-founder of Sears.

To See and Do

ART AND ARTISTS. Northern Indiana Art Center. 5446 Hohman (931-0018). Changing exhibits of local artists and an art fair the second weekend in May.

HISTORICAL COLLECTION. Calumet Room, Hammond Public Library. 566 State (931-5100). Local and Indiana memorabilia and artifacts.

MOVIES. Hammond 41 Out-Door Theatre. 2500 Calumet (WE2-2180).

Hammond Outdoor Theatre. Indianapolis Boulevard and Tri-State Expressway (844-0219).

Kennedy Theatre. 6735 Kennedy (TI4-9769).

Paramount Theatre. 5404 Hohman (WE2-8168).

Parthenon Theatre. 5144 Hohman (WE2-0431).

RECREATION.

BOWLING. Bowl-Era Lanes. 6530 Calumet (WE1-4800).

Calumet Bowling Center. 5851 Caumet (WE1-2641).

Kenwood Lanes. 6311 Kennedy (TI5-0980).

Pin Bowl Lanes. 6716 Kennedy (844-9810).

Stardust Bowl. 167th and Columbia (932-5010).

ROLLER SKATING. Roller Dome Rink. 730 Goslin (933-9401).

PARKS. Dowling Park. Kennedy and Bohrman Expressway. Picnicking, tennis.

Lake Front Park. Calumet at Lake Michigan (931-2760). Fishing, picnicking, boating, public boat ramp, water skiing.

Riverside Park. Calumet and Bohrman Expressway. Picknicking alongside the Little Calumet River in thick woods.

Wolf Lake Park. 121st and Calumet (WE2-0093). A park extending over the Illinois State line. Swimming, fishing, picnicking, boating, water sports, ice-skating, ice-fishing, public boat ramp.

RELIGIOUS SITE. First Baptist Church of Hammond (Independent). 523 Sibley (WE2-0711). Operates world's largest fleet of Sunday school buses for one of the largest Sunday school classes in the nation.

RESTAURANTS. Barton's Pizza. 6819 Indianapolis (844-1000).

Cam-Lan. 132 Sibley Street (931-5115). Chinese food.

Purdue-Calumet Campus. 2233 171st (844-0520). An excellent cafeteria.

SHOPS. Hessville Sporting Goods. 6637 Kennedy (844-2205).

Indiana Botanic Gardens. 626 177th (WE1-2480). Herbs imported from all over the world.

Johann Sports. 6942 Indianapolis (844-8000).

J.W. Millikan Sports. 449 State (WE1-2760).

Pla-Time. 441 State (931-3512).

Sportsman's Store. 7112 Calumet (WE1-6999).

THEATRE AND ENTERTAINMENT CENTER. Civic Center. Sohl Avenue between Carroll and Highland (WE2-0093). Events such as professional basketball games, cat and dog shows and the circus are held here.

SPECIAL FACILITY. Chamber of Commerce. 429 Fayette (931-1000). Open Monday–Friday, 9–5.

St. Margaret Hospital. 25 Douglas (932-2300).

HIGHLAND (24,819 population)

Self-styled as the largest town in Indiana, Highland is a bedroom suburb of the Calumet industrial district. Settled by Hollanders in 1847, it was once a thriving truck farm area. Today the Dutch influence lingers mainly in the Town Hall building decorations. Highland's name refers to its elevation which was caused by the drainage of Old Lake Chicago.

To See and Do.

MOVIE. Jerry Lewis Cinema. 3022 45th (838-1417 or 838-1478).

RECREATION.

BOWLING. Plaza Lanes. 8101 Kennedy (WA3-3800).

GOLF. Wicker Memorial Park Golf Course. Rt. 6 at Rt. 41 (838-9809). Eighteen holes. Open according to weather.

PARK. Wicker Park. Rt. 6 at Rt. 41. (838-9809). 282 acres. Swimming pool, picnicking. Small amusement park.

SHOOTING RANGE AND INDOOR TENNIS COURTS. Hansen's Sports. 3750 Ridge (838-7495).

SHOPS. Arctic Ski Shop. 9636 Forrest (923-8700). Ski equipment rental.

C-K Sports and Hobby Service. 9553 Indianapolis (923-6809).

Hansen's Sports. 3750 Ridge (838-7495).

Highland Sports Center. 2820 Highway (838-2212).

SPECIAL FACILITY. Chamber of Commerce. 8536 Kennedy (WA3-3666).

HOBART (21,485 population)

Situated on a rise of land through which the Deep River meanders, the Hobart area was for centuries an Indian berrying and hunting area and relics of their dancing and burial grounds have been discovered here.

The development of modern Hobart began with George Earle who platted the town in 1845. Damming the Deep River, he built a grist and saw mill which made the town a commercial center for pioneer farmers. Timber cut at the mill was used for Chicago's first paved street, Lake Street. Earle also built an art gallery in his home, the first in northern Indiana. The town soon became a stop on the important stagecoach routes and eventually Lake County's first railroad center. Deposits of clay found nearby led to the establishment of thriving brickyards—and even today the high school football team is known as the "Brickies."

Hobart is now predominantly a residential community with a few small industries. Prominent among the latter is Midwest Products, a leading supplier of model airplanes.

To See and Do

ARCHITECTURE. Hobart Public Library. 100 Main (942-2243). A handsome modern glass and concrete building overlooking the Deep River.

The Pennsylvania Railroad bridge over the Deep River (1854). Listed in the Historic American Engineering Record.

AUCTIONS. Mac's Auction. 150 Illinois (942-1915).

FARMS AND FARM PRODUCE. Johnson, Rt. 6 (962-1383). An abundance of home grown fruits and vegetables. There are a number of other farm stands along Rt. 6 between Portage and Hobart.

MOVIE. Art Theater. 230 Main (942-1670).

MUSEUM. Hobart Historical Museum. 4th and East Streets (942-2724). Saturdays, 10–3. Call to arrange tours at other times. Housed in one of the last Carnegie libraries to be built, it displays some Indian relics and memorabilia of Hobart history.

RECREATION.

BICYCLE RENTAL. Hobart Schwinn. 201 South Illinois (942-3942).

BOATS-RENTAL. Bowman's Landing. 603 South Wisconsin (942-7765).

BOWLING. Cressmoor Bowling Lanes. Wisconsin Avenue (942-1212).

Hobart Lanes. Rt. 130 (942-6248).

Kirk's Cressmoor Lanes. 620 North Wisconsin (942-3213).

New Chicago Pla Bowl Lounge. 3617 Michigan (962-9059).

GOLF. Cressmoor Country Club. 601 North Wisconsin (942-7424). 18 holes.

Indian Ridge Lake Country Club. 6363 Grand (942-6850). Mid–March to first snow. 18 holes.

PARKS. Lake George. South Lake Park Avenue, south of 3rd and Wisconsin (942-7765). 270 acres with fishing, picnicking, boat rental, skating, public boat ramp, marina, ice fishing.

Robinson Park*. 53rd Street and Liverpool Road (942-5498). June–August. Swimming, fishing, picnicking, boating, archery, camping.

ROLLER SKATING. Oak Ridge Roller Dome. 143 South Hobart (942-2416). Wednesday, 7–10; Friday, 7:30–10:30; Saturday, 2:30–4:30 and 7:30–10:30; Sunday, 2–4:30 and 7–10.

RESTAURANT. Country Lounge. 37th Street east of Rt. 65 (942-6074). Daily, 11 a.m.–12:30 a.m. Bar.

SHOP. Hobart Sports. 437 East 3rd Street (942-4014).

SPECIAL EVENT. Hobart holds a bang-up, old-fashioned celebration on the Fourth of July weekend. Art show, watermelon and pie-eating contests, canoe races, ice cream social, carnival, barbecue, flea market, parade, fireworks.

SPECIAL FACILITIES. Chamber of Commerce. 18 East Ridge (942-5774).

Hobart Sky Ranch. 3426 North Lake Park (962-1189). Charter flights.

St. Mary's Medical Center. Lake Park Avenue (942-5015).

LEROY (350 population)

To See and Do

RECREATION.

HORSEBACK RIDING. Bill Cottingham. 5507 East Rt. 8 (663-4647). Daily except Mondays. Also gear, feed.

PARK. Stoney Run County Park. East on Rt. 8 to County Line Road, north to 450S, left one-half mile. 287 acres, picnicking, hiking.

LOWELL (4,300 population)

Lowell, Indiana, is named after Lowell, Massachusetts. Tucked between the Kankakee River and the Cedar Lake area, this handsome old town, once a small residential community surrounded by rich farm country, is now in the midst of a great population surge. Belanger racing cars which won countless championships were made here. Today, there are many antique stores in its environs.

To See and Do

ANTIQUES. Evergreen Shop. I-65 and Rt. 2 (696-0707). A gold mine of music boxes.

Hitzeman's Country Haus. 135 West Commercial. (696-7121).

Livery Stable. Washington Street (696-9395). Open Saturdays and Sundays only, noon to 6. This converted stable has thirty-seven stalls, each rented to an antique dealer. While a nickelodeon plays, you can buy clothes, antiques, candy, and even have lunch.

ARCHITECTURE. Lowell Senior High School. East of town on Rt. 2. Built for 1,000 children in 1969 by the Shaver Partnership of Michigan City. The school is laid out in modules, has the latest in facilities, yet manages a friendly atmosphere.

RECREATION.

BOWLING. American Legion Post. 1108½ East Commercial Avenue (696-7401).

HORSEBACK RIDING. Barbara Henry Stables. 2708 West 165th (696-8655).

Candlestick Farm. 15807 Morse (696-8650).

SHOP. Blythe's Sport Shop. 1330 East Commercial (696-7010).

SPECIAL FACILITY. Chamber of Commerce. 603 East Commercial Street (696-7321).

MERRILLVILLE (15,918 population)

Merrillville, once an important Indian village, is now one of the fastest growing towns in Indiana, with shopping centers and new franchises springing up all around.

To See and Do

ANTIQUES. Stagecoach Antiques. Broadway and Rt. 6 (769-5986). Owner Harry Brown salvages, restores and re-leads old stained glass, terra cotta, fret and iron work.

ARCHITECTURE. Lake County Reference Library. Rt. 30 east

of Rt. 55 (769-6123). A modern glass building with a large collection of Indiana historical materials. Film series.

HISTORICAL MARKER. Homer Idding School. 7249 Van Buren (769-6373). Commemorates the Great Sauk Trail's route through Merrillville.

MOVIE. Y & W Twin I and II. 6600 South Broadway (769-2203).

MUSIC. Northwest Indiana Symphony Orchestra.* Merrillville High School, 276 East 68th (769-2401). Sunday afternoon concerts with well-known soloists. Call for schedule.

RECREATION.

BICYCLE RENTAL. Area Rental. 5449 Broadway (887-7388). Tandems only.

BOWLING. Merri-Bowl. 7610 Broadway (769-2449). Monday, Tuesday, Friday, 1–6; Saturday, 6–11; Sunday, 1–11.

GOLF. Broadmoor Country Club. Rt. 30 and Whitcomb (769-5444). 18 holes.

Turkey Creek Country Club. 6400 Harrison (887-9479). 7 to dusk. 18 holes. Lunch and bar.

SQUARE DANCING. Promenade Hall. Rt. 55, one block north of Rt. 30 (769-5074). Tuesday and Thursday evenings. Only for experts and interested viewers.

SHOP. Merrillville Sporting Goods. 7199 Broadway (769-7031).

SPECIAL FACILITY. Chamber of Commerce. 47 West 67th Place (769-8180).

MILLER (included in Gary population)

Miller is really a part of Gary. It was once a stop on the Chicago-Detroit stagecoach line when the area was so desolate that an eagle perched on every sand hill. Among the first settlers were a fisherman and his wife, whose heirs fought the United States Steel Company for forty years over the land on which they squatted, and a Black man, Davey Crockett, who fled to the dunes dur-

ing the Civil War. Later Miller became a distribution center for fish when sturgeon and white fish were abundant
in the Lake; for sand mined from the dunes; and for ice
from the Lake.

Miller dunes won lasting fame in 1896 when Octave
Chanute made the world's first successful flight in a
heavier-than-air craft there. Orville Wright credited
Chanute with building the prototype of the plane which
the Wright Brothers flew four years later at Kitty Hawk.
Chanute has often been called the father of aviation. A
marker commemorating Chanute's flights is located in
the grassy area south of the pavilion in Marquette Park.

The wild Miller sand dunes were also the locations for
making the silent films "The Conquest of Mexico" and
"Lost in the Desert."

To See and Do

ART AND ARTISTS. Clyde and Belva Ball (938-5580). Sculptors.

Toby Balter (938-8262). Macrame.

Dale Fleming (938-3834). Dunescapes.

Gard Gallery, 396 South Lake (938-6860).

Gary Artists League Gallery. Located in old church at
400 South Lake (938-3356). Open Sundays, 1–5. Invita-
tional shows.

RECREATION.

BEACH. Lake Street Beach. Lake Street at Lake Michigan.
Parking charge.

BOATS-LAUNCHING. Lake Street at Lake Michigan. Public
ramp. Parking charge.

LAKES AND PONDS. Miller Ponds. A beautiful sand dune
area laced with small ponds proposed for addition to the
National Lakeshore. Owned by the United States Steel
Company, it is open to hikers and nature enthusiasts by
special arrangements. Call the Public Relations Department of U.S. Steel (944-4925).

PARK. Marquette Park. Marquette and Grand Boulevards (944-6677). 165 acres bordering Lake Michigan. A

statue of Father Marquette in the park commemorates his travels along Lake Michigan in 1675. Picnicking, tennis, lagoon for fishing, toboggan slide.

RESTAURANT. Golden Coin. Rt. 20 and Clay Street (989-5357). Monday–Saturday, 11 a.m.–midnight. Steaks. Bar.

SHOP. Wilco. 6300 Miller (938-6631). Good Greek bakery in a supermarket.

MUNSTER (16,514 population)

Travelers to and from Fort Dearborn often stopped at the Brass Tavern located in what is now Munster. This hostelry built in 1847 by Allen and Julia Brass had the first telegraph station in Lake County. It was here that news of President Lincoln's assassination was sent in 1865.

Munster's early Dutch settlers became prosperous truck farmers and the area remained predominantly farm country until the end of World War II. Then Munster rapidly changed to a residential bedroom community.

To See and Do

ART AND ARTISTS. Town Gallery. 117 Ridge (836-6230). Open Wednesday–Friday, 9–5. Features local artists.

HISTORICAL MARKER. Columbia Avenue and Rt. 6 marking the site of the Brass Tavern.

MUSIC. Northwest Indiana Symphony Orchestra. Munster High School, 8808 Columbia (836-1450). Saturday evening concerts. Also open rehearsals on Saturday afternoons. Call for schedule.

RECREATION.

  BOWLING. Munster Lanes. 8000 Calumet (TE6-9161).

RELIGIOUS SITE. Carmelite Monastery. 1628 Ridge (838-5050). Old church with Byzantine-type murals. Grotto in gardens.

RESTAURANTS. New Moon Restaurant. 8250 Calumet (836-5464). Monday–Thursday, 11–11; Friday and Saturday, 11–midnight. Chinese food.

  Vince's. 1734 45th (838-6660). Monday–Thursday, 11–midnight; Friday and Saturday, 11 a.m.–1 a.m. Bar.

Shop. Rothstein Sports. 8937 White Oak (838-9734).

Special Facility. Chamber of Commerce. 719 Ridge (836-5096).

SCHERERVILLE (3,363 population)

Schererville was the crossroad for several Indian trails. Later pioneer settlers in covered wagons followed these same trails westward. One of these settlers was A. N. Hart who purchased 18,000 acres of swamp lands. He began a project of road building. Wherever Hart built a road, he also dug a ditch, and wherever there was a ditch eventually there would be Hart, travelling in his one-horse buggy, hoe in hand, to keep his ditches free of obstructions. Sadly and ironically the ditch builder lost his life when one of his ditches collapsed on him.

To See and Do

Antiques. Landmark Antiques. 1619 Junction (322-4534 or 923-0429). Thursday–Sunday, noon–5. Country antiques. Located in converted rail station.

Architecture. Nicholas Scherer Home. 33 Wilhelm. Original house of the town's founder.

Recreation.

amusement park. Sauzer's Kiddie Land. Rts. 41 and 30 (865-8160). May–September, Monday–Friday, noon–10; Saturday and Sunday, 10–10. September and October, Saturday and Sundays only, noon–10.

golf. Scherwood Golf Club. 600 East Joliet (865-2554). 18 holes.

horseback riding. Lakehill Downs Riding School. 85th Street and Cline Avenue (365-8253).

Logal's. Rt. 41, one mile north of Rt. 30 (865-3131). Also hay rides.

roller skating. Omni-41. Rt. 41 (865-6600).

stock and drag car races. Illiana Speedway. 7211 West Lincoln Highway (322-5311). Friday and Saturday nights. Also midget racing.

Restaurant. Teibel's. Ridge Road at Rts. 41 and 30 (865-

2000). Daily, 11–10. Famous for chicken. Huge crowds. Bar.

SHOP. Schererville Clock Shop. 105 East Joliet (322-5433). Tuesday–Saturday, 10–5. Large variety of old and new time pieces.

WHITING (7,247 population)

Until 1884 when the Standard Oil Trust built its refinery, Whiting was an isolated area of swamps and sand dunes, almost entirely encircled by water. Standard had built a pipeline from its Lima, Ohio, oil fields to Chicago to capture the mid-west market. But the Lima crude had a high sulphur content and the citizens of South Chicago wanted no part of its stench. So the company looked for an alternate site along the pipeline and found an ideal location at Whiting's Crossing.

Cheap land, low taxes, plenty of railroad service, no citizens to complain about the smell, and best of all an unlimited amount of free water from Lake Michigan to cool its distilleries, made the location of the refinery in Whiting ideal. At this plant scientists invented the thermal cracking process which doubles the amount of gasoline derived from crude oil. Although Standard Oil has operated here for eighty four years, Whiting never became a true company town, since the company neither built housing for its employees nor controlled the commercial establishments. In later years, the Union Carbide and American Smelting & Refining companies also built major plants in Whiting. For years the community had many foreign-born residents who worked at the refinery, including the largest Turkish settlement in the United States. Today Whiting remains an industrial community whose miles of gas tanks and piping are well-known to drivers entering or leaving Chicago.

To See and Do

ARCHITECTURE. Memorial Community House. 1938 Clark (659-0860). John D. Rockefeller and Standard Oil contributed a half million dollars in 1923 to erect this building.

RECREATION.

PARK. Whiting Park. 117th Street at Lake Michigan. Tennis, picnicking, and fishing.

RESTAURANTS. Condes. 1440 Indianapolis (659-1052). Daily, 11–midnight. Bar. Greek night annually in late September. By reservation only. Greek foods, bands, dancing, but you don't have to be Greek to come.

Fonda del Lago. 1423 Indianapolis (659-4738). Daily for breakfast, lunch and dinner. Bar.

Phil Smidt and Son. 1205 North Calumet (659-0025). Monday–Saturday, 11:30–11. For generations one of the best-known restaurants in the Calumet Region. Fish and frog legs are specialities. Bar.

Vogel's. 1250 Indianapolis Boulevard (659-1250). Daily, 11–midnight. Bar.

SHOP. Whiting Sport Shop. 1601 121st (659-2600).

THEATER. Marion Theatre Guild. 1844 Lincoln (659-2118). A good community theatre group which gives weekend performances in its own theatre. Call for schedule.

SPECIAL FACILITY. Chamber of Commerce. 1905 New York (659-0292).

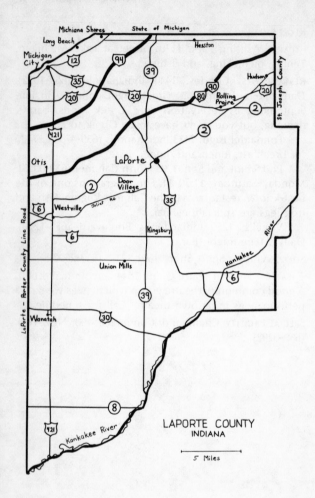

LAPORTE COUNTY
INDIANA

5 Miles

LAPORTE COUNTY
(105,342 population)

LaPorte, The Gateway, was named for the opening in the forest through which the westward-bound pioneers first glimpsed a twenty mile stretch of incredibly rich prairie. Originally covering all of northern Indiana, today La-Porte County extends from the Michigan state line on the east to the Kankakee River on the south, the Lake Michigan shoreline on the north and Porter County on the west. Its 607 miles include a heavily settled area built on levelled sand dunes, a moraine section where small lakes are interspersed with rolling hills covered with orchards and vineyards which produce millions of pounds of fruit annually, a large prairie band, and vast acres drained from the Kankakee marshes now transformed into superb farms.

The LaPorte County Fruit Growers Association publishes a handy map and guide listing the locations and harvest schedules of most of the big farms. Be sure to pick one up when you visit one of them. Fresh apples, cherries, pears, peaches, plums, blueberries, apricots, strawberries, cider, honey and grapes are available from mid-July through October. Many of the owners will let you pick your own at substantial savings.

DOOR VILLAGE (40 population)

Tiny Door Village was the spot where the early pioneers of northern Indiana first saw the opening from woods to prairie. So high were the grasses and flowers that a man on horseback could hardly be seen.

To See and Do

ARCHITECTURE. Octagonal Barn. Left side of Rt. 35, 1.8 miles south of LaPorte County Court House. Huge Door Village sign on the barn. May be viewed only from road.

CEMETERY. Door Village Cemetery. South on Rt. 39 from LaPorte, west on Joliet Road for two miles. A marker commemorates the messenger sent from Fort Dearborn to warn the early settlers of an Indian uprising.

HESSTON (30 population)

In this crossroads hamlet, the only store, a grocery and bar, is locally referred to as "State and Madison." For a dot on the map however, the town has four attractions well worth visiting.

To See and Do

CEMETERY. Posey Chapel Cemetery. 1000N, two miles east of Fail Road, north side of road. This old cemetery is set on a high knoll from which you get a glorious view of both dune and orchard country. In the last century the church on this site was served by a monthly circuit-riding preacher. It burned in 1972.

GARDEN. Hesston Gardens. 1000N and 215E (778-2421). The gardens are the labor of love of Father Joseph Sokolowski who for fifty years has worked to create this charming place. He welcomes visitors, sells antiques to support his avocation and also holds Sunday Mass at 10 in a tiny Greek Orthodox chapel in the woods. Ask to see his special collection of ikons. Free-will offering.

MUSEUM. LaPorte County Steam Society*. 1000N east of Rt. 39 (no phone). Open weekends, June–October. Local farmers and summer residents have joined together to develop this nostalgic steam museum on a 155 acre site. They've collected a bevy of old-time steam engines and cars, laid track for the little "Flying Dutchman" railroad. The public can ride the authentic narrow gauge railroad. On July 4th and Labor Day weekends there are also demonstrations of old-time steam driven farm machinery and other steam powered equipment. On these days, old-fashioned farm dinners are served.

RESTAURANT. Heston Bar, Fail Road at 1000N (778-2938). Tuesday–Saturday. Lunch, dinner, 5–9. Bar.

HUDSON (1,538 population)

This town was the first to be settled in LaPorte County. Among its pioneer inhabitants was Rev. Isaac McCoy, who established a Baptist mission to the Potawattami Indians nearby.

Located nearby is Hudson Lake*, once owned by the South Shore Railroad. In the early 1900's excursion trains brought thousands of Chicagoans to the lake for giant picnics. Today, a substantial summer resort, fishing, boating, boat rental and picnicking are available to the general public.

KINGSBURY (no residential population)

During World War II, a large army ordinance complex was located here on a 23,000 acre site. Part of the buildings have now been converted into an industrial park.

To See and Do

Tours. LaPorte Egg Ranch. Industrial Park (393-3531). Call to arrange a tour of a mammoth egg factory where 300,000 chickens produce for market. Wildlife Area. Kingsbury State Fish and Wildlife Area. East on Rt. 6, north on Rt. 35 (393-3612). Indiana has acquired 5,000 acres and maintains here the only fenced-in wildlife area in the State. Reason? To protect visitors from the un-detonated shells beyond the fences. Camping, hiking, a shooting range and hunting (in season) for teal, pheasant, rabbit, quail, squirrel and deer. Bucks by bow and arrow only. Training for rabbit and bird dogs. Coho salmon fishery.

LAPORTE (22,140 population)

The county seat since the town's founding in 1832, its red stone court-house has a large gold dome and a bell tower erected in 1848. In early years, whenever the bell rang the residents would gather to hear the news, especially during the Civil War. LaPorte is a manufacturing and commercial center. The surrounding residential areas are lovely, with large avenues, huge old-fashioned mansions and five lakes.

LaPorte University, the first medical school in the midwest, was founded in 1842 by four local men including the father of the Mayo brothers. The school no longer exists but the medical tradition continues. A ten million dollar, 191 bed Community Hospital opened in 1972.

LaPorte's largest employers include Allis Chalmers which produces farm equipment, a Whirlpool parts distribution center, and an American Home products canning plant.

Local history includes the grim tale of Mrs. Belle Guiness who in 1902 lured thirteen men to her farm north of town with the promise of marriage and killed them all.

To See and Do

ANTIQUES. Tulip Tree Antiques. 700N off Fail Road (778-2662). By appointment.

ARCHITECTURE. 815 Division (1840). The first frame house in LaPorte. Moved to this location at a later date.

Charles Finlay Farm. Johnson Road at I-80-90 overpass. A sport tycoon's spread.

Garwood House. Small Road, .6 miles west of 500W. Tan brick and gabled home on the south side of the road. The first house in the county to be built with a furnace. Its top floor is a ballroom which used to take two days to heat up before a dance.

Methodist Church. Harrison and Clay Streets. Originally a Quaker meeting house.

Orr-Richter House (1875). Small Road, .8 miles east of 500W. A red brick home on the south side of the road, it was built by the son of Indian fighter, General Joseph Orr. This Victorian Gothic mansion has a central tower and pointed arch windows.

Swan-Anderson House (1870). 1020 Indiana. A white frame Italianate home with lovely tall windows.

ART AND ARTISTS. Judith and Lee Rein (362-3738). Painters.

CEMETERY. Union Chapel cemetery. North side of Rt. 6 between Rts. 39 and 421. The first white settler of LaPorte County, Miriam Benedict, is buried here.

FARMS AND FARM PRODUCE. Bernacchi Farm Market. 2429 Monroe (362-7416). Fresh produce grown locally.

Garwood Orchards. North of Rt. 2 between Rt. 421 and city (362-4385). July 1–November 1, 8–7:30 p.m.; November 1–February 15, 8–5:30. Especially popular. Has operating cider mill.

John Hancock Fruit Farm. Fail Road (778-2096). For apples. Has lovely gardens. Also sells apple dolls, vegetables and plants.

MOVIE. LaPorte Deluxe Drive-In. Rt. 2 East (362-4013).

MUSEUM. LaPorte County Historical Museum. In basement of the County Court House (362-7061). Monday–Friday, 10–4. A cluttered but fascinating potpourri of pioneer and Indian artifacts, the Edward Vail collection of native Kankakee birds, and antique firearms.

RECREATION.

BICYCLE-RENTAL. Area Rental. 602 East Lincolnway (362-7038). Tandems, single speeds.

BOATS-LAUNCHING. Stone Lake, Rt. 35 (362-9746). Public ramp.

BOATS-MARINES. Holiday Boat Sales. 1270 Pine Lake Avenue (362-4423). Boat rentals, launching ramp, bait, fishing equipment.

Pine Lake Marina. 816 Pine Lake Avenue (362-8455).

BOATS-RENTAL. D & D Boat Mart. 908 Pine Lake Avenue (362-1491).

BOWLING. Civic Auditorium, Ridge Avenue (362-7422).

Idle Hour Lanes. 610 Colfax (362-1751).

Thunderbird Lanes. 1251 Pine Lake Avenue (362-3555).

CAMPING. Cutty's Campground Rt. 39 (362-5111). Open year round.

GOLF. Beechwood Golf Course. Woodlawn Drive (362-2651). April 1–November 1. 18 holes.

Char-Mar Hills Golf Club. Rt. 39 at I-80-90 (no phone). 18 holes.

HORSEBACK RIDING. Colonial Stables. 100W (362-3675).

Richard Fritz. Fail Road (778-2614).

Elwin Ames. 400N off Fail Road (325-8368). You can watch this blacksmith and horse trainer at work on summer evenings.

LAKES. Clear Lake.* Truesdale Road (362-2434). 106 acres, fishing, ice fishing.

Fishtrap Lake. Off McClurg Road (325-0290). 102 acres, fishing, ice-skating and ice fishing.

Lower Fish Lake*. Rt. 4, (324-6401). Southeast of La-Porte. 134 acres. Fishing.

North and South Pine Lakes. On either side of Waverly Road (362-9746). Particularly beautiful 564 acres, swimming, fishing, picnicking, water skiing, ice skating.

Stone Lake. In Soldiers' Memorial Park (362-9746). Picnicking, camping, swimming, tennis, boat rental, fishing.

Upper Fish Lake.* Rt. 4 (325-8385). Southeast of La-Porte. 139 acres, swimming, fishing, boat rental.

ROLLER SKATING. LaPorte Casino Rink. 115 West McClurg (362-6765).

SKIING. Ski Valley. Five miles west of city and north of Rt. 2 (362-1212). Six rope tows, beginning, intermediate, advanced trails; lighted night skiing.

RESTAURANTS. Oriental. 610 Colfax (362-1571). Daily, 11:30–midnight. Bar. Chinese food. Entertainment, Thursday, Friday, Saturday. Bar.

The Timbers. 444 Pine Lake Avenue (362-4585). Daily, 6 a.m.–10 p.m. Entertainment nightly. Bar.

SHOPS. Bernacchi Greenhouses. 1010 Fox (362-6202). Thousands of plants growing in thirteen buildings. Popular varieties, mostly for the wholesale and retail holiday trade. Tours on May 1 and December 1. Retail shop open Monday–Saturday, 9–5.

Garr Hardware and Sports. 505 State (362-3474).

Gun Shop. 925 East Lincolnway (362-3038).

LaPorte Sporting Goods. 816 Lincolnway (362-3447).

Lee Jax Sports. 910 Lincolnway (362-2332).

SPECIAL EVENTS. Independence Day Parade. A rousing 100 unit celebration down Lincolnway, the main street. Call the Chamber of Commerce (362-3178) for details.

LaPorte County Fair.* Rt. 2 at 150N (362-2647). Held annually the second week in August. An old-fashioned fair with animals, produce and amusements.

SPECIAL FACILITIES. Chamber of Commerce. 509 State (362-3178). Monday–Friday, 8:30–5.

LaPorte Hospital. Lincolnway, across from County Court House (362-7541).

LaPorte Municipal Airport. 250S east of Rt. 39 (362-9925). Charter flights.

LONG BEACH (2,740 population)
MICHIANA SHORES (449 population)

After World War I developers began building summer communities east of Michigan City. Today the area up to the Michigan state line includes Long Beach, Duneland Beach, Shoreland Hills and Michiana. The latter straddles Michigan and Indiana and has a predominance of log cabin type homes, many of them year-round residences. Drive east on Lake Shore Drive to see the area and view the ever-changing lake.

To See and Do

ARCHITECTURE. Bavarian-style house. 2704 Lake Shore Drive, Long Beach. This gingerbread, gabled home was built by an eighteen year-old German architect. Note the stones on the roof to fend off wind damage.

ARTS AND ARTISTS. Gertrude Harbart (874-6894). Painter.

Helen Miller (874-5767). Macrame

Karl Warren (872-8550). Painter.

RECREATION.

HORSEBACK RIDING. Michiana Riding Stables. 3848 Academy (872-2114). Daily from 9 to dusk, year round. Pleasant wooded trails. Also hay and sleigh rides. Horse auctions on Friday nights.

RESTAURANTS. Tinker's Dam. Rt. 12 east beyond Michigan City to Karwick Plaza. One block north on east side of Karwick Road (879-7373). Monday–Saturday. Lunch, 1:30–3:30; dinner, 5:30–10. Bar. Thursday–Saturday, music. Beautiful site with animals grazing in summer.

THEATERS. Barlo Playhouse. In Tinker's Dam complex, North Karwick Road, Long Beach (872-0941). Thursday–Saturday, 8 p.m., year round. Mostly stock and comedies.

Dunes Art Foundation Summer Theater. Oakdale Road. Michiana Shores (879-9782). Summer stock during July and August. Also children's plays and classes for children in the arts and the theatre.

MICHIGAN CITY (39,369 population)

Once larger than Chicago, this community at the mouth of Trail Creek along Lake Michigan has successively been a booming port, a railroad and manufacturing center and a well-known resort town. It is now a commercial and industrial center for northern Indiana.

Michigan City's history has been tied to the changing patterns of transportation. For centuries Indians came to its lakefront by paddling up Trail Creek. Father Marquette met here with Potawattamis on his explorations in the 1670's. After Indiana became a state in 1826, the Trail Creek outlet to the Lake was developed and a road was built from the harbor all the way to the Wabash River. (A marker on the County Courthouse lawn at the corner of Rt. 12 and Washington Street shows where this road began.) In 1832 Michigan City was platted and soon became a thriving community and a stagecoach stop on the Detroit to Chicago run. Beginning in 1836 Federal funds helped to make the town a busier harbor than Chicago and, during the days of sail and steam ships, millions of feet of lumber, vast quantities of farm produce and thousands of pounds of fish were shipped from Michigan City piers.

In the mid '50's the railroad era began. With three railroad lines, cheap prison labor (from the nearby state prison) and the nearness of such raw materials as sand, clay, marl and lumber, Michigan City became an important manufacturing center. A major railroad car manufacturing plant which became part of the Pullman empire was in operation for over a century. In 1907, it was the largest manufacturer in Indiana as well as the largest freight car plant in the country.

By 1900 the community was also a playground city. Excursion boats brought Chicagoans across the Lake to scores of summer cottages and hotels through the '20's. From the Lake, the visitors saw a spectacular natural landmark, the Hoosier Slide, a 184-foot high sand dune on the western side of the harbor. Once the largest sand mountain in the United States, it was mined over the years to feed Indiana's glass factories, for other industrial uses, and even to serve as the base for the Illinois Central Railroad tracks in Chicago. By 1920, the Slide had been levelled, and on that site a public utility cooling tower now dominates the landscape.

Today the port is only active as a haven for pleasure boats, and an extensive redevelopment project is underway to spruce up the harbor area. The city's many industries include plants of such national firms as Dr. Scholl's, Clark Equipment and Jaymar-Ruby. Coho fishing is now the prime tourist attraction.

To See and Do

ANTIQUES. Five Gables. 217 Rice (872-9315). By appointment. For plates and dolls.

The Gypsies of Canterbury. 110 West 9th (879-9713). Next to the Canterbury Playhouse. Summer, Tuesday–Saturday, 6–8; Wednesday–Saturday, noon–4; Sundays, 10:30–2:30; all winter and spring, Tuesday–Sunday, 10–4. Closed Mondays. Several antique dealers have collections for sale including furniture, glassware, silverware, and primitives.

Phase II. 915 East Michigan (324-7881). Monday, Tuesday, Thursday, Friday, 9–5; Sunday, 1–6. Collectables, Avons, primitives.

ARCHITECTURE. The Barker Center. 631 Washington (872-0159). Mondays and Tuesdays, 10–2. Call to arrange tours at other times. Free will offering. The home of a turn-of-the-century railroad magnate, who hosted Vanderbilts, Clays and Fricks in his opulent mansion, is furnished in late Victorian style with Aubusson tapestries and a remarkable continuity of design in plaster, marble, and wood. The house is now owned by the city and is open to visitors.

The Brewery. East Michigan Boulevard. An imaginative complex of shops and offices in an old beer plant which has been remodelled by architect Ken Fryar.

Franklin Square. The downtown business area between Fifth and Ninth Streets has been turned into a pedestrian way with plantings and pools.

Mullen School. 100 Manny Court, in the Sheridan Beach section (872-5783). Designed by The Shaver Partnership, this lovely school is nestled in a spectacular dunes setting. The school has open classrooms radiating off a central library pit and bright graphics on the walls.

Porter-Kerrigan House (c. 1875). Corner of Washington and 10th Streets. A Romanesque Revival home with a varied skyline of dormers, roof peaks and chimneys. Battered by the years but still showing signs of its original excellence.

Waterford Inn. Johnson and Wozniak Roads at I-94 overpass. Old stagecoach hostelry on the Detroit to Chicago route.

ART AND ARTISTS. The Brewery Gallery. 600 9th (872-4395). Monday–Saturday, 10–5. Mostly a bookstore but with some works by local painters, weavers, and potters.

Elizabeth Fleming (879-9446). Figure painting, oil, ink.

AUCTIONS AND FLEA MARKETS. Anxious Al's Rt. 20, one-and-a-half miles east of Franklin Street (874-4130). Sundays at 2:30. Everything from antique nails to fire trucks.

Nationwide Flea Market. Rt. 20, one-and-a-half miles east of Franklin Street (879-5288). Saturdays and Sundays, 8 to dusk.

Nationwide Sales. Rt. 20, one-and-a-half miles east of Franklin Street (879-5288). Fridays at 6:30 p.m.

The Junk Shop. 1620 Columbia, The Pines (south of Rt. 12) (874-3161). Open daily. Extensive collection of used items of all kinds.

20 Grand. West side of Rt. 20 past I-94 overpass (874-5054). Thursday, 7–11; Sunday, 2–11.

FARMS AND FARM PRODUCE. Arndt's Orchards. Wozniak Road (872-0122). Apples and cider.

Kintzeles. Earl Road (874-4779). One of several truck farms on the street. Fresh and inexpensive vegetables.

N.W.D. Blueberry Ranch. Fryar Road (872-7477). Blueberries and grapes.

Radke. 200N (872-3140). Apples, pears, vegetables.

GARDENS. Allison, LaPorte-Porter County Line Road, five miles south of Rt. 20 (872-5004). Wild flower plants native to the area and herbs.

International Friendship Gardens.* Liberty Trail (874-3664). Daily, 9–9. This memorial to world peace occupies 100 acres east of the city and has a large variety of flora planted in the styles of various countries, including specimens given by such celebrities as the late King Gustav of Sweden, Paderewski, and Mussolini. Occasional concerts and operettas during summer. Run-down but showing remnants of its original beauty.

MOVIES. Lido. 814 Franklin (872-3414).

Marquette. Marquette Mall (872-9101).

212 Outdoor Theater. Rt. 212 (872-1472).

MUSEUM. Lighthouse Museum. At the bend of the harbor to the west as you enter Washington Park (872-6133). Once used to guide ships in and out, the building has been restored by the Michigan City Historical Society. A fascinating collection of memorabilia of an older Indiana. The displays include books, maps, photographs, period clothing and jewelry. Summer, Tuesday–Sunday, 1–5; winter, 1–3:30. Freewill offering.

RECREATION.

BOATS-CHARTERS. (For fishing on Lake Michigan.) B & E Marine. 500 Center (879-8301).

Bob's Sport Shop. 1705 Franklin (872-1720).

BOATS-LAUNCHING. Georg Boats and Motors. 83 North Franklin (872-8608).

Great Lakes Marine. 6th Street (872-7201).

Michigan City Port Authority. Washington Park Basin (872-1712).

BOWLING. Rose Bowl Lanes, 2309 Franklin (872-9930).

Suburban Lanes. 2820 East Michigan (879-9445).

CAMPING. KOA Campground. Rt. 421, four miles south of Rt. 20 (872-7600).

DANCING. Polka Dot. 926 Chicago (879-9017). Fridays and Saturdays, 9:30–midnight.

St. Joseph's Hall. 2001 Franklin (879-9454). Polka bands on alternate Saturday nights, 9:30 p.m.–midnight.

Side Door. 5518 Rt. 421 (879-7388). Nightly, 10 p.m.–12:30 a.m.

FISHING. Hot line for coho fishing information (872-7311). Daily, 8–8, April 1 until ice comes.

GOLF. Michigan City Municipal Golf Course. Wolf Avenue and East Michigan Boulevard (872-2121). March 15–December 1. 18 holes.

THE LAKEFRONT. Michigan City has developed its Lake Michigan shoreline over the years for a large variety of recreational uses. There is a mile long clean and safe swimming beach at the eastern end.

Adjoining the beach is Washington Park (879-8393) which has lovely picnic grounds and is the setting for old-fashioned band concerts which are given on Thursday evenings during the summer months at 8 p.m.

Across from the park is a small, friendly city zoo.* Summer daily, 10–8, winter, Monday–Friday, 10–4, Saturday and Sunday, 1–4. Free on Thursday.

Next door to Washington Park is the private Michigan City Yacht Club and its basin where sailing races can be seen on summer weekends.

Facing the water is the Coast Guard Station and the Michigan City Port Authority's 315 slip marina, the largest on the southern and western shores of the Lake.

A parking fee is charged non-city users of the Park's facilities during summer weekends.

RESTAURANTS. Canterbury Inn Buffet. 110 West Ninth, Upstairs next to the Canterbury Playhouse (874-4269). Summer, dinner and Sunday brunch; Tuesday–Friday, 6–8; Saturday, 7–10:30; Sunday, 10:30 a.m.–2:30 p.m. Fall, winter and spring, dinner only on nights of Canterbury playhouse performances.

Maxine and Heinie's. 521 Franklin (879-9068). Daily except Sunday, 4–midnight. Bar. German food in a tavern setting.

Robin Hood. Marquette Mall (872-8629). Daily, Monday–Thursday, 11–8:30; Friday–Saturday, 11–10:30; Sunday, 12:30–8:30. Bar.

SHOPS. Bobs Sports Shop. 1705 Franklin (872-1720).

Eastmoor Factory Outlet. Chicago and Ford Streets (874-5231). Monday–Friday, 10–4. Women's sportswear at less than retail prices.

Great Lakes Duck Farm. Rt. 35 south of Rt. 212 cloverleaf (874-6642). Baby ducks galore at Easter time.

Hayloft. 909½ Franklin (874-6833). Handwork items displayed in lovely antique pieces.

Heritage Gun Shop. 105 East Barker (879-5717).

Indiana State Prison Store. Chicago Avenue (874-7258). Wednesday–Sunday, 9–5. This trailer in prison parking lot sells dolls, leather and knit goods made by prisoners.

Michigan City Sports Center. 1716 Franklin (879-0907).

Old Towne Crafts. 1410 Franklin (874-7588).

The Patchwork Shop. Deutscher Road, west of Rt. 421 (874-7054). Modest selection of home-made dolls, pillows and quilts.

Ritter. 118 West Fifth (874-7635). Here one of the few remaining Lake Michigan fishing families sells fresh local trout, salmon and perch in season as well as delicious smoked fish.

Society Lingerie Factory Store. North Roeske Avenue (872-7206). Monday–Friday, 9–5; Saturday, 9–noon. Thrifty buyers can purchase ladies loungewear at much less than department store prices in a tiny salesroom.

Tuholski. 519 Chicago (874-4188). Monday–Saturday, 8–5:30. Also Sundays in May and June when they have great quantities of flower plants in flats. An old fashioned feed and seed store at the same location for forty years.

SPECIAL EVENTS. Miss Indiana Pageant finals. Held annually the last weekend in June. (Call the Chamber of Commerce (874-6221) for exact date and location.)

Summer Festival. Four weeks of events every July: sidewalk sales, a huge parade, entertainment, athletic contests, the largest drum and bugle corps competition in the midwest drawing top bands from all over the country, tours and band concerts are among the activities. (Call Chamber of Commerce (874-6221) for schedule.)

THEATER. Canterbury Playhouse. 907 Franklin adjoining the Franklin Mall (874-4269). Offers concerts and dance performances during the fall, winter and spring. Semiprofessional resident summer stock in an attractively remodeled 102 year old church.

Dunes Art Foundation. 600 East 9th (872-3912). In The Brewery. Sponsors adult and childrens' plays using local talent during fall, winter and spring at various locations. Moves to Michiana Shores in summer.

SPECIAL FACILITIES. Chamber of Commerce. 719 Franklin (874-6221). Monday–Friday, 9–5.

Memorial Hospital. 5th and Pine Streets (879-0202).

St. Anthony's Hospital. 301 West Homer (879-0661).

Joe Phillips Airline. Michigan Road (872-5571). Charter flights as well as regularly scheduled flights to Valparaiso and Chicago's O'Hare and Meigs Airports.

Municipal Airport. South Franklin Street (879-0291). Charter flights.

OTIS (250 population)

A tiny hamlet with a population of Polish descended farmers who live in the surrounding countryside. Otis has an attractive Catholic Church, and nearby, on the La-Porte-Porter County Line Road south of Burdick Road, is the old 8-Square Cemetery.

ROLLING PRAIRIE (500 population)

Three Indian trails crossed near this town on the southwest fork of the Sauk Trail. On one, Indians walked from

Illinois to Detroit to collect their annuities from the British for their support in the Revolutionary War and the War of 1812. Another route connected Fort Wayne and Fort Dearborn, and the third went north to Michigan City and then east to the mouth of the Chicago River. (A historical marker on Rt. 20 commemorates all three.)

The community was settled in the early 1830's and has remained a thriving farm town ever since.

To See and Do

ARCHITECTURE. Foster-Shuck House (c. 1833). Jimmerson Shores Road, north of Rt. 20. Greek Revival style.

Provolot-McGuire House (c. 1843). Byron Road north of Rt. 20. Built by Ezekial Provolot, the town's founder. With its center entrance and pronounced pilasters, it is representative of many homes built in this area by settlers from Ohio.

FARMS AND FARM PRODUCE. Sunacre Fruit Farm. 300E, 4.2 miles north of Rt. 20. (778-2483).

RECREATION.

DANCING-FOLK. 2 South Maple (778-2669). Third Sundays.

GOLF. Valley Hills Golf Course. Rt. 2 (778-2823).

LAKES. Hog Lake*. 300E east of Rt. 2 (778-2241). Fifty-nine acres, public fishing, boat rental, tent camping, public launching ramp, ice fishing.

Rolling Timbers Lake.* Two miles east of town, south of Rt. 2 (778-4107). Fishing, picnicking.

Saugany Lake.* East on Rt. 2, near intersection of Rt. 20 (778-2936). Seventy-four acres, swimming, fishing, boat rental.

UNION MILLS (400 population)

Once the center of Indian Mound country, Union Mills is now a small town in the midst of farm lands.

To See and Do

SHOP. Ed Klein's Saddle Shop. South on Rt. 39, between Rts. 6 and 30 (767-2640). Tuesday, Wednesday, Thursday,

8–5; Monday and Friday, 8–9; Saturday, 8–noon. One of the vanishing breed of leather craftsmen who learned his trade from an old harness maker.

WANATAH (800 population)

A center for farm equipment and supplies, this community was settled in 1865 and for a while thrived as a railroad hub.

The name is Indian, means "knee-deep-in-mud" and to this day Hog Creek periodically overflows its banks.

To See and Do

FARMS AND FARM PRODUCE. Pinney-Purdue Experimental Farms. North side of Rt. 30 at 100N (733-2379). Indiana University's College of Agriculture conducts agronomy research on this 450 acre farm with its century-old farmhouse. Open House Day in July with demonstration of farming techniques and crafts. (Check exact date by calling farm.)

Siegesmunds. Four-and-a-half miles south of town on Rt. 421, one mile east on 900W (733-2259). Blueberries.

Tidholm. Three-and-a-half miles south of town on 1050W (733-2560). Forty acres of strawberries and blueberries. Ring bell for assistance.

RECREATION.

CAMPING. KOA Campground. Rt. 30, Hanna (797-2395).

SPECIAL EVENT. Summer Festival.* Annually, third weekend in July. Pit-beef barbeque, horsepulling contest, art show, rides for children, sports.

WESTVILLE (2,614 population)

Home of Beatty Memorial Hospital, one of Indiana's state mental institutions, and of the Purdue-North Central campus (north on Rt. 421). There are two historical markers in Westville: one north of town on Rt. 421 indicating the old Sauk Trail, and the other on West Main Street at the railroad tracks, commemorating a stop of the Lincoln funeral train.

To See and Do

ART AND ARTISTS. Tony Popp (785-2464). Metal sculptor.

ARCHITECTURE. Forrester House. East of town on Rt. 2. An old red brick home with a handsome cupola and two staircases, one for men and one for women.

RECREATION.

HORSEBACK RIDING. Red Rock Ranch. Snyder Road (785-2622). Also hay rides.

LAKE. Clear Lake.* North of Rt. 2 on Porter-LaPorte County Line Road (872-9363). Seventeen acres with swimming, fishing, picnicking, boat rental, launching ramp. Open only to season subscribers.

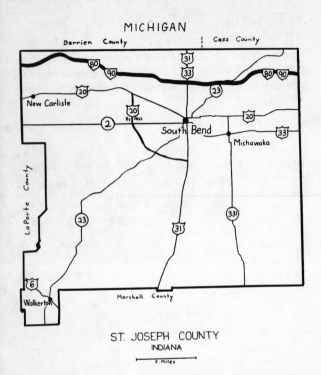

MICHIGAN

Berrien County   Cass County

New Carlisle

South Bend

Mishawaka

Walkerton

Marshall County

ST. JOSEPH COUNTY
INDIANA

5 Miles

ST. JOSEPH COUNTY
(246,045 population)

The first county in Indiana seen by a European, St. Joseph County was visited by Father Marquette in 1675 when, on his last and fatal expedition, he portaged near South Bend from the Kankakee River to the St. Joseph River. The two rivers have dominated the county's development from Indian days. They were the main transportation routes for tribes from Canada and the northern United States to the south. Both the Kankakee and the St. Joseph originate in St. Joseph County, the former flowing to the Gulf of St. Lawrence and the latter to the Gulf of Mexico.

The northern portion of the county is the valley of the St. Joseph River and the southern section the valley of the Kankakee. The Valparaiso Moraine's eastern edge extends into St. Joseph County accounting for its many glaciated lakes and rolling countryside dotted with fruit farms.

The county's fertile valley soil attracted its pioneer settlers. Many originate to the Terre Coupe Prairie, north of South Bend. Today this rich farm area yields bumper crops of corn and soy beans. Other pioneers were traders with the Indians who became merchants and small businessmen.

St. Joseph was organized in 1830 and originally covered all of northern Indiana to the Illinois border; today its 468 square miles extend from Elkhart County on the east to LaPorte County on the west and from Marshall County on the south to Berrien County, Michigan on the north.

The waters of the St. Joseph River were an early source of power for the industry which developed in the Mishawaka-South Bend area, the county's only urban center, after the discovery of bog iron close to the river bed. The two cities, on opposite banks of the river, have continued for more than a century as a major manufacturing center, especially in the transportation field.

MISHAWAKA (35,517 population)

Mishawaka was a lovely Shawnee Indian princess who chose as her suitor, "Dead Shot," a white man, over his Potawattomi rival. Tribal wars followed as a result, but in the end "Dead Shot" won the lady and eventually gave Mishawaka's name to the town which sprang up on the St. Joseph River.

The Potawattomi and Miami Indians built villages along the banks of the St. Joseph River. French explorers came through the area and much later, trappers and traders.

When iron ore deposits were discovered in Mishawaka, the first blast furnace in the new State of Indiana was built here. The blast furnace attracted industry, the industry attracted workers, and soon waves of migration brought Italians and Poles and Belgians. (Mishawaka today has the nation's second largest Belgian-American community.) Variously plows, wagons, farm implements, windmills, woolens, and Amplex and Simplex cars have been produced here. Today it is home to US Rubber, Dodge, Wheelabrater, Bendix.

To See and Do

ARCHITECTURE. Beiger Home. 117 Lincoln Way West.

Hutcheson-Schindler Home. 810 Lincoln Way East.

Merrifield-Cass Home (c. 1837). 816 Lincoln Way East. Originally one story, this house was expanded during the Civil War. Porch with Gothic carpentry added in 1871.

Niles-Weiss Home (c. 1860). 410 Lincoln Way East. Renaissance-type house with handsome curved staircase and marble fireplaces. Currently the Mishawaka Children's Museum.

St. Joseph Church (c. 1893). Corner of Third and Mill Streets. Gothic and German influence. Oldest Catholic congregation in city. Hand-carved communion rail. Stained glass window of Last Supper which was displayed at Chicago's Columbian Exposition.

MOVIES. Boiler House Flix Twin Theaters. 100 Center, 700

Lincoln Way (255-9575).

    Cinema Art. 208 West Main (255-0697).

    Town and Country. 2340 Hickory (259-9090).

MUSEUM. Mishawaka Children's Museum. 410 Lincoln Way East (259-3475). Labor Day to Memorial Day, Monday-Friday, 1–5; Saturday, 2–4. Small collection of pioneer and Indian relics.

MUSIC AND LECTURE SERIES. Bethel College. Goodman Auditorium, 1001 McKinley Avenue (259-8511).

NATURE CENTER. South Bend Audubon Society Nature Sanctuary. Clover Road off Dragoon Trail (291-2830). June–September. Guided tours on Sundays only, 1–5.

RECREATION.

    BOWLING. Jefferson Manor Lanes. 1504 North Chestnut (255-5424)

    Parkway Lanes. 2806 Lincoln Way West (255-4277).

    Regal Lanes. 1121 West 8th Street (259-5209).

    Rose Bowling Lanes. 107 East 1st (255-8611).

    GOLF. Eberhart Petro Municipal Golf Course, North State Street (255-0550). March 15 to first snow. 18 holes.

    PARKS. Battell Park. Mishawaka Avenue, four blocks west of Main Street (255-6610). Beautiful rock garden around steps leading to St. Joseph River. Gold fish pond. Band concerts.

    Izaak Walton League Park. 2400 Darden (272-3660). Woods, stream, picnic area, archery.

    Marine Stadium. East Jefferson Road (255-6610). Fishing, camping, public boat launching ramp.

    Merrifield Park. East Mishawaka Avenue (255-6610). Swimming pool, picnicking, ice skating, public boat ramp.

    ROLLER SKATING. Mishawaka Roller Rink. 506½ West Main (255-0451).

    Rainbow Roller Rink. 1705 East 12th (259-9642).

    SWIMMING POOL. Mary Gibbard Park. 1024 Somerset (255-0854). Daily in season, 6–9.

SHOPS. 100 Center. 700 Lincoln Way West (Rt. 33) (259-

7861). The old Kammes Brewery was built in 1853 and turned into a large and interesting shopping complex. The old boiler house is now the movie theater; storage rooms that once held hops and malt are now art galleries, craft shops, and stores too many to mention. The stalls of the stables now have been converted into exhibit space and are occupied on weekends by antique dealers sporting their wares. There are also two restaurants in the Center.

TOURS. Southhold Restoration Tours. 112 South Lafayette, South Bend (232-4284); or call Chamber of Commerce (234-3431). A group of St. Joseph County residents are in the process of preserving and restoring fine old homes and historic buildings. The Mishawaka Southhold Restoration Division runs three or four tours a year.

SPECIAL FACILITY. St. Joseph Hospital, 215 West 4th (259-2431).

NEW CARLISLE (1,434 population)

Once a stop for stagecoaches on the Chicago-Detroit run, New Carlisle is now a trading center for farmers in the surrounding area. A Philadelphian, Richard Carlisle, in 1830 gave the town his name, and named its streets after his native city. Schuyler Colfax, the nation's Vice President under Ulysses Grant, lived here as a teenager. Elias Baldwin lived here for a while too. Then in the 1849 Gold Rush, he went West, hit it big in the Comstock Lode, and country-wide became known as "Lucky Baldwin."

New Carlisle also enjoyed a bit of fame because of its Opera House, built in 1873. The census of 1870 listed the town's population as 500, but a New York drama agent mis-read or mis-copied the figure as 5,000. New Carlisle, as a result, was included on the touring circuit of New York opera companies for a number of years.

To See and Do

ARCHITECTURE. Hamilton Church (c. 1830). Walnut and Old Chicago Roads. Greek Revival.

Hubbard House (c. 1881). Southwest corner of Cherry and Front Streets. Notice ceiling-to-floor windows.

Methodist Church (now Apostolic) (c. 1870). Front Street.

Olive Chapel (c. 1870). Two miles south of town at junction of Timothy Street and Rt. 2.

CEMETERIES. Hamilton Cemetery. Old Chicago Road. Graves of soldiers dating back to Revolutionary War. Joseph Hursh, whose life spanned three centuries, 1793–1903, is buried here.

Town Cemetery. Rt. 20, west of town. Organized in 1863.

FARM. Homer Fitterling Farm. Five miles east of Bendix Park, on north side of Rt. 2. Lovely white farm buildings with a herd of buffalo wandering through meadows.

RESTAURANT. Miller's Cafe. 110 East Michigan (654-3431). Monday, 8–2; Tuesday–Saturday, 8–8; Sunday, 11–8. Thursday–Saturday, 4:30–8, smorgesboard. No bar.

RECREATION.

Camping. Mini-Mountain Campground. Rt. 2 (654-3302). Open year round.

Park. Bendix Woods County Park. Rt. 2, south of town (654-7658). Once the Proving Grounds for the Studebaker Company, then sold to the Bendix Corporation who in turn gave it to the county, this lovely area includes prairie and a hardwood forest. The churches of Michiana raised the money for a "whispering woods trail" for the handicapped and blind. There are ramps, plants selected for their delicious smells, and casettes to inform blind visitors. Today the park also has four miles of trails, a fine nature center offering varied activities, picnic areas, ski slopes, ponds, horseshoe courts, ice skating and toboggan runs. Summer: 9–dusk on weekdays; 10–dusk on weekends. Winter: 9–5 weekdays; 10–5 weekends. Winter sports from 6–10 p.m. on weekdays; 10–10 on Sundays.

SHOP. Railroad Salvage. East Michigan Street (654-3533). Monday–Thursday, 9–7; Friday and Saturday, 9–5.

SOUTH BEND (125,580 population)

The fifth largest city in Indiana lies in the south bend of the St. Joseph River. Once there were Indian villages along the St. Joseph River and various tribes paddled up and down it and portaged over to the Kankakee, thus connecting the two major water systems of North America. In 1679 Robert LaSalle arrived here with the Jesuit, Father Louis Hennepin, and saw this connecting link between the St. Lawrence basin and the Mississippi River.

The first settlers in the area were two of John Jacob Astor's fur traders, Pierre Navarre and Alexis Coquillard. Coquillard and Lathrop M. Taylor founded Southhold as the city was first called.

When iron ore was discovered in the Mishawaka area, South Bend got its first real growth spurt. Five young brothers named Studebaker opened their wagon works in 1852, which became the largest of its kind in the world. They built carriages for the White House and covered wagons for the pioneers and wagons for the Union Army. From 1902 to 1963, they built automobiles for everyone.

James Oliver also built the chilled plow in South Bend. This plow played a vital role in breaking the prairie of the midwest and the plains.

During the Civil War, South Benders helped runaway slaves on their escape route to Canada. In addition to a large influx of Blacks, South Bend has had repeated waves of ethnic migration: Germans, Poles, Hungarians, Russians, Belgians and Irish.

Headquarters for the Irish, of course, is the University of Notre Dame du Lac, the college founded in 1842 by Father Edward Sorin. (His log chapel has been reproduced and stands on the campus next to the original College building.) When the "Fighting Irish" football team is at home on fall weekends, Rt. 31 is jammed with traffic, sun-up to sun-down. The football fury probably reached its zenith under Knute Rockne, the late great coach who, in his prime, was said to walk through South Bend arguing football strategy with everyone from barbershop personnel to clothing store clerks. In the past decades, particularly under Chancellor Hesburgh, Notre Dame has become an intellectual center of importance.

The university's role in the life of the city has been important, giving it a sophistication and a regional influence which extends beyond Indiana well into the Michigan area. South Bend has undertaken major urban renewal projects, including a handsome new mall and an important convention center. South Bend is today home for many major industrial concerns; it is also home for St. Mary's (sister college to Notre Dame), Holy Cross Junior College, and the regional campuses of both Indiana University and Indiana Vocational and Technical College. And finally, and perhaps a bit bumpily, South Bend is the last stop on the South Shore Railroad.

To See and Do

ANTIQUES. Thieves Market. 2309 Edison (233-9820). Saturday and Sunday, 10–6. Forty antique dealers display their collections in individual stalls.

ARCHITECTURE. Bartlett House. 720 West Washington (1850). Marker on front lawn. Tree here was bent by Indians to mark their ancient trail. Bartlett was a grandson of a signer of the Declaration of Independence. Federal style, one of oldest brick houses in the city. Two-foot thick foundations, hand-hewn walnut beams, half-inch thick aprons, sills of cast iron. Unique. There are secret passages in case of Indian attack. When Bartlett retired he used brick from the oven in his commercial bakery to pave the walk.

Chapin-Willis House (1855). 407 West Navarre Street. Frame with arched windows. Gothic Revival. There are only fifty examples in the United States.

Cushing House (1882). 508 West Washington. Front doors of this house took first prize at Chicago World's Fair of 1893. Italian style house, long narrow windows, fine woodwork. Currently houses a boutique and beauty salon. Doors were displayed in 1920 at Democratic National Convention because they are similar to Jefferson's Monticello.

Northern Indiana Hstorical Museum (c. 1855). 112 South Lafayette. Greek Revival. One of few remaining examples of Chicago architect John Van Osdel's work. Moved to this site in 1897. Museum since 1907. This building was originally a court house and is listed in the National Register.

Saint Paul's Memorial United Methodist Church (1901). 1001 West Colfax. Gothic Revival. Gift of Clement Studebaker and his wife who bought the stained glass windows while visiting the Mayer and Company glass works in Munich. Note the window of St. Paul preaching from Mars Hill. Baptismal font is by Roman marble workers of the twelfth or thirteenth century.

Clement Studebaker Mansion (called the Tippecanoe House). 620 West Washington (232-4284). Designed by Henry L. Cobb, this Romanesque house is a showplace dating from 1889. It has especially fine detail in exterior stone, wood, marble and tile. Local craftsmen did most of the work but materials came from around the world. There are forty rooms, twenty-one fireplaces, a feeling of great opulence. The house is only open when the Southhold Restoration conducts tours (234-3431). Or call the Chamber of Commerce (234-0051 or 232-4284) for schedule.

Frank Lloyd Wright houses:

Avalon Grotto-De Rhoades house (1906). 715 West Washington. Long low Prairie School eaves. Windows are finely leaded glass.

Herman T. Mossberg House (1951). 1404 Ridgedale. Example of late Wright work.

A drive up West Washington Street gives an unusually fine view of the late Victorian as well as the early twentieth century mansions of South Bend's industrial barons.

ART AND ARTISTS. Baldoni Fine Arts. 1314 Mishawaka (287-6661).

Moreau-Hammer Galleries. St. Mary's College (284-4854). Monthly exhibits. Tuesday–Friday, 11–9; Saturday, 1–5.

O'Shaughnessy Hall Art Gallery. Notre Dame University (283-6011). Monday-Friday, 10-5; Saturday and Sunday, 1-5.

South Bend Art Association. 121 Lafayette (233-8201). Tuesday–Saturday, noon to 5; Sunday, 2-5. Painting, sculpture, photography, crafts exhibits. Film series.

AUCTION. Mayflower Auction. 55266 State Road 123 (233-1021). Friday, 7:30.

FARM. Martin Blad Mint Farm. Rt. 2 to Rt. 23 then go south (287-9022). This 2,500 acre peppermint farm is one of the largest in the country. July is the perfect month to visit, but call for an appointment first. Peppermint is a big and growing industry. The next farm has an old-fashioned mint press, so it's possible to compare the highly mechanized methods at Blad with the older ways. Blad farm has bright yellow mint wagons, specially designed to haul the newly harvested mint into the mint press building. The wagons act as cook pots for fifty minutes while the oil is separated, picked up like steam, guided through coils and pumped into fifty-five gallon containers. These containers, or drums, are bought by a company in Kalamazoo which, in turn, sells them to the big chewing gum manufacturers.

GARDENS. Fragrance Garden. Leeper Park, 900 block of North Michigan Street (284-9405).

Morris Conservatory and Muessel-Ellison Tropical Gardens. 2105 Mishawaka Avenue (284-9442). Daily, 10-5. Seasonal floral shows.

HISTORICAL SITES. Highland Cemetery. 2557 Portage. Here is the oak tree called the Council Oak, said to be 700 years old. On this site, during the French and Indian War, LaSalle convinced the Miami and Illinois tribes to side with the French against the Iroquois.

Leeper Park. 900 block of North Michigan Street (Rt. 31) (284-9405). Pierre Navarre's cabin has been moved here, and visitors can get a real flavor of what life was like for the settler of 1820. Visitors can also see the Powell Home, the dwelling of South Bend's first Black settler.

MOVIES. Avon Theater. 307 South Michigan (288-7800).
Colfax Theater. 213 West Colfax (233-4532).
Moonlight Drive-In Theater. 4000 South Main (291-5191).
River Park Theater. 2929 Mishawaka (288-8488).
State Theater. 214 South Michigan (233-1676).
Western Drive-In. 56445 Peppermint Road (288-1727).

MUSEUMS. Northern Indiana Historical Society Museum.
112 South Lafayette (284-9664). Tuesday–Saturday, 9–5.
Housed in the former St. Joseph County Courthouse,
there are exhibits of pioneer tools, toys, powder horns,
newspaper presses, fire engines and Indiana lore.

Studebaker Antique Car Collection. 635 South Main
(234-4121). Open first Sunday every month, noon–5. Historic vehicle collection of wagons, military cars, autos
manufactured from 1901–1963.

MUSIC. Notre Dame University. Check for monthly
schedule (283-7367).
St. Mary's College. Check for monthly schedule
(284-4176).
South Bend Symphony, Morris Auditorium, 211
North Michigan. For schedule call South Bend Symphony Orchestra Association (282-1392).

RECREATION.

BICYCLE RENTAL. United Rental. 2022 South Bend (272-5482).

FISHING. Pleasant Lake for public fishing.

FOOTBALL AND OTHER ATHLETIC SCHEDULES. Notre Dame
University (283-7367).

GOLF. Elbel Park Municipal Course. 26595 Auten, seven
miles west of city (272-4048). April–November. 18 holes.
Erskine Park. 4600 Miami (291-0156). April 1–November 1. 18 holes.
Playland Golf Center. 1721 Lincoln Way East (288-0033). March 15–December 1. Night lighted. 9 holes.
Robin Hood. 20099 New Road, seven miles south of
city (291-2450). March 15–December 1.

Studebaker Golf Course. 718 East Calvert (289-0041). March 15–November 30. 9 holes.

LAKES. Bass Lake. Rt. 20, five miles northwest of city (232-7026). Rental boats, private landing, swimming, ice skating, fishing.

Goodman Lake. Myrtle and Kern Roads, seven miles southwest of city. Swimming, fishing, picnicking, boat rental.

Szmanda Lake. North on Quince Road from Rt. 2 for three-quarters of a mile. Rental boats, private landing, fishing.

BOATS-LAUNCHING. For St. Joseph River. A Darden Road State Public Boat Landing, three miles north of South Bend.

MEMORIAL PARK. North Drive. Swimming, fishing.

STOCK CAR AND MIDGET RACING. Speedway, Rt. 20 (287-1704). Fridays, 8 p.m.

SWIMMING POOLS. Bendix Park (284-9424). Daily in season, 1–4:30.

Natatorium. 1044 West Washington (284-9413). September 1–November 30. Indoor pool.

Pinhook Park. 2801 Riverside (284-9421). Daily, 11 to dusk, June 12–Labor Day. Lagoon.

Potawattomi Park. 2000 Wall (284-9438). Daily in season, 1–4:30, 6:30–9:30. Outdoor.

RELIGIOUS SITE. Lourdes Grotto. Notre Dame University.

RESTAURANTS. Boar's Head. 52855 Rt. 31 (277-5478). Daily, 11:30; open Saturday and Sunday at 5. Bar.

Eddie's. 1345 North Ironwood (232-5861). Monday-Friday, 11–11; Saturday, 4–11. Closed Sundays and holidays. Bar.

Morris Inn. Notre Dame campus (234-0141). Monday–Saturday, 7 a.m. to 8:30 p.m.; Sundays and holidays, 8–8. Bar.

Wooden Keg. 1611 South Main (289-4824). Tuesday-Saturday, 3:30–12:30.

SHOPS. Farmers Market. 760 South Eddy (282-1259). Tuesday, Thursday, Saturday, 7–2. Large and colorful market with fruit, vegetables, meat, fowl, hickory smoked bacon, mushrooms, flowers, and even rocks, fossils, and some pets. In the coldest weather the Amish plain people come in with their apples and tomatoes, protected by individual newspaper wrappings.

Midwest Athletic. 517 West Hill (232-9550).

Sonneborn's Sports. 115 West Colfax (232-1451).

Sportsman's Paradise. 254 Dixie Way West (272-9755).

SPECIAL EVENT. St. Joseph County 4-H Fair, Jackson and Lakewood Streets (291-3400). First week of August.

THEATERS AND ENTERTAINMENT CENTERS. Morris Civic Auditorium. 211 North Michigan (232-6954). Touring companies in Broadway plays. One night celebrity stands.

Notre Dame Athletic and Convocation Center (283-7354). Two and one-half acres. Seats 12,000 for trade shows, football games, hockey, dances.

South Bend Civic Theater. 701 Portage (233-0683).

Laughlin Theater. St. Mary's College (284-4141) or (284-4176).

TOURS. Associated Investment Company. 1700 Mishawaka (288-9141). Call a week in advance for a red carpet tour of the sumptuous headquarters of the company which O. C. Carmichael, Jr. built.

Avanti Corporation. 765 South Lafayette (287-1836). Watch the fabrication of deluxe custom cars; only ten are built each month.

Notre Dame Campus (283-7367).

Southhold Restoration Tours. 112 South Lafayette (232-4284). The South Bend division sponsors several tours to benefit its preservation projects.

UNIVERSITY CAMPUSES. University of Notre Dame du Lac. Rt. 31 (283-7367). Largest Roman Catholic university for men in United States. Guided tours available. Special things: famous Golden Dome, Lobund sterile laboratory, original chapel, Knute Rockne mementoes, Lourdes Grotto reproduction, the Convocation Center with its geodesic dome (largest building of its kind in the world), two million volume library with its exterior murals and the 1,700 handsome acres.

St. Mary's College. Opposite Notre Dame on Rt. 31 (284-4854). Has especially fine mosaics in its Church of Loretto.

Zoos. Pottawattomi Park. 2000 Wall (288-8133). Conservatory and small collection of animals.

Storyland Zoo*. 1304 West Ewing (284-9434).

SPECIAL FACILITIES. Chamber of Commerce. 320 West Jefferson (234-0051).

Memorial Hospital. 615 West Michigan (234-9041).

St. Joseph's Hospital. 811 East Madison (234-2151).

St. Joseph County Municipal Airport. 22965 Rt. 20 (233-2185). Direct flights to Chicago and Cleveland via North Central, United, Allegheny. HUB flies to Meigs Field in Chicago.

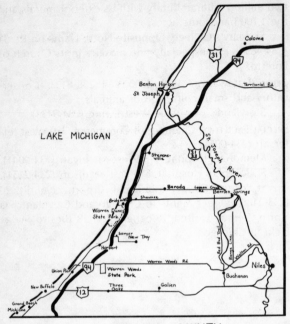

LAKE MICHIGAN

BERRIEN COUNTY
MICHIGAN

5 Miles

BERRIEN COUNTY
(163,875 population)

Michigan's most southwestern county, Berrien, extends from the Indiana border northward twenty-five miles along Lake Michigan. Its 600 square miles include an enormously productive fruit growing region of rolling country dotted with inland lakes and a level plain used for wheat growing. Berrien's lake shore has sandy bluffs and is dotted with summer colonies. There are good harbors at New Buffalo and St. Joseph.

Berrien County was once the home of the Miami Indians and later from 1710 to 1838 of the Potawattomi Indians. But white men knew the area 150 years earlier. The famous French explorers, Marquette and LaSalle, visited the St. Joseph area in the 1670's, and here a large French trading post was established to which the Indians brought furs to sell. At the start of the nineteenth century Berrien County still belonged to the Potawattomi, but it was taken from them because they sided with the British during the War of 1812. Berrien County was organized in 1829 and named after John M. Berrien, a Georgian who served as Attorney-General under President Andrew Jackson.

Pioneer settlers in the county's western section found a forest of heavy timber so that logging became an important industry and wood working plants were established throughout the area. Settlers in the interior found that the combination of soil and climate produced high yields of fruit. The first orchards were planted in the late 1820's and the industry has continued to flourish.

By the time the lands along Lake Michigan had been lumbered out near the turn of the century, Berrien County began its resort business. Daily excursion boats from Chicago brought visitors to the hotels which lined the Lake and summer home colonies, both modest and opulent, were developed. Today Berrien County continues to attract a large tourist business with its beaches, harbors, resorts and tourist attractions. The county also has an expanding industrial base in the St. Joseph-Benton Harbor area.

BARODA, MICHIGAN (439 population)

One of the loveliest drives in the whole area is through rolling countryside along Lemon Creek Road, from Baroda to Berrien Springs. The vineyards and orchards, beautiful any time of the year, are at their best at blossom time in May and harvest time in the fall.

To See and Do

RESTAURANTS. Bill's Tap. First Street (422-1141) Fish fry on Friday night.

SHOP. Tabor Hill Vineyard and Winecellar. Mt. Tabor Road (422-1515). From I-94, Exit 16 (Bridgeman) turn right on Lake Street and continue through Bridgeman. (Lake Street becomes Shawnee Road outside of town.) Follow Shawnee to Hill's Road. After cemetery, turn right onto Mt. Tabor Road. There are many blue and white signs to guide you. Monday–Saturday, 10–5:30; Sunday, noon–5:30. (422-1515). The vineyard was begun in 1948 by four Chicagoans who chose this area for its temperate growing season, abundant moisture, and sandy-clay soil. For their fourteen acres under cultivation, they imported grape vines from France. They make both red and white wine, and visitors can taste and buy all they like, at the same time getting a spectacular view of the area. The tours and tasting go on year-round, and during late August and early September you can watch the actual wine production.

BENTON HARBOR-ST. JOSEPH, Michigan (27,523 population)

These towns are look-alikes and act-alikes. Both have an abundance of blossoms in the spring and tourists in the summer. They are separated by the St. Joseph River, and a bridge leads the traveller from Benton Harbor's Main Street to St. Joseph's Wayne Street.

Their history is almost three centuries old. Father Marquette came up the St. Joseph River in about 1675, and the explorer Robert de LaSalle arrived soon after and built Fort Miami at the river's mouth. Over the years the fort became an important trade center with the Indians of southwestern Michigan and in turn four flags flew over it: Spanish, French, British and American. Eventually the Fort became a trading post, the trading post became St. Joseph. Settlers who couldn't afford land at St. Joseph built a new community, Benton Harbor.

As they grew, Benton Harbor and St. Joseph had periodic feuds over size, boundaries and settlers. Their friendship was finally cemented when they realized they shared such economic interests as tourists, resorts and orchards. Today the area also is a booming industrial center, the major manufacturing hub of southwestern Michigan. It has the national headquarters of the Whirlpool Corporation. It is also the home of Lake Michigan Community College, 2755 Napier Street, Benton Harbor (927-3571).

One of the most colorful of local citizens was Benjamin Franklin Purnell (King Ben) who arrived in 1903 and bought 130 acres in Benton Harbor for a commune. In time his House of David became a smashing success, well known for its baseball team.

To See and Do

AMUSEMENT PARK. House of David. Britain Avenue, Benton Harbor (926-6446). Mid-June–Labor Day. Faded memory of former glory, but square dancing, steam railroad, ponies, amusement rides.

ART. St. Joseph Art Association. 600 State, St. Joseph (983-0271).

The association has classes and changing exhibits in its new building, and sponsors the St. Joseph Art Fair.

FARMS AND FARM PRODUCE. Benton Harbor Fruit Market. 1891 Territorial (925-0681). May 1–November 1, Monday–Friday, 9–6. The largest non-citrous cash-to-grower market in the world. Each grower is his own auctioneer. The farmers of three counties bring their produce, consisting of many kinds of fruits, vegetables and plants.

MOVIES. Fairplain Cinema 1 & 2. Fairplain Plaza, Benton Harbor (927-4862).

Liberty. 212 East Main, Benton Harbor (WA6-2216).

Southtown Twin. 815 St. Joseph, St. Joseph (983-3233).

St. Joseph Auto. Rt. 12 (GA9-3946).

Starlite Drive-In. M-139, Benton Harbor (WA5-3682).

State. 148 West Main, Benton Harbor (925-7002).

MUSEUM. The Josephine Morton Memorial House. 501 Territorial Road, Benton Harbor (WA5-7011). Built in 1849, this large white frame house (with adjoining barn) now is furnished in various historical periods. It has a large collection of old fire trucks. Note particularly the porch which was called the Indian Hotel because the Potawattomi were allowed to sleep there as they came through town selling their baskets. The Morton House is the museum of the Ft. Miami Heritage Society. Tours from mid-April to October on Thursdays and Sundays, from 2–4.

MUSIC. Band concerts. Lake Front Park, Lakebluff Avenue, St. Joseph. Every Sunday in summer. Sponsored by Community Concerts Association. Call Chamber of Commerce (925-0040) for schedule.

NATURE CENTER. Sarett Nature Center. Benton Center Road, Benton Harbor (927-4832). This is a beautiful 175 acre wildlife sanctuary and educational center of the Michigan Audubon Society. It was named for poet, teacher and nature lover Lew Sarett, and offers lectures, Sunday films, a nature shop, craft classes and exhibits. There are observation platforms from which one can view the beautiful acreage, and children can watch a variety of birds and small mammals feeding. There are hikes through swamp, forest, grasslands, tamarack bog and along the Paw Paw River. No pets, picnics or radios. Self-guided walks and organized tours on Sundays at 2.

RECREATION.

BEACH. St. Joseph Public Beach. Sunset Drive. Here Augustus Herring was reported to have managed the first flight of a power-driven heavier-than-air craft, five years before the Wrights. Herring's daring lasted seven seconds. He went on to discover several principles which became vital to the development of aeronautics.

BOATS-LAUNCHING. Benton Harbor Boat Ramp. Riverview Drive (925-7061).

Benton Township Ramp. For access to Lake Michigan via the St. Joseph River. Take I-94 to Exit 27, Niles Avenue to 1725 Territorial Road (925-0616).

BOATS MARINAS. Whispering Willow Marina. 2383 Niles, St. Joseph (983-9963). Take I-94, Exit 27, (Niles Avenue). Go 1.7 miles north on Rt. 33. Boat rentals, fishing boat charters.

Gardner's Favorite Sports and Marina. 741 Riverview Drive, Benton Harbor (925-3247). Rents sail boats, fishing boats and canoes for St. Joseph and Paw Paw Rivers. Boat landing on Riverview Drive. Ski equipment rental.

Chaney's Wharf. Industrial Island, St. Joseph (983-3681).

West Basin Marina. 273 Prospect, St. Joseph (983-5432).

BOATS-RENTALS. Walt Wolf Enterprises. 205 Wayne, St. Joseph (983-1008).

BOWLING. Blossomlanes. 2305 M-139, Benton Harbor (927-3174).

Gersonde Brothers. 2705 Cleveland, St. Joseph (983-3034).

Temple Lanes. 520 Broad, St. Joseph (YU3-9071).

CAMPING. House of David. Britain Avenue, Benton Harbor (927-3302).

GOLF. Blossom Trails. 1565 East Britain, Benton Harbor (925-4951). 18 holes. Sport-o-rama. 33 Rt. 33, St. Joseph (429-3800).

Wyndwicke Country Club. 3711 Niles Road, St. Joseph (429-7007).

HORSEBACK RIDING. Stockbridge Farms. 1995 Dickerson, St. Joseph (429-9892).

PARKS. Lake Front Park. Lakebluff Avenue, between Park and State Streets, St. Joseph. Beautiful view, well maintained; band concerts in summer.

RIVERVIEW PARK. Rt. 31, St. Joseph (983-6341).

RESTAURANTS. Holly's Landing. 105 North Main, St. Joseph (983-2334). Monday–Saturday, 11–midnight; Sunday, noon–midnight. Bar.

House of David. Britain Avenue, Benton Harbor (926-9710). May 1-Labor Day. Vegetarian restaurant. Belgian and potato pancakes are specialties.

Bill Knapp's. M-139 at I-94, Benton Harbor (925-3212). Monday–Thursday and Sunday, 11–10; Friday and Saturday, 11 a.m.–midnight.

Lobster Lounge. 221 North Wayne, St. Joseph (between bridges) (983-5031). Monday–Friday, noon–11; Saturday, 3 p.m.–1:30 a.m.; Sunday, noon –midnight. All kinds of well prepared fish. Inexpensive, unpretentious. Bar.

The Flagship. 100 Main, St. Joseph (983-3212). Daily, 6 a.m.–10 p.m. Entertainment, Tuesday–Saturday. Bar.

SHOPS. Grootendorst. 2450 Red Arrow, Benton Harbor (925-2535). Wholesaler of bulbs and flowering perennials but will sell to travelers at retail.

Heath Company Factory Store. Hilltop Road, Benton Harbor (983-3961). Monday–Friday, 8:30–5; Saturday, 9–3. World's largest manufacturer of electronic kits. Some models at reduced prices.

Jim's Bait and Tackle Shop. 942 South Crystal, Benton Harbor (926-2544).

Midwest Athletic Equipment. 507 Pleasant, St. Joseph (983-7905).

SPECIAL EVENTS. Art Fair. Lake Front Park, Lakebluff Avenue, St. Joseph (983-0271). Second Sunday in July. Considered one of the better regional art shows.

Blossomtime. Don't miss it. It lasts a week beginning the last Sunday in April and includes the Blessing of the Blossoms; an elaborate parade with floats and bands and pretty girls; concerts; dancing; baton twirling. The Blossom Trail which is actually four·motor trails or 125 miles

BLOSSOM TRAILS

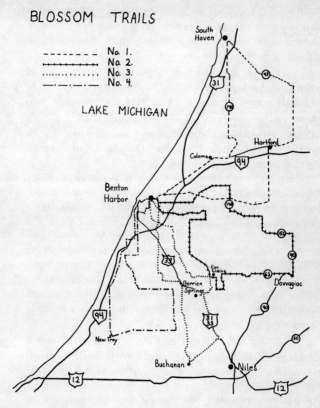

- - - - - -	No. 1.
-·-·-·-·-	No. 2.
··········	No. 3.
—··—··—	No. 4.

LAKE MICHIGAN

South Haven

Hartford

Coloma

Benton Harbor

Eau Claire

Berrien Springs

Dowagiac

New Troy

Buchanan

Niles

BERRIEN and VAN BUREN COUNTIES

MICHIGAN

5 Miles

and 52,000 lovely acres, wanders through orchards of apples, peaches, pears, plums, grapes and every kind of berry. Maps are available at Blossomtime Headquarters, 311 Colfax, Benton Harbor (925-7019).

THEATER. Twin City Players. Playhouse, 4681 South Red Arrow, St. Joseph (429-9402). Amateur theatricals. Call Chamber of Commerce (925-0044) for schedule and times.

TOURS. Heath Company. Hilltop Road, Benton Harbor (983-3961). Memorial Day–Labor Day, 10–2. Other times, group tours by appointment.

Musselman's. 3515 Red Arrow St. Joseph (983-3901). A Monday to Friday cannery where you can see, in season, canning of asparagus, cherries, crab apples, apple rings and tomato juice. Call ahead for appointment.

Nye's Apple Barn. 4716 Hollywood, St. Joseph (983-6602). They grow and sell apples and take visitors on tours of their orchards.

Whirlpool Company. Upton Road, Benton Harbor (926-5000). There are several divisions of this appliance company which can be toured. Call in advance to make specific arrangements.

SPECIAL FACILITIES. Twin Cities Area Chamber of Commerce. 777 Riverview Drive, Benton Harbor (925-0044).

Memorial Hospital. 2611 Morton, St. Joseph (983-1551).

Mercy Hospital. 960 Agara, Benton Harbor (925-8811).

Ross Field. West Main, Benton Harbor (927-3194).

North Central Airline has daily scheduled flights to Chicago, Detroit, Grand Rapids and points north.

Blue Star Aviation. 1681 Reeder, Benton Harbor (927-2954). Charter flights.

BERRIEN SPRINGS, Michigan (1,951 population)

Today this area is the heart of the fruit growing belt. One hundred and thirty years ago Indian tribes travelling the Sauk Trail, passed through here on their way to Detroit.

To See and Do

ARCHITECTURE. Berrien County Courthouse (1833). North Cass and West Union Streets, This Greek Revival red brick and white wood building with handhewn timbers is beautifully preserved in its elegant simplicity. Open weekends in July and August.

MOVIE. Berry Theatre. Ferry Street (471-1931).

RECREATION.

BOATS-LAUNCHING. Ramp to St. Joseph River available for all but largest boats.

HAY RIDES. Country Hideaway. Range Line Road (683-7290). Tractor-driven. Bon fire picnics. Fall and Spring only. Reservations necessary.

Red Bud Trails. Three miles north of town on Red Bud Trail (695-6405).

LAKE. Lake Chapin, Range Line Road.

SPECIAL EVENT. Berrien County Youth Fair. (473-4251). Mid-August. Call fairgrounds for schedule and dates. Livestock, thousands of flowers, vegetables and fruits grown by county youngsters; tractor and horse pulling contests, and entertainment by well-known rock and stage stars.

UNIVERSITY CAMPUS. Andrews University. Rt. 31 (471-7771). Open daily except Sunday. A Seventh Day Adventist School. The University operates its own College Wood Products Company on campus (473-5511). Monday–Friday, 7:30–noon, and 1 to 5; Sunday, 10–5; Thursday until 9. You can watch early American-type furniture being made. The University also operates its own grocery store on campus (471-7442). Since Seventh Day Adventists are vegetarians, this store features a wide variety of natural foods—soy and peanuts in endless varieties, fresh grated coconut, grains galore, and many special breads. (Cheese and onion in particular available on Tuesdays).

SPECIAL FACILITY. Berrien General Hospital. 1250 Deanhill, Berrien Center (471-7761).

BRIDGMAN, Michigan (1,579 population)

Bridgman has fine high dunes and according to the natives, whispering sands. Unfortunately, some of the dunes in the area have been stripped by industry. During the first World War this remote area became a secret meeting place for members of the famous illegal labor group, the International Workers of the World.

To See and Do

PARK. Warren Dunes State Park. Red Arrow Highway, west of town (462-4013). 1,500 acres with two miles of splendid lakefront, fine beaches and large high dunes. The park has facilities for swimming, camping, picnicking, hiking. Camping is limited to fifteen days in July and August.

RECREATION.

BEACH. Weko Beach. Lake Street at Lake Michigan (465-5407). From Exit 16 (Bridgman) on I-94 go one mile north of town. Swimming, picnicking and boat launching facilities. Municipally owned.

BOWLING. Bridgman Country Club. 9794 Jericho (465-5611).

GOLF. Bridgman Country Club. 9794 Jericho (465-5611). 18 holes.

RESTAURANTS. D'Agostino's Navajo. Red Arrow Highway (465-3434). Monday–Saturday, 5–midnight. Closed holidays. Bar. Reservations needed Saturday.

Hyerdall's. Red Arrow Highway (465-5546). Lunch, 11:30–3; dinner, 5–8. Closed Monday. Chicken and dumpling specialty. Good home cooking. No bar.

SHOP. Rainbow Gardens. 9394 Red Arrow (465-3191). A choice small family business with perennials, rock garden plants and sedum of many varieties.

TOUR. Donald C. Cook Nuclear Center. Red Arrow Highway (465-6101). Tuesday–Saturday, 10–5; Sunday, noon–6. Closed Monday. The story of nuclear energy is presented with sound effects, on a moving stage. Next to the theater is a spectacular garden.

BUCHANAN, Michigan (4,645 population)

Once called McCoy's Creek, Buchanan is one of the oldest cities in the county; its first settlers arrived in 1833. Now a town with several industrial plants, Buchanan also boasts the only cave in all of Michigan. The first phonograph needles were manufactured here.

To See and Do

CAVE. Bear Cave. Red Bud Trail, four miles north of town (OX5-3050). Daily from Memorial Day to Labor Day; weekends only from April 7 to Memorial Day, and from Labor Day to November 1. Boat rentals, fishing, swimming pool, camping. The cave was formed by action of water on a porous rock base, which in turn rests on glacial drift more than 50,000 years old. Stalactites, petrified vegetation, much of it colored by metallic oxides. Guided tours.

CEMETERY. Oak Ridge Cemetery. Front Street. Notice monument marking grave of one Joseph Coveney, an atheist whose tomb, erected during his lifetime, bears inscriptions from atheistic writings. The tomb was made in England because no local God-fearing stonecutter would do the job.

RECREATION.

BOWLING. Poorman's Recreation. 708 East Front (695-5521).

CAMPING. Fuller's Camp Ground. Clear Lake Road, three miles west of town. (695-3785). Swimming, camping, fishing, boat rentals. Friday night square dancing.

Three Braves Campground. Madron Road to Wagner Lake, five miles northwest of town (695-9895). Swimming, camping, fishing, boat rentals. Bands on holiday weekends.

GOLF. Brookwood Golf Club. Niles-Buchanan Road (695-9193).

SKIING. Royal Valley Ski Resort. West Main Street, three miles north of town. (695-3847). Monday–Friday, noon–10; Saturday, 10–10; Sunday, 10–6; Christmas week, 10–10; Christmas and New Year's Day, 2–10. Seven electric tows, eight runs, beginners, intermediate, advanced trails. Night skiing. Ski reports (684-1000).

RESTAURANT. Meadowbrook. 1207 Red Bud (695-3811). Lunch, daily 11:30–1:30; dinner, Wednesday–Saturday, 6–9. Bar.

SHOPS. Gambles Sporting Equipment. 226 East (OX5-6891).

Thompson Archery. 315 Liberty (695-3379). Daily, 9–9. Indoor and outdoor testing ranges and all equipment for hunting and target practice.

TOUR. Clark Equipment Company, Automotive Division, 324 East Dewey (697-8385). Call in advance. Very large axle plant with foundry, forge and punch press.

SPECIAL FACILITIES. Buchanan Community Hospital. 1301 Main (695-3851).

Buchanan Area Chamber of Commerce. 119 Main (695-3291).

COLOMA, Michigan (1,814 population)

A canning center for the rich Michigan farm crops in the surrounding countryside, Coloma is situated in beautiful rolling country. First settled in 1840 by New Yorkers, the town was originally called "Dickersville" because money was a scarce commodity and the first store operated almost entirely on the barter system. Coloma, Spanish for a flower that grows on the Pacific slopes, is the name given by a town father who tried his hand in the gold rush and returned.

To See and Do

AMUSEMENT PARK. Deer Park. Paw Paw Lake (468-4961). Open May 25 to Labor Day, 10–6. Deer, llama, bears, monkeys, camel, seals and birds are on display. A natural setting for children to see, pet and enjoy a wide variety of animal life, and animal shows.

ANTIQUES. Millstone Antiques. Martin Road (HO8-6667). Daily, 10–5. On a farm with a children's playground. Two big barns filled with finished furniture, china, glass, toy trains, gloves and other country items.

ARCHITECTURE. Community Church (1855). Church Street. Volunteers for the Civil War gathered here to join the Army of the Republic. The church bell comes from a steamship wreck.

SPECIAL EVENT. Coloma Gladiolus Festival. First weekend in August. Largest gladiolus show in Michigan. Parade, water ski and air shows, arts and crafts display. Call Coloma Chamber of Commerce for schedule (468-6601).

GRAND BEACH, Michigan (165 population)

There are probably as many beach communities as there are subdividers, but Grand Beach's claim to fame is one resident: Chicago's Mayor, Richard J. Daley. Along with him come an enclave of Chicago politicians who weekend and summer here. Grand Beach also has a Frank Lloyd Wright home on Station Street, an early example of Wright's work, built originally as a summer house.

HARBERT, Michigan (600 population)

Harbert is one of a series of old summer colonies primarily settled by Chicagoans of Swedish descent. The poet Carl Sandburg once lived here. The Prairie Club of Chicago has its permanent camp here.

To See and Do

SHOPS. Harbert Bakery. 13746 Red Arrow (469-1777). Open daily except Monday during July and August; weekends only in March and April; closed January and February. Swedish specialties.

Molly Pitcher Winery. 13581 Red Arrow (469-0700). Manufacturers of cherry jubilee wine.

Swedish Bakery. Red Arrow Highway (469-4202). Daily except Thursday. Closed, November to May. Swedish breads and pastries.

LAKESIDE, Michigan (400 population)

In its early days, Lakeside was a center for the shipment of timber logged nearby and carried to Chicago and other Great Lakes ports. For the past fifty years, Lakeside has been a summer resort colony. Though the large resort hotels are gone, the town is replete with summer homes owned by second and third generation Chicago families who come here for a quiet, cool summer.

Lakeside is proud of its ancient sassafras tree outside the old firehouse. The property owners' association has planted thousands of bulbs along Main Street, a delight in the Spring, and has painted the water tower blue.

To See and Do

ANTIQUES. Heritage House. 15300 Red Arrow (469-1412). Victorian and country items, old glass, farm tools, kitchen utensils.

What-Not Shop. 15154 Lakeside Road (469-3113). Hand-knit items and a small collection of better-than-average country items.

ART AND ARTISTS. Lakeside Studios, 150 South Lakeshore (469-0675). Call in advance for an appointment. Museums, collectors and universities are regular purchasers of prints by famous artists produced here. Very fine items but expensive. Also art courses for serious professionals during summer. Housed in an old hotel overlooking the lake.

SHOP. Arts and Crafts of Lakeside. 14876 Red Arrow (469-2771). Monday–Saturday, 9–6.

NEW BUFFALO, Michigan (2,784 population)

New Buffalo was first settled in 1835 and got its name because a ship captain from Buffalo, New York, wrecked his boat on Lake Michigan. While searching for it, he found the harbor. It became a lumbering center and a ship terminus for Lake Michigan travellers. Today the town has a fine natural harbor and a beach front which offers fishermen and boatsmen a summer paradise. It has also long been prominent as a center for youth and welfare camps.

To See and Do

ART AND ARTISTS. The Atelier. 10 North Barton (469-1643). Classes, local paintings, art fair.

GARDEN. David Holmes. 13128 Lubke (469-2330). Fine geranium garden. Lake with Canada geese and mallards.

PARK. Warren Woods State Park. Turn east off Red Arrow Highway on County Highway 735 and go north for two miles. 320 acres of dense primeval forest with giant beeches and maples. A meandering river and lovely walking trails, picnicking, natural spring water to drink. Bird and game sanctuary.

BOATS-LAUNCHING. Public ramp. Red Arrow Highway, east of town. For smaller boat access to Galien River.

BOATS-MARINAS. New Buffalo Marina. 245 Whittaker (469-0010).

Oselka Snug Harbor Marina. 514 West Water (469-2600).

BOWLING. Theo's Lanes. Rt. 12 (469-0400). Opens at noon. Good sandwiches and pizza.

DANCING. Blue Chip Lounge. Red Arrow Highway (469-9828). Polkas, Friday and Saturday evenings.

ROLLER SKATING. Scotty's Roller Bowl. 27 North Whittaker (469-3750). Thursday–Saturday, 7:30–10:30; Sunday, 2–5.

RESTAURANTS. Czech Hospudka Villa. Red Arrow Highway (469-3330). Tuesday–Saturday, 5–10; Sunday, noon–8. Closed Monday. Bar. Good native Bohemian food. Hearty and inexpensive.

Golden Door. I-94 and Rt. 12 (469-1191). Tuesday–Saturday, 5:30–11; Sunday, 1–9. Closed Monday. Bar.

Little Bohemia. 115 South Whittaker (469-1440). Tuesday–Thursday and Sunday, 11–11; Friday and Saturday, 11–midnight. Closed Monday. Bar. Also caters to boats and provides transportation from harbor to restaurant.

Redamak's Tavern. Rt. 12 (469-9866). Daily, 8:30 a.m.–2:30 a.m. Sunday opens at noon. Good hamburgers.

Scotty's Place. Rt. 12 (469-1353). Monday–Wednesday and Thursday, 5–midnight; Friday and Saturday, 5–2; Sunday, noon–2. Bar.

SHOPS. Decor. Red Arrow Highway (469-2745). Objets d'art and a few hand-made wood carvings.

Skipper's Landing. 244 North Whittaker (469-1120).

Fishing equipment and guns. Also rent boats.

THEATER. Scotty's Dinner Theater. Rt. 12 (469-1353). Year-round repertory; revivals, mostly light comedy. Dinner, 6:30 p.m.; curtain, 8. Bar.

NEW TROY, Michigan (385 population)

This tiny hamlet, settled in 1836, once had four operating mills. Today it is the home of one of the few original grist mills still in operation with new-fangled electricity to grind the grain, but a sod roof and an old sign advertising "Marley's wheat germ for constipation and nervousness." Corn meal and buckwheat, graham, whole wheat and pancake flour are produced and sold on the premises. Open daily (426-3422).

NILES Michigan, 12,988 population)

Niles calls itself The City of the Four Flags, since it has been under the control of the French, the British, the Spanish and finally the United States. Situated on high bluffs overlooking the St. Joseph River, Niles has been settled for over 300 years. Its Indian history goes back even further. The Sauk Trail forded the St. Joseph River at Niles.

At the French Jesuit mission here, the first in the lower Michigan, Wisconsin or Indiana area, thousands of Indians were instructed and baptized. Fort St. Joseph, south of the city, was built by the French in 1697. Notre Dame archeologists are trying to uncover remains of the fort.

Today there are thirty-five manufacturing plants in Niles. The Dodge Brothers of auto fame hailed from Niles, as did Ring Lardner and Montgomery Ward.

To See and Do

ANTIQUES. Lois Sherer. 1008 Oak (683-7224). Tuesday–Saturday, 10–5. Housed in the city's first bank building which was moved to this location.

AUCTION. Niles Community Auction. 510 North Front (684-1263). Fridays, 7:30 p.m.

ARCHITECTURE. City Hall. 508 East Main (MU3-4700). Monday–Friday, 8–5. This elegant mansion was built in 1882 by Henry Austin Chapin and was given to the city by his grandchildren. It has fourteen rooms, an early elevator, a ballroom, beautiful fireplaces and stained glass windows. Each room is decorated in a different wood.

Greek Revival homes of the 19th century line Oak Street.

Ring Lardner House (c. 1860). 519 Bond. A Hudson River Gothic, the house perches on a high bluff overlooking the St. Joseph River. Ring Lardner grew up in this home and began his writing career on the Niles Sun.

CEMETERY. Bertrand Catholic Cemetery. Madalene Street. Many old tombstones.

HISTORIC MARKERS. The Grave of Father Allouez, the Jesuit missionary, is on Bond Street, on a bluff overlooking the St. Joseph River.

Fort St. Joseph, Bond Street. A boulder marks the approximate site of the fort and gives dates of its checkered history.

Sauk Trail Crossing. On the west side of St. Joseph River on Rt. 31, the old Sauk Trail forded the river.

Catholic Mission. Clay and Lincoln Streets. Here on the grounds of the Roman Catholic Church the Jesuits ministered to the Indians.

Carey Mission. A boulder at the crossroads of Phillips Road and the Niles-Buchanan Road, on the west bank of the St. Joseph River, commemorates the Rev. Isaac McCoy's aid to the Pottawattomi Indians.

MOVIES. Outdoor 31 Theater. 2131 South 11th (683-4272).

Ready Theater. 420 East Main (683-7272).

MUSEUM. Fort St. Joseph Historical Museum. 508 East Main (MU3-4702). Tuesday–Sunday, 1–5. Closed Mondays and holidays. Call for tours. Self-guided tour sheets to Fort St. Joseph and the Summerville Mounds provided. Located behind City Hall in what were once the stables of the Chapin Mansion. Displays of Indian and local history.

MUSIC. Band concerts. Ella Champion Park, Main and Fifth Streets. Wednesday evenings during the summer.

NATURE CENTER. Fernwood. 1720 Range Line northwest of the city (695-6491). Tuesday–Sunday, 10–5. Closed Monday. An unusually beautiful hilly nature preserve, with springs, pools and streams, along the St. Joseph River. Formal gardens, herb and rock and bog gardens, a river trail, an eighteen acre wilderness trail, and a self-guided nature trail. Gift shop.

RECREATION.

BOWLING. Shula's 31 Bowling. 2732 South 11th (684-2270).

Timber-Lanes. 517 North 2nd (MU3-6122).

White's. 530 South 11th (683-8484).

BOATS-LAUNCHING. Municipal boat dock. St. Joseph River at Marmont Street.

CAMPING. Spaulding Campground. Bell Road (684-1393).

GOLF. Plym Park. East of Rt. 31 (684-1928). Municipally owned. 9 holes.

Kelly's Sports Land. 2107 South 11th (MU3-5421). Two 18 hole miniature golf courses.

HORSEBACK RIDING. Diamond D Ranch. 3232 Dunning (683-5892). Also hay rides.

Laughin' Place Stable. 2140 Niles-Buchanan Road (683-8813). Monday–Friday, 2–4; Saturday, 10–noon. These elegant facilities and grounds will thrill any horselover. Visitors welcome.

Wild Bill Plott Riding Stable. 3165 Portage (683-2923). Daily except Friday. Also rents pony hitches, coaches and wagons.

RESTAURANTS. Franky's. 1033 Lake (683-7474). Daily except Tuesday, 11–midnight. Bar. A pleasant and inexpensive restaurant featuring Italian food.

Portofino's. Rt. 31 (683-5000). Daily except Monday, 11–2. Italian specialties. Bar.

SHOPS. Hully's Bait and Tackle. 12215 11th (684-1444).

Paris Candy Company. 220 East Main (MU3-9792). An old-fashioned ice cream parlor selling home made candies and ice cream.

W.S. Leisure Center. 2607 South 11th (684-0750).

Twelve Oaks Sport Shop. 2610 South Rt. 31 (684-1743).

SPECIAL EVENT. Four Flags Area Apple Festival. The second week in October. Call Chamber of Commerce (683-3720) for schedule and locations. Seven days of activities to celebrate the apple harvest, including French, Spanish, British and pioneer dinners and historical, agricultural and industrial tours. Indian dancers, flea market, parades, street dances, square dancing, raft races, antique and art shows. The first Sunday is for the children with clowns, games, train rides. Plenty of apples and apple pie available all week.

TOUR. Clark Equipment Company, Tyler Refrigeration Division. Call Chamber of Commerce to make arrangements (683-3720).

SPECIAL FACILITIES. Chamber of Commerce of Greater Niles. 103 North 4th (683-3720). Monday–Friday, 9–5.

Air Michiana. 191 Fir (683-2078). Charter flights.

Niles Airways. 2020 Lake (683-3434). Charter flights.

Pawating Hospital. 31 North St. Joseph (MU3-5510).

SAWYER, Michigan (500 population)

Sawyer is another old Lake Michigan summer community with a heavy Swedish influence. There are still many summer residents but the town's year-round population is growing as workers in the Benton Harbor-St. Joseph area settle here.

To See and Do

RESTAURANT. Anderson's. Red Arrow Highway (426-4904). Monday–Saturday, 11–3 and 5–8; Sunday, noon–8. A simple, clean restaurant with homecooked food.

SHOPS. Drier's. Red Arrow Highway. This branch of a well known New Buffalo meat store is open only during July and August. Cheese and sausage are sold in a little store right on the highway.

Haalga's. Red Arrow Highway (426-4233). Monday–Saturday, 10–6. During December, July and August, open daily. A gift shop which stocks a large selection of Swedish items.

STEVENSVILLE, Michigan (1,070 population)

Stevensville, in the midst of the Michigan dune country, is a bustling community that provides many activities for the visitor.

To See and Do

RECREATION.

BOWLING. Lakeshore Lanes. 6201 Red Arrow (429-5421).

NATURE CENTER. Grand Mere Nature Study Preserve. From Stevensville exit on I-94 go north to Thornton Drive. Turn west to first road and then north to preserve (no phone). 22 acres of beautiful dunes. Operated by the Kalamazoo Nature Center. The State of Michigan is developing the surrounding area as a state park to be opened in several years. Call 381-1574 to arrange tours.

RESTAURANTS. Ritter's. Red Arrow Highway (GA9-3591). Monday–Saturday, 11:30–11. Bar.

Win Schuler. 5000 Red Arrow (429-3273). Monday–Friday, 11–11; Saturday, 11–midnight; Sunday, 10–10. Decorated like an old English inn. Specializes in fish, seafood, beef. Very popular. Bar.

Tosi. 4337 Ridge (429-3689). April 1–December 31; Monday–Friday, 5–11; Saturday, 5–midnight. Closed Sundays and holidays. Food is Italian and excellent. Always a crowd. No reservations ever on Saturday nights or any night during July and August. Worth the wait. Bar.

SHOPS. Emlong Nursery. Red Arrow Highway (GA9-3431). Monday–Saturday, 8–6; Sunday, 9–6. A large nursery. Field grown trees and shrubs.

Mrs. Halby's Jellies and Jams. Red Arrow Highway, north of town (429-1813). In this little brick building Mrs. Halby personally sells her homemade preserves.

Paris Flea Market. Grande Vista area, Red Arrow Highway (429-7501). Saturday and Sunday, 11–7. A large selection of farm items and Americana.

A Bit of Swiss Bakery. On premises of Tosi's restaurant, 4337 Ridge (429-1661). Monday–Saturday, 8:30 a.m.–9:30 p.m. Excellent pastries.

THREE OAKS, Michigan (1,738 population)

In the park at the entrance to Three Oaks stands the first cannon to be captured by Admiral Dewey at the battle of Manila in 1898. The residents raised more money per capita than any town in the nation and won the cannon —and a dedication speech by President McKinley. The town was named for three oaks which stood close together near the site of the present post office. Trainmen coming through would look out their locomotives and say, "There now's the three oaks."

To See and Do

ANTIQUES. The Depot. Oak Street (756-9366). The Rev. Reginald Dryden bought the old Michigan Central Railroad depot to house his collection of old and new books, china, glass, and furniture.

Rainbow's End. 1000N (756-9291). Excellent selection.

RECREATION.

BOWLING. Three Oaks Bowling Alleys. 17 South Elm (756-9131) Daily, 9–11.

SHOP. Drier. 14 South Elm (756-3101). Three generations have been involved in this very expensive excellent store featuring aged cheeses, smoked meats and home-made sausages. The home store is a treasure house of old pictures, knives, butcher blocks and generational mementos. Drier also has a country store on Rt. M-60.

SPECIAL EVENT. Annual Flag Day Parade. On the Sunday nearest to June 14. A small town gala with bands, marching units, batons and bugles and fun.

SPECIAL FACILITY. Oselka Field. Forest Lawn (756-9252). Charter flights.

CROP PICKING CALENDAR

There are dozens of orchards and farms in the Indiana-Michigan area. Only some are listed in this book. The La-Porte County Fruit Growers Association publishes a more comprehensive listing and a map showing their locations. You can obtain a copy by writing Garwood Orchards, Rt. 1, Box 460, LaPorte, Indiana or by stopping at any member orchard.

A large number of orchards are located in Berrien County, Michigan. Check with any of the Chambers of Commerce listed in the Categorical Guide.

Confirm with the individual orchard whether their crop is ready. These are approximate dates.

June	1-30	Strawberries
	20-July 20	Cherries
	24-July 15	Gooseberries
July	1-25	Red Raspberries
	4-20	Black Raspberries
	4-30	Sour Cherries
	6-25	Red Currants
	10-20	Dewberries
	15-September 12	Blueberries
	20-August 30	Summer Apples
August	4-October 5	Cantaloupes
	6-September 25	Peaches
	10-October 30	Pears
	12-September 25	Plums
	25-October 31	Grapes
September	15-November 5	Fall Apples

THE KANKAKEE AREA

The Kankakee River begins at Mud Lake near South Bend and winds through Indiana and Illinois in a southwesterly course, joining the Illinois River and finally flowing into the Mississippi.

The Kankakee got its name from the Indian A-ki-ki, meaning wolf, because a band of Mohicans lived on its banks and terrified other tribes of the area.

LaSalle and Marquette and countless other missionaries and explorers moved through this land. Indian tribes lived and hunted and left their burial grounds here. And thousands of settlers followed trails first marked by the Indians.

The most famous stretch of this river was the 500,000 acre Grand Marsh, between English Lake, Indiana and Momence, Illinois, an immense sponge that for centuries attracted millions of migrating birds and made the area one of the greatest concentrations of waterfowl in the world. Prairie chickens once abounded in this hunter's paradise, as did otter, mink and deer. Wolves, fox and raccoons are the major wildlife survivors today.

Around the turn of the century gentlemen hunters from as far away as England began coming to the Kankakee. These sportsmen, whose wives were known as "Kankakee widows", built a number of clubhouses for themselves in the English Lake and Baum's Bridge areas; a few abandoned buildings remain. Among the most famous of the sportsmen was General Lew Wallace who, idling down the river on his houseboat, conceived his most famous book, *Ben Hur*.

Over the years, through constant draining of the Kankakee flood plains, farm land was uncovered for raising peppermint, corn, potatoes, onions, blueberries and asparagus. But with the draining and clearing of 600,000 acres, and straightening of the river, the natural flood control which the Kankakee had provided for the areas south and west was sacrificed. The hunters blasted the wildlife; the great marshy sponge which had attracted

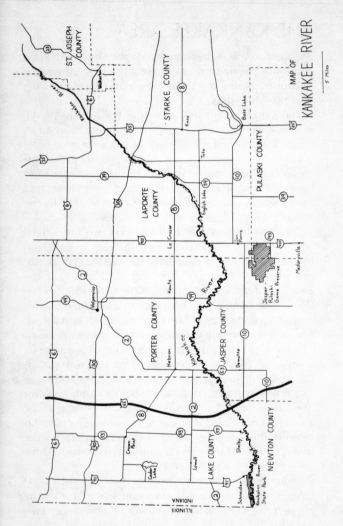

MAP OF
KANKAKEE RIVER

5 Miles

the waterlife was gone and the migrating birds stopped coming; lumbermen timbered the woodlands almost bare. It was, in short, a devastation so terrible and so complete that by the early '20's the hunters, fishermen, conservationists, legislators and agronomists finally united and began the slow and painful work of partial restoration of the marsh.

Now the Kankakee is again a storm center. This time violent opposition is building up toward the plan of the Army Engineers to use 300,000 acres of the Kankakee Valley as an experimental dumping ground for various kinds of waste matter from the Chicago and Calumet areas.

DEMOTTE (1,697 population)

DeMotte is the asparagus capital of the country, and each year farmers harvest 800 acres of this choice crop. The farmers have names like DeVries and Walstra and all of them are descendants of "wooden shoe" Dutch settlers, a term used to distinguish them from the Amish Dutch. They work hard, they pray devoutly, and they close up tight on Sundays.

DeMotters have been raising asparagus for fifty years. In May and June visitors can watch the asparagus carts in the fields. These carts, designed by a local blacksmith, hold four to ten pickers who sit backwards, feet raised, fingers gloved. As they swing on swivel seats, they snap the vegetable spears from the ground. Until very recently asparagus time meant the children were needed in the fields, so school started late each morning. Now, with a consolidated school system, which ranks arithmetic as more important than asparagus, the farmers are trying to replace the youngsters with agile housewives.

To See and Do

FARMS AND FARM PRODUCE. Eenigenburg. Rt. 231, one-half mile north of town (987-3500). The Eenigenburg family have several asparagus farms of their own, and in addition haul half of the whole local crop. Visitors are welcome to watch the operation, and at very reasonable prices can buy asparagus, plants, and flowers.

HISTORICAL MARKER. Rt. 231 at Kankakee River. Commemorates spot where LaSalle's expedition stopped en route from South Bend to Mississippi River.

RECREATION.

CAMPING. KOA Campground. I-65 and Rt. 10 (987-3132).

RESTAURANT. Forest River Lodge at Ramsey's Landing. South side of Kankakee River off Rt. 231. Mooring dock for boaters. Sandwiches and beer.

SPECIAL EVENT. Town and Country Day. The last Saturday before the Fourth of July, after the asparagus harvest and before the blueberry season begins. A grand parade, antique cars, floats, Dutch dances, a pork roast at the local school, and a tour of local farms. For details call (987-2537).

ENGLISH LAKE (60 population)

This tiny hamlet is located where the Yellow and Kankakee Rivers meet. Trout, walleye and channel fish abound beginning in early March. Deer drink at the river's edge and wild flowers bloom everywhere.

This is the area where tycoons had their game clubs. There is good duck and goose hunting still, and the Kankakee Wildlife Area is a mile or two to the east. However, since blinds are at a premium at the Area before dawn, private blinds (owned by Gumps, Christianson and Chesak) are available.

To See and Do

BOATS-LAUNCHING. Public ramp, Rt. 55 at Kankakee River.

BOATS-RENTALS. English Lake: Mrs. James Wickizer, 650W (754-2174).

Shelby: Mrs. Eleanora Ballard, Rt. 55 at Kankakee River (552-0188).

HEBRON (1,624 population)

This town is named for Abraham's Biblical village in Canaan. Hebron lies in the valley of the Kankakee, near the once great marshland, and was originally a Potawattomi settlement. The last library built by the Carnegie Foundation is here. So is the Porter County Herald, the only Democratic paper in the county, and the best source of farm auction ads.

To See and Do

HISTORICAL MARKER. Rt. 2, two miles south of Hebron. "Huakiki" (Indian Town Village) was the winter home and oldest and largest village of the Potawattomi. It was abandoned when the tribe moved to Kansas.

MUSEUM. The Alyeas, a pioneer family, have spearheaded several restorations, among them the Stage Coach Inn, an 1849 hostelry on Main Street (996-2700). The key to this small museum must be obtained from the Alyea auto agency directly across the street.

RESTAURANTS. Country Kitchen. Main (996-5241). Monday–Saturday, 6 a.m.–8 p.m.; Sunday, 7 a.m.–8 p.m. Plain but excellent cooking. Home-made pies.

Old Heritage Inn. Main (996-9010). Weekdays, sandwich lunch; dinner, 4:30–10; Saturday until 2 a.m. with dancing. Closed Sunday. Bar. One hundred years old.

KNOX (3,519 population)

To See and Do

FISH HATCHERY. Bass Lake Fish Hatchery. South of Knox on Rt. 35 to Toto Road. Turn east for two miles to Lake Road. Follow Lake Road south to Bass Lake and turn east one-half mile (772-2353). Open daily to sunset. Eighteen acres, fifteen ponds. This is the only bass hatchery in midwest.

CEMETERY. Crown Hill Cemetery. East Lake Street, north of town. Reputedly the smallest man in the world was buried here. Che Ma was two feet four inches, three inches shorter than Tom Thumb. He came from China in 1881, spent his working life with a circus, and retired to Knox where he lived to the ripe old age of eighty-eight.

RECREATION.

PARK. Bass Lake State Park (same directions as hatchery) (772-2243). 1,600 acres. Water skiing, swimming, picnicking, boat launch, camping.

SHOP. Toto's. West on Rt. 3 to Toto Road (772-4533). Vast discount store in the middle of nowhere.

KOUTS (7,388 population)

Kouts got its name during the period when the Panhandle Railroad was building a new route from Valparaiso down to the Kankakee River. One evening after a hot day's work, the surveyors stopped at a farm and asked for food and shelter. The lady of the house was making apple butter in the yard and asked to be excused. At the next farm, however, the latchstring was out and Bernhardt Kouts and his wife offered them bed, board and a full larder. Later when a townsite had to be named, the Kouts were honored by the surveyors.

Kouts was settled by Germans, Poles, and Irish who came to work on the railroads and stayed on to farm. It was also an early gathering place for hunters, sportsmen and fishermen because it was not far from the Kankakee River. In 1889 an eighty round world's featherweight boxing championship was held here.

To See and Do

HISTORICAL SITES. Baum's Bridge. Take Rt. 8 east from Kouts till you come to Baum's Bridge Road. Head south to the river. This bridge was built in 1863 where the old Potawattomi Trail forded the river and it is on the site where Father Marquette preached Christianity to the local Indians.

Boone Grove. 350W and 650S. This tiny hamlet is largely remembered as the site of the Wark Mound, one of the oldest Indian burial tombs in the area. In 1912 an excavation team from the University of Illinois dug up a circle of seated skeletons holding tools and weapons, and the archaeologists removed every prehistoric relic.

Dunn's Bridge. Rt. 8 to 500S. Turn south to Kankakee River. This walking bridge was made from part of a ferris wheel used in 1893 at the Chicago World's Fair.

Tassonong Grove. Baum's Bridge Road and Rt. 49. This tiny settlement, named for Tassements (French for trade post), was probably the site of an old French post as early as 1673. All that remains of this oldest village in northern Indiana is a marker.

RECREATION.

CAMPING. Donna Joe Campground. 1200S and 350E (462-1545). Swimming, fishing, hiking, picnicking, boat rental, boat ramp.

RESTAURANTS. Hilliard's. Main (766-3851). Open daily, 11–8. Reservations necessary Sunday. Family style.

John's Corner Tap. Main (766-9930). Fish fry, Fridays, 4:30-10. Walleye, perch, or other fresh water fish.

SHOP. Horn's Chocolate Factory. Four and a half blocks east of Rt. 49 on Rt. 8 (766-2241). Saturday and Sunday, 1–6. The chocolate store is housed in an A-frame next to factory. Company makes chocolate bars, cocoa crisp, white bark, and their products are used for fund raising by organizations all over the United States.

TOURS. Heinold fertilizer plant. Rt. 8, four and a half miles west of Kouts (766-2234). Of interest to young chemists.

Heinold grain elevator. Rt. 49 south past two railroad tracks (766-2234). Visitors are welcome five and a half days a week. See wheat being brought to elevators in July and soy beans and corn in the fall.

Heinold hog yards. Down street from grain elevator. (766-2221). Call for arrangements. Heinold is the largest independent hog buyer in the world, and there are always from two hundred to a thousand hogs in the yard. Visitors should bring boots for walking in the yard and a plastic bag to bring them home.

SPECIAL FACILITY. Chamber of Commerce. 406 Main (766-2228).

LA CROSSE (697 population)

La Crosse is named for the "crossing" of two railroads, the Monon and the Pennsylvania. Actually at one time five railroads came through town. In 1868 when the Pennsy wanted to reroute several miles of its right-of-way, this engineering feat was accomplished in thirty-six hours by hundreds of men and horses carrying and relocating ties and track. La Crosse was also a gathering place for hundreds of sorrowing Americans as the Lincoln funeral train came by the Monon depot on its way to Michigan City.

In early La Crosse many homes were built on stilts to avoid the flooding that came at every rise of the Kankakee River.

To See and Do

ANTIQUES. Jackson Antiques. Rt. 421 in town (938-5018). Country items.

Das Anttikaus. One mile south of intersection of Rts. 421 and 8. Turn three-quarters mile west on 2100S (754-2265). Daily, 9–5; Sunday, 1–5. Ring great outside bell.

FARM. LaVern Krueger's angus farm. 2100S (754-2402). Call for appointment and family will be delighted to show children their breed herd.

MUSEUM. Miller's Museum*. Three miles south of town on Rt. 421 (754-2255). Open Sundays during summer, 9–6. Old tractors, steam engines and antiques.

RECREATION.

BOATS-RENTAL. Miller's Landing. Rt. 421 at the Kankakee River.

WILDLIFE AREA. Kankakee State Game and Fish Area. Rt. 8 near Rt. 39 (754-2237). In 1927 farmers of Starke and LaPorte Counties donated tracts of their swampland to the state, and that gift was to mark the beginning of this preserve which is one of the oldest in Indiana. 2,000 acres. Camping, boat launch; migrating ducks and deer in season; fishing for walleye, muskie, channel fish.

SHOP. Railroad Salvage. South on Rt. 421 to 2300S. Turn one-quarter mile west (285-2515). Damaged and unclaimed freight including groceries and building supplies.

MEDARYVILLE (732 population)

To See and Do

TREE NURSERY. Jasper-Pulaski Tree Nursery. Rt. 421, north of Medaryville (843-4827). Indiana residents can purchase seedlings of many varieties at bargain prices, and everyone can visit black walnut orchards from which genetically healthy specimens are grown.

WILDLIFE AREA. Jasper-Pulaski State Wildlife Area. Five miles north of Medaryville on Rts. 421 and 143 (843-3641). 7,585 acres with full camping and picnic facilities. Fishing, hunting in season, hiking trails, archery, skeet shooting; buffalo, a deer herd, hundreds of pheasants, and an observation platform for viewing rare sandhill cranes which stop at Jasper-Pulaski on their migrations from Canada to Florida. Bring binoculars.

SCHNEIDER (426 population)

RECREATION.

CAMPING. Duncan's Lake* (693-7328). Picnicking, boating.

WILDLIFE AREA. LaSalle State Game and Fish Area. Northeast corner of Rt. 41 and 150N (992-3019). 800 acres. Fishing, hunting, picnicking, camping, ice skating, ice fishing, boat ramp.

WALKERTON (2,006 population)

Walkerton is the mint capital of the nation. Ninety percent of all oil of peppermint and spearmint, used for flavoring everything from chewing gum to juleps, is grown here.

To See and Do

AUCTION. Walkerton Sale Barn. Rt. 23, three-quarters of a mile north of town (586-3159). Pony and horse auctions on the third Saturday of each month. Also a flourishing livestock auction and market is held here in a cowboy atmosphere.

FARMS AND FARM PRODUCE. Carl Webb's gladiola farm.

Rt. 4 southeast of Walkerton to blinker and take Rt. 104 for three miles. Second turn to right. The house is on left side of road (325-9659). Webb grows 20,000 gladiola bulbs of some 100 name varieties, has an acre or two of organic vegetables and sells both crops to the public.

HISTORICAL MARKER. In the center of town, a placque honors native son, Harold Urey, 1934 Nobel Prize winner for the discovery of deuterium.

BEYOND

In this section we bend our firm rule: "places listed are within an hour's driving distance of the National Lakeshore." What follows are the exceptions, the places BEYOND which, for one reason or another, are worthy of notice.

CULVER, Indiana, Rt. 117.

Home of famed Culver Military Academy, now co-ed. The campus borders beautiful Lake Maxinkuckee, one of Indiana's largest. You can watch the Black Horse Troop on parade. Culver Inn (842-3331) overlooks the lake and is open to the public for dinner daily from 6–9 (except Mondays); and for lunch from noon to 2 on Saturdays and Sundays. Reservations necessary. Also try the ice cream at The Shack on campus, open daily, 7:30 to 7:30. Public swimming and water skiing on the lake and sailboat rentals too.

ELKHART Area, Indiana, Rt. 80-90, Exits 9 and 10

Amish Livestock Auction. Rt. 13, three miles east of Middlebury. Every Wednesday, the Amish livestock auction begins at 8 a.m. This is an old-fashioned market day, very lively and colorful.

Krider Nurseries. One-half block north of Rt. 13 in center of Middlebury (825-5714). Spring and fall, Monday–Friday, 7–5; Saturday, 7–4. Open Sunday without assistance. Closed: Saturdays during December and January; June 15–August 15. 350 acres of plant and nursery stock. Three generations have been operating this huge wholesale and retail business for nearly eighty years.

Michiana Mennonite Relief Sale. County fairgrounds in Goshen. Yearly in late September. Call Elkhart Chamber of Commerce (293-1531) for exact date. Hand-pieced quilts and hand-made clocks sold at auction. Expensive. Huge crowds. Food in plain folk style: hog sausage, pancakes, applebutter, barbecued chicken and rosettes

(Mennonite doughnuts) cooked before your eyes.

Patchwork Quilt Restaurant. Rt. 80-90, Exit 10. Take Rt. 13 north to County Road 2, one mile west (825-2417). This is a first-class restaurant located on a beautiful 350 acre working farm. Reserve a couple of days in advance, because in season they pick and cook vegetables to order. Charming checkered table cloths, flowers and cats and piglets everywhere.

The River Queen. A real stern wheeler river boat which can be chartered to cruise up and down the St. Joseph River. Contact Mr. Macumber, 110 Bower Court, Elkhart (524-0264).

HOLLAND, Michigan, Rt. 31.

The Tulip Festival, four days in mid-May, is well worth the long drive to Holland. The town, the day, the events are Dutch to the core, with scrubbed streets, traditional Dutch dances in costume, parades, antiques, bands, floats. See the DeKlomp Wooden Shoe Factory, windmills, Netherlands Museum, and tulips, tulips, tulips. If you can't get to Amsterdam this year, then call the Holland Chamber of Commerce and arrange a Dutch treat (392-2389). Make reservations early. Mobbed.

NAPPANEE, Indiana, Rts. 6 and 19.

Amish Acres.* (773-3611). Tours, 9–5; Sunday 1–6. Four day art festival in August. This is Amish and Mennonite country (the latter are called "Jump the Fence" because they are less strict). Great chance to see how life was led a century ago by our grandparents, and is still led by some Americans. There's a twelve room farm house, a summer kitchen, pump, barn with animals, kitchen garden, smoke house, root cellar, drying sheds. There are "bonnet and britches" tours for the young, horse and buggy rides, a picnic grove. There's also an Amish restaurant where you can "eat till it ouches" daily, Memorial Day to Labor Day, 11–4.

In downtown Nappanee don't miss the old Market Street where the horse and buggies still come. Also a maple sugar grove, a buggy shop. Please don't take pictures of the Amish people. It is offensive to them.

PAW PAW Area, Michigan, I-94, Exit 60.

The Paw Paw area has an annual Grape and Wine Festival the third weekend in September. Wine tasting, a carnival, an art show and a grape stomping demonstration are part of the fiesta atmosphere. One can also tour the local wineries, which are also open year-round. Call Paw Paw Chamber of Commerce for specifics (657-5627). Be prepared for crowds and lines.

TOURS. Bronte Champagne and Wine Company. County Road 687 (Keeler Road), Hartford, five miles south of Exit 46 on I-94 (621-3419). Monday–Saturday, 10–4.

Frontenac Wine Company. West Red Arrow, Paw Paw (657-5531).

St. Julian Wine Company. 716 South Kalamazoo, Paw Paw (657-5568). Monday–Saturday, 9–11:30 and 1–4.

Warner Vineyards. 706 South Kalamazoo, Paw Paw (657-5765). Film on wine making shown in Ye Old Wine Haus. Visitors can sample a large variety of the locally produced wines and champagnes.

Welch Grape Company. South four miles on M40 from Paw Paw exit, I-94 to Laughton. (624-4141). Reservations necessary. Only groups can tour this huge plant. The grapes are not fermented, but you can see jams, jellies and grapejuice in the making.

PERU, Indiana, Rt. 124.

This is the town which bills itself as Circus Capital of the World, and in its heyday Peru was winter headquarters for seven major circuses. The aura is still there. On Rt. 31, six miles south of town, you can see circus animals on the Paul Kelly farm. Each summer during the third week of July the community puts on a three-ring circus, amateur, but very good. Trapeze work, aerial artistry, all topped by a magnificent parade. Also the Circus Museum on the grounds is open from June to September. Group tours.

There are two other museums rich in circus lore: Miami County Historical Museum, on the fourth floor of the court house, 9 till noon except Sundays and holidays; and Peterbaugh Museum, 11 North Huntington, 1–5 except Sundays, Wednesdays, and holidays.

Peru Chamber of Commerce (317-473-6653).

PLYMOUTH, Indiana, Rt. 30 to Rt. 17.

Marshall County Blueberry Festival. Saturday–Monday, Labor Day weekend. A real country outing with garden tractor pull, thieves' market, antiques, horse show, arts and crafts, bands, ball games and B-L-U-E-B-E-R-R-I-E-S. For details call Plymouth Chamber of Commerce, 120 West Washington (936-2323).

SAUGATUCK Area, Michigan, I-94 to I-196.

The well-known summer resort village of Saugatuck has fourteen antique stores and nine art galleries in the area.

S.S. Keewatin.* Berthed in Kalamazoo Lake, off Center Street, Douglas. Open daily, 10–5, June 1–October 1 (857-2158). This 1907 boat plied the Lake Huron-Lake Superior waters until 1965 and now houses a marine museum. Guided tours.

Island Queen.* Berthed at Anchor Park, Water Street, Saugatuck (857-2453). Mid-June–Labor Day. Cruises on the Kalamazoo River and Lake Michigan. Four trips daily.

Mt. Baldhead. Across Kalamazoo River from downtown Saugatuck. A 282-step climb gives a superb view of the Lake Michigan coastline. Radar installation on summit.

Willowbend Farm. Ganges Exit, I-196 (227-3400). Saturday–Sunday, spring and fall. Daily, July and August. A potpourri of pottery, baskets, craftwork and antiques housed in a lovely three-story barn.

SOUTH HAVEN, Michigan, I-94 to I-196.

South Haven is one of the larger resort areas in southwestern Michigan. Just over an hour's driving distance from the National Lakeshore, it is mid-way between

Benton Harbor and Saugatuck.

National Blueberry Festival. Thursday-Sunday, the third week in July. Parade, pie-eating contest, flea market, bakeathon, ox roast, sports events, entertainment.

Clothesline Art Show. Johnson Park. First Sunday in July. One of the better regional arts and crafts sales in a lovely setting overlooking Lake Michigan. Plenty of blueberry pie and ice cream available.

Black River Orchids. 77th and Blue Star Memorial Highway (637-5085). Largest wholesale grower of orchids in Michigan opens greenhouses by appointment. Guided tours.

Chamber of Commerce. 556 Phoenix (637-1450).

BEYOND REASON

Shambarger's. Redkey, Indiana, Rt. 1, one hour south of Fort Wayne (317-369-2216). Indiana's most famous restaurant, known both for gourmet food and entertainment by owner. Open Thursday to Sunday only for dinner at seven sharp. Located in a tiny hamlet close to the Ohio border, this whacky establishment caters to enterprising souls who drive from all over the mid-west and wait at least six months for reservations. The tab is $18.50 per person plus tip and the surroundings are unpretentious and cluttered. But an evening at this dining spot is really worth the wait and the drive. Owner John Shambarger cuts up in a five hour solo show, changing outfits, singing, dancing and cooking up a storm. The patrons are stuffed with delicious food including home-made dill bread, shrimp cocktail, cheese fondue, soup, prime rib au flambeau and gargantuan fresh strawberry pie. No liquor is served. The menu is fixed, the dishes are mismatched and the ninety guests are squeezed together at round tables.

Calendar
of Events

DATE	EVENT	LOCATION	PHONE*
First Week in May	Blossomtime Festival	Benton Harbor, Michigan	925-7019
Mid-May	Tulip Time	Holland, Michigan	392-2389
Sunday nearest June 14	Flag Day Parade	Three Oaks, Michigan	no phone
Last Weekend in June	Miss Indiana Pageant	Michigan City, Indiana	874-6221
July	Pinney-Purdue Field Day	Wanatah, Indiana	733-2379
July	Summer Festival	Michigan City, Indiana	874-6221
First Sunday in July	Clothesline Art Show	South Haven, Michigan	637-1450
Last Saturday before July 4	Town and Country Day	DeMotte, Indiana	987-2537
July 4th	Parade	Whiting, Indiana	659-0292
Fourth of July Weekend	Old Fashioned Celebration	Hobart, Indiana	942-5744
Second Sunday in July	Art Fair	St. Joseph, Michigan	983-0271

DATE	EVENT	LOCATION	PHONE*
Third Week in July	Circus Festival	Peru, Indiana	317-473-6653
First Weekend in August	Gladiolus Festival	Coloma, Michigan	468-6601
First Week in August	Porter County Fair	Valparaiso, Indiana	462-1105
First Week in August	St. Joseph County 4-H Fair	South Bend, Indiana	284-9604
Second Week in August	LaPorte County Fair	LaPorte, Indiana	362-2647
Early August	Art Fair	Chesterton, Indiana	926-5513
Mid-August	Art Fair	Nappanee, Indiana	773-3611
Mid-August	Berrien County Youth Fair	Berrien Springs, Michigan	473-4251
Third Week in August	Lake County Fair	Crown Point, Indiana	663-0428
Labor Day Weekend	Blueberry Festival	Plymouth, Indiana	936-2323
Labor Day Weekend	Steam Show	Hesston, Indiana	no phone
Early September	Mexican Independence Day	East Chicago, Indiana	398-1600
Third Weekend in September	Grape and Wine Festival	Paw Paw, Michigan	657-5627
Late September	Michiana Mennonite Relief Sale	Goshen, Indiana	293-1531
Second Week in October	Apple Festival	Niles, Michigan	683-3720

*Remember the southwestern Michigan area code is 616 and northern Indiana's area code is 219.

Tours

This is a section of outings. Some are planned for rainy days; some for kids; some for antique buffs. We've tried to provide variety. Don't be scared off by the mileage given for each tour; it's round trip. In many cases, the hours spent will depend on you and your interest. We've listed an approximate time. The routings have been carefully worked out, but governors create detours. Remember that all directions start and end at the Lakeshore Visitor Center. Adjust your plans if you are coming from elsewhere. Keep in mind the Michigan time change. Use the phone numbers included in each tour to make sure nothing has changed. If you should get lost, we consider the entire area beautiful and/or interesting. Serendipity breeds new tours.

In Search of Antiques   MILES : 90
(A Saturday in Late May)   HOURS: 6

Take a look at the old Tratebas Mill near Valparaiso, charmingly restored as a home, with fine gardens. Then drive down Old Suman Road and enjoy the countryside. Stop in to see the elegant antiques at the Marc Nielsen

Country Store. Continue on to the Uphaus Shop for country antiques. In Hebron have a simple, home-cooked lunch at the Country Kitchen (996-5241). End up browsing through the thirty-five antique stalls at The Livery in Lowell.

DIRECTIONS: From the Lakeshore Visitor Center, take Kemil Road .8 miles south to Rt. 20. Turn right (west) on Rt. 20 for 2½ miles to the turn on your right marked Rt. 49 south. Follow Rt. 49 south for 5 miles to Tratebas Road. Turn left (east) for a mile on Tratebas Road to see the Tratebas Mill. Then continue on Tratebas Road, jogging south and east for a mile. Turn right (south) at the top of the hill and cross Rt. 6. You are on Old Suman Road. Continue for a mile jogging south and west, to the Marc Nielsen Country Store. For Uphaus Shop, head north on Old Suman Road to Rt. 6. Turn left (west) on Rt. 6 and continue 2 miles to Rt. 49. Turn left (south) on Rt. 49 for 6 miles to the junction with Rt. 2. Follow Rt. 2 southwest for 5 miles to 300W. Turn right (west) for ½ mile to Uphaus. For the Country Kitchen, head east on 300W to Rt. 2. Turn right (southwest) and continue for 8 miles on Rt. 2 to Hebron. The Country Kitchen is on Rt. 2 in the middle of town on the right (west) side of the road. After lunch, continue on Rt. 2 south for 2 miles. Then Rt. 2 turns directly west. Follow it for 11.6 miles to Lowell. The Livery is on the right (north) side of Washington Street immediately after crossing the Monon Railroad tracks. To return to the Visitor Center, proceed east on Rt. 2 to Rt. 49. Go north on Rt. 49 to Rt. 12 and east on Rt. 12 to Kemil Road and the Visitor Center.

Ladies' Day Out   MILES : 30
(Second Saturday in August)   HOURS: 5

Enjoy a guided tour through the sumptuous home of a 19th century railroad car magnate, the Barker Mansion in Michigan City. Prior arrangements are necessary (872-0159). Lunch at The Spa in Porter (926-1654), where you can watch raccoons and birds feeding in the woods while you eat. Then on to Chesterton, just a ten minute drive, for the Chesterton Air Fair where works of Michigan, Illinois and Indiana painters, sculptors and craftsmen are on display. Admission charge.

DIRECTIONS: From the Lakeshore Visitor Center, take Rt. 12 (east) for 7.2 miles to Washington Street (Rt. 421) in Michigan City. Turn right (south) for four blocks. The Barker Mansion is on the northwest corner of 7th and Washington Streets. After your tour, drive one block west on 7th Street to Wabash Street. Turn right (north) on Wabash and return to Rt. 12. Turn left (west) on Rt. 12 and continue for about 12 miles to Mineral Springs Road. Turn left (south) on Mineral Springs Road and continue for .8 miles, crossing Rt. 20, to The Spa which is on the left side of the road. When you've finished lunch, turn right (north) on Mineral Springs Road to Rt. 20. Turn right (east) on Rt. 20 and proceed for 1.8 miles to Rt. 49. Turn left (south) on Rt. 49 for about 2 miles to the first stop light which is Indian Boundary Road. Turn right (west) for ¼ mile to the first stop sign (Indian Boundary Road dead ends here) and turn right (north) on to old Rt. 49. The Art Fair is held on the grounds of the St. Patrick's School which is .1 mile north. To return to the Lakeshore Visitor Center, retrace your route to Rt. 49 and go north to Rt. 12. Take Rt. 12 right (east) to Kemil Road and the Visitor Center.

Pick, Shovel and Beat   MILES : 46
(A Thursday in July)   HOURS: 8

Try your hand at picking pears or apples at the Anderson Orchards near Valparaiso. Be sure to call ahead (462-8568) to check picking conditions. Then take your fruit along for a picnic supper on the beach at Beverly Shores, perhaps after a swim in Lake Michigan. If you plan to have a barbecued meal, be sure to get a permit at the Lakeshore Visitor Center. About 7:30 p.m., pack up and drive over to Michigan City to enjoy the outdoor band concert in Washington Park at 8 p.m.

DIRECTIONS: From the Lakeshore Visitor Center take Rt. 12 (west) for 3 miles to Rt. 49. Turn left (south) on Rt. 49 for 6.7 miles to Rt. 6. Turn left (east) on Rt. 6 for 4.5 miles to Anderson's which is on the left (north) side of the road. When you've finished picking, retrace the route to the Lakeshore Visitor Center. Cross Rt. 12 onto State Park Road. (Don't be confused—State Park Road is a continuation of Kemil Road but changes its name at Rt. 12). Continue on State Park Road almost to the Lake. About 500 yards before the beach, there is a marked beach parking lot on the east side of the road. Leave your car here and walk down to the beach. When it's time for the concert, return to Rt. 12 and turn left (east). Continue on Rt. 12 for 7.2 miles to Pine Street in Michigan City. Turn left (north) on Pine Street and proceed .5 miles and you'll be entering Washington Park. Turn right on the park road and continue ¼ mile to the parking lot which is on your left, across from the zoo. Leave your car here and it's a short walk back to the band shell in the middle of the park. There is a parking charge. After the concert, return to Rt. 12 and go west to Kemil Road and the Lakeshore Visitor Center.

An Architectural Potpourri
(Any Day in June)

MILES : 85
HOURS: 8

This tour will take you to visit a variety of church buildings ranging from a log cabin structure to a towering modern chapel. You will finish with a visit to the oldest house still standing in Lake County. You'll begin by seeing the Augsburg Svenska Skola, the smallest church in Porter County. Then visit the Chapel of the Resurrection in Valparaiso. Be sure to look behind you as you proceed up to the altar to examine the inset windows. Next stop off at the Seven Dolors Shrine near South Haven. After lunch at the Country Lounge in Hobart (942-6074) where the strudel is excellent, spend some time at the Capuchin Seminary near Crown Point. Be sure to see the stained glass windows in the chapel. If you're lucky the monks will be singing in some far off room. On the monastery grounds is a log cabin building, the first Catholic house of worship in Lake County. End your day at the Old Homestead in Crown Point, built in 1847. Call to arrange for your tour (663-0456 or 663-0590) of this charming and well-preserved house.

DIRECTIONS: From Lakeshore Visitor Center, go south for .8 miles on Kemil Road to Rt. 20. Turn right (west) on Rt. 20 for 3.5 miles to Oakhill Road. Angle right and stay west on Oakhill for 2.75 miles to the Svenska Skola church which is on the right side of the road. The church can only be viewed from the road. Then turn around and return to Rt. 20. Angle left (east) on to Rt. 20 and continue for a mile to Rt. 49. Turn right (south) on Rt. 49 and continue for about 13 miles to Lincolnway in Valparaiso. Turn left (east) on Lincolnway for 2 miles to the Valparaiso University entrance on the right. The Chapel of the Resurrection is the tallest building on campus. Park in front of the Moellering Library. For the Seven Dolors Shrine, stay on Lincolnway, and drive through town for 3 miles until Lincolnway merges with Rt. 130. Continue west on Rt. 130 for 3 miles to Rt. 149. Turn right (north) on Rt. 149 for 3 miles to 700N. Turn left (west) on 700N for ¾ miles to the Seven Dolors Shrine. For lunch in Hobart, return to Rt. 149 and turn right (south) for a mile to Rt. 6. Turn right (west) on Rt. 6 and continue for about 9.6 miles to the Country Lounge, which is on the left (south) side of the road. (Rt. 6 is also called 37th Street.) After lunch, proceed a block west on Rt. 6 to I-65 (which is an elevated highway). Take the entrance ramp marked I-65 South on your right and continue approximately 5½ miles south on I-65 to Rt. 30. Exit at Rt. 30 and head right (west) for about 3.1 miles to Burr Road. Turn left (south) on Burr Road for a mile to the Capuchin Seminary. Then return to Rt. 30, turn right and continue east for a mile to Rt. 55. Turn right (south) on Rt. 55 for 4 miles to Courthouse Square in Crown Point. Make a U-turn around the Square. The Old Homestead is at 220 South Court.

  To return to the Visitor Center, head north for 4 miles on Rt. 55 to Rt. 30. Turn right (east) on Rt. 30 for 2.3 miles to Rt. 65. Proceed north on Rt. 65 for 6.3 miles to Rt. 94. Turn right (east) on Rt. 94 for about 13 miles to the Chesterton exit. Turn north from exit ramp on to Rt. 49. Continue for 4.9 miles to Rt. 12. Turn right (east) on Rt. 12 and continue for 3 miles to Kemil Road and the Visitor Center.

An Autumn Drive
(A Sunday Afternoon in October)

MILES : 90
HOURS: 5

For a fall day in the country, start by seeing masses of chrysanthemums in bloom outside of Michigan City. Then try apple picking at the Garwood Orchards near LaPorte (362-4385). Your choice of macs, pippens or delicious. They taste better plucked from the tree. Be sure to try their free apple cider. You might even want to take home a gallon. On your way to dinner at The Timbers in LaPorte (362-4585), see the lovely countryside in the Small Road area.

DIRECTIONS: From the Lakeshore Visitor Center, go south .8 miles on Kemil Road to Rt. 20. Turn left (east) on Rt. 20 for .8 miles to the second railroad crossover on your right (south). Cross the tracks and bear sharp left on Old Chicago Road. In about a mile you'll see a fine chrysanthemum grower's display. You can stop for plants, gourds and dried fall flowers. Continue on Old Chicago Road for 1.6 miles to Brown Road (500E). Turn left (north) on Brown Road for ½ mile to Rt. 20. Turn right (east) on Rt. 20 and continue through the outskirts of Michigan City for 10.4 miles to Rt. 35. Turn right (south) on Rt. 35 for 17 miles to the junction with Rt. 2. Turn right (west) on Rt. 2 for 4.7 miles to Pinola (500W). You'll see the Garwood sign at this intersection. Turn right (north) on 500W for ½ mile to 50S. Turn left (west) on 50S for a mile to the Garwood Orchards. After you've picked your fill, return to 500W and turn left (north). Continue to the first crossroad which is Small Road. Turn right (east) and continue on winding Small Road through the rolling back country to Orr Lake Road. Turn left (north) on Orr

Lake Road and proceed to 150N past Orr Lake. Turn right (south) on 150N to Rt. 2. Turn left (east) on Rt. 2 and return to Rt. 35. Continue north on Rt. 35 to The Timbers, 444 Pine Lake Avenue, on the left hand side of the road. (Within LaPorte, Rt. 35 is called Pine Lake Avenue). To return to the Visitor Center, continue north on Rt. 35 to Rt. 20. Turn left (west) on Rt. 20 to Kemil Road. Turn right (north) on Kemil Road and the Visitor Center.

A Bus Tour to the Wine Country
(A Saturday in late September)

MILES : 165
HOURS: A Day

Winelovers, summon up your thirst, hire a bus and sample six Michigan brands. The drive is beautiful and the variety ample enough for any taste. End up the day at a first rate restaurant in many a mile, Tosi's in Stevensville, which has its own large wine cellar. Reservations are advised (429-3689). Take home some delicious pastry from the Bit of Swiss Bakery on the premises.

DIRECTIONS: From the Lakeshore Visitor Center, take Kemil Road .8 miles south to Rt. 20. Turn left (east) for 6.7 miles to Rt. 421. Turn right (south) on Rt. 421 for a little less than a mile to the I-94 entrance ramp. Go east on I-94 toward Benton Harbor for about 25 miles to Exit 16 (Bridgman). Take the right hand ramp to the stop light. Turn right on Lake Street and follow the Tabor Hill Vineyard's blue and white signs through Bridgman. (Lake Street becomes Shawnee Road). Follow Shawnee through the lovely rolling countryside to Hill Road. Turn right (south) on Hill Road to the Vineyard. There's wine testing in the Tabor Hill A-frame headquarters and if you're lucky you can go out and pick some ripe grapes. Then return to I-94 for a further 20 minute trip of about 22 miles of Exit 46 (Hartford). Turn right on County Road 687 for about 4 miles to Keeler Road where the Bronte Wine Company is located. They conduct tours and have wine tasting too. Save some space for the next four wineries, about 16 miles further along I-94 at exit 60 (Paw Paw). Turn left (north) on Rt. 40 for a mile to Paw Paw. You'll come first to the Frontenac Wine Company on the

Red Arrow Highway and just around the corner are the Michigan Wineries at 706 Kalamazoo Street and the St. Julian Wine Company and the LaSalle Wine Company at 716 Kalamazoo Street. All four have tours and wine-tasting too. For dinner return to I-94 and go south about 35 miles to Stevensville, Exit 17. Go right (west) for a mile crossing Business I-94 to Tosi's at 4337 Ridge Road. To return to the Visitor Center, retrace your route to I-94 and continue southwest to the Chesterton exit. Turn north onto Rt. 49 and continue to Rt. 12. Follow Rt. 12 east to Kemil Road and the Visitor Center.

A Day for the Kids
(The Third Saturday in July)

MILES : 100
HOURS: 6

Load your youngsters into the car for a day in the country. First stop at Bendix Woods Park in New Carlisle—just a half hour drive for a picnic and a walk along the trails. Drive on for another half hour to the Martin Blad Farm near South Bend. Call ahead (287-9022) and they'll take you and your brood on a tour of one of the biggest peppermint farms in the country. See the mint crop being harvested and pressed for the Wrigley gum of the future. Bring along boots if the weather has been rainy. Then it's another short drive to the Walkerton Pony Barn where you can watch a real live auction in progress.

DIRECTIONS: From the Lakeshore Visitor Center, take Kemil Road south .8 miles to Rt. 20. Turn left (east) and continue 21 miles on Rt. 20 toward South Bend. At this point Rt. 20 turns north and Rt. 2 continues east. Stay on Rt. 2 for 7 miles. The entrance to Bendix Woods Park is on the right (south) side of Rt. 2 just beyond the turnoff to New Carlisle. For the peppermint farm, continue east on Rt. 2 for 8 miles to the Rt. 20 bypass. Turn right (south) and continue for 2 miles on the bypass to Rt. 23. Turn right (southwest) on Rt. 23. The Martin Blad Farm is on the right (west) side of the road a few miles beyond the bypass. Look for their bright yellow wagons. For the Walkerton Pony Barn, continue south on Rt. 23 for 14

miles. The barn is on the right (west) side of the road,
three-quarters of a mile before Walkerton. To return to
the Visitor Center, head northeast on Rt. 23 to the Rt. 20
bypass. Go north on the bypass to Rt. 2. Turn left (west)
on Rt. 2 and continue until Rt. 2 joins Rt. 20. Continue
west on Rt. 20 to Kemil Road. Turn right (north) on Kemil
Road and the Visitor Center.

Another Day for the Kids
(Any Summer Day)

MILES : 114
HOURS: 6

Start out after breakfast with everyone's boots stowed in
the trunk and plastic bags for bringing them home.
You'll be in Kouts in less than an hour. First stop is the
Heinold Hog Yards. Call ahead (766-2221), to arrange a
tour. After the youngsters have seen and smelled their
fill of pigs about to go to market, down the street at the
Heinold Grain Elevator they can watch wheat being
loaded in July and soybeans and corn in the fall. It's quite
a sight. If there's a young chemist in your crew, drive on
to the Heinold Fertilizer Plant. Then on to the Jasper-Pulaski State Wildlife Area for a picnic, a climb up the observation tower and glimpses of buffalo, deer and thousands of pheasants.

DIRECTIONS: From the Lakeshore Visitor Center, take
Kemil Road .8 miles south to Rt. 20. Turn right (west) on
Rt. 20 for 2½ miles to Rt. 49. Turn right at the Rt. 49 south
entrance ramp. Cross over Rt. 20 and continue south for
24 miles to Kouts. The Heinold Hog Yard is on the left
(east) side of Rt. 49, past the railroad tracks. You can see
the grain elevator from the yard. To get to the Heinold
Fertilizer Plant (called the Alysworth Elevator) return to
Rt. 49 and go north a block to the intersection with Rt. 8.
Turn left (west) on Rt. 8 for 4.5 miles. The plant is on the
left (south) side of the road. For lunch turn around and
go east on Rt. 8 for 17½ miles to Rt. 421. Turn right
(south) on Rt. 421 and continue for 13 miles to the Jasper-Pulaski Wildlife Area. The entrance is on the right
(west) side of the road just north of Medaryville. To re-

turn to the Visitor Center head north for about 44 miles on Rt. 421 to Rt. 20. Turn left (west) on Rt. 20 for 6.7 miles to Kemil Road. Turn right (north) on Kemil Road for .8 miles to the Visitor Center.

Highlights of South Bend
(A Summer Saturday)

MILES : 77
HOURS: All Day

Begin your day in South Bend by visiting the Notre Dame campus. Student guides will take you on a personally conducted tour. Just leave your car in the Visitor Parking Lot near the main gate and meet your guide at the information booth. In about an hour you will see the highspots of the campus and return to the main gate. Just across the street is the Morris Inn (234-0141) where you can have a pleasant lunch. Then go on to the Thieves Market where forty antique dealers display their collections in individual stalls. End up the day at the Farmers Market where a profusion of fresh produce is on sale.

DIRECTIONS: From the Lakeshore Visitor Center, take Kemil Road south .8 mile to Rt. 20. Turn left (east) on Rt. 20 for 6.7 miles to Rt. 421. Turn right (south) on Rt. 421 for 6.7 miles to the Indiana Toll Road entrance on the right. Be sure to use the ramp marked Ohio and East. At Exit 8, South Bend (37.7 miles) turn right (south) on Rt. 33 for about a mile to Angela Boulevard. Turn left (east) on Angela and continue to the first traffic light which is Notre Dame Avenue. Turn left (north) and continue for a block to the main gate. After your tour and lunch, drive south on Notre Dame Avenue to the traffic light at Angela Boulevard, which becomes Edison Road at this intersection. Turn left (east) on Edison Road and continue for 2 miles. The Thieves Market is at 3309 Edison Road. To reach the Farmers Market which is at 760 South Eddy Street, turn around and go west on Edison Road for 2 miles to the stoplight, which is Eddy Street. Turn right (south) and continue for a mile on Eddy to South Bend Avenue. Turn right (west) on South Bend Avenue and continue for about a mile until the road turns left. At this

point South Bend Avenue becomes Hill Street. Continue
on Hill for several blocks to Jefferson Street. Turn right
(west) on Jefferson for a block to Frances Street. Turn left
(south) on Frances and continue for 2 blocks. At this
point Frances becomes Northside Drive. Continue on
Northside around the bend of the St. Joseph River and
you will see the Farmers Market on your left. To return to
the Visitor Center retrace your route to Rt. 33 and continue north to the Indiana Toll Road. Drive west on the
Toll Road to the Michigan City exit. Continue north on
Rt. 421 to Rt. 20. Turn left (west) on Rt. 20 to Kemil Road.
Turn right (north) on Kemil Road to the Visitor Center.

Industry at Work   MILES : 115
(Weekdays from Memorial Day   HOURS: A Day
to Labor Day)

Want to see an industrial research laboratory in operation? Or watch the manufacture of washing machines or
electronic kits? Or visit a fruit auction? You can combine
all these experiences and have a delicious dinner to boot
in a day in Benton Harbor. The Whirlpool Company
opens both its research and manufacturing divisions to
visitors. Call (926-5000) a week in advance to arrange
your tours. The Heath Company (983-3961), world's largest manufacturer of electronic kits, offers tours at 10 a.m.
and 2 p.m. The Benton Harbor Fruit Market is a fascinating place to see farmers selling their crops of fruits and
vegetables. On your way back stop in for dinner at Win
Schuler's in Stevensville (429-3273), where the food is
hearty and the atmosphere pleasant.

DIRECTIONS: From the Lakeshore Visitor Center, go south
.8 mile on Kemil Road to Rt. 20. Turn left (east) on Rt. 20
for 6.7 miles to Rt. 421. Turn right (south) on Rt. 421 for a
little less than a mile to the I-94 East entrance ramp on
your right. Take I-94 for 37 miles to Exit 27 (Niles Avenue). To visit the Whirlpool Research Laboratory: turn
left (north) on Niles Avenue (Rt. 33) and continue for 5
miles to the center of downtown St. Joseph. Turn right

(east) at the second traffic light which is Main Street. Continue on Main Street, crossing the Blossom Land Bridge for 3 miles. The Whirlpool Administration Center is on your right. To visit the Whirlpool Manufacturing Division: turn left (north) on Niles Avenue (Rt. 33) and continue for 5 miles to the center of downtown St. Joseph. Turn right (east) at the second traffic light which is Main Street. Continue on Main Street and cross the Blossom Land Bridge. Immediately after crossing the bridge, turn right (south) on Upton Drive. Follow Upton Drive which curves several times and the visitor's parking lot will be on your right.

After you have visited either or both of the Whirlpool operations, return to Main Street and head west recrossing the Blossom Land Bridge. Turn left (south) at Ship Street and continue for ¼ mile at which point Ship Street becomes Wayne Street. Follow Wayne Street to downtown Benton Harbor. After you cross a bridge, Wayne Street becomes Main Street. Continue on Main Street through downtown Benton Harbor. Main Street then becomes East Main Street. Follow East Main Street to its junction with M-139. Turn left (north) on M-139 to first traffic light which is Territorial Road. Turn left on Territorial for ¾ mile. The Fruit Market is at 1891 Territorial Road on the left hand side of the road. To reach the Heath Company, which has its plant on Hilltop Road in Benton Harbor, retrace your route to Main Street, St. Joseph and head west. Continue on Main Street past the Niles Avenue stoplight to next stop light which is Hilltop Road. Turn left (east) on Hilltop and continue for 500 feet to the Heath Company plant.

When you're ready to head back for dinner, retrace your route to the intersection of Hilltop Road and Main Street. Turn left (south) on Main Street which becomes Lakeshore Drive and follow Lakeshore 4.5 miles to Exit 27 of I-94. The entrance ramp is on your right. Now head south on the lane marked I-94 Chicago. At the Stevensville exit (9 miles) turn left and cross over I-94 to the first intersection, the Red Arrow Highway. Turn left (north) to Win Schuler's which is just a few yards away at 5000 Red Arrow Highway. To return to the Visitor Center, go southeast on the Red Arrow Highway through Bridgman and Lakeside until it becomes Rt. 12 north of New Buffalo. Continue on Rt. 12 to Kemil Road and the Visitor Center.

For Eager Gardeners

MILES : 70

(A Summer Day)

HOURS: 5

Start out with a visit to the Bernacchi Greenhouses, 1010 Fox Street, LaPorte. Their shop is open year round, but on May 1 and December 1 you can tour the greenhouses. Then go on to see the herb garden and the begonias at the John Hancock Orchards. Drive on to Heston Gardens. The charming landscaped premises have been lovingly fashioned by a Greek Orthodox priest. There's also a tiny chapel in the woods. Lunch at the Golden Door (469-1191) in New Buffalo. End the day with a visit to the Rainbow Gardens in Bridgman. Enjoy their perennials, rock garden and extensive sedum plantings.

DIRECTIONS: From the Lakeshore Visitor Center, go south .8 mile on Kemil Road to Rt. 20. Turn left (east) on Rt. 20 and drive 10.4 miles to Rt. 35. Turn right (south) at green sign "To LaPorte." Travel on Rt. 35 for 9 miles to the LaPorte courthouse. Stay on Rt. 35 (Indiana Avenue) for 1.1 miles. Then make a right turn on Fox Street and go a block to the greenhouses. After your visit, return on Rt. 35 to Rt. 2, turn left (west) and go 2.6 miles till you come to Fail Road (the American Home Foods plant will be on the left). Turn left (west) into Fail and proceed 5.9 miles till you see the John Hancock sign on your right. To reach the Heston Gardens, make a right turn to Fail Road and go .9 miles on Fail to the Heston Bar. Make a right turn here and take 1000N for a block. Turn left (north) at 150E; Heston Gardens will be on the left. Leaving Heston Gardens go back to the Heston Bar. Instead of returning to Fail Road, continue northwest on 1000N for several miles until it crosses Rt. 39. Turn right (north) on Rt. 39

and continue for 3.1 miles to New Buffalo. Turn right (east) on Rt. 12 and continue for 1.6 miles. Turn right at the first Golden Door sign which is on your right. After lunch turn left (northwest) on Rt. 12 for .4 miles. At the Red Arrow Highway turn right (east) and continue for 12 miles to Rainbow Gardens, 9394 Red Arrow. The Gardens are on the left side of the road. Return to the Visitor Center (about 27 miles) via the Red Arrow which joins Rt. 12 at the east end of New Buffalo.

Blossoming Out
(A Spring Weekday)

MILES : 110
HOURS: An Afternoon and Evening

Blossom time is really special in the Benton Harbor area. We suggest a tour through pear, apple and grape orchard country. Then a visit to Andrews University and its interesting vegetarian shop (471-7442). Marvelous breads (specials on Tuesdays), soy beans converted into every edible form, grains, nuts, and fresh shredded coconut. Closed Saturdays (the sabbath for the Seventh Day Adventists who run the University). Also visit the University's furniture factory (471-7771). On your way to dinner, take a beautiful drive on Lemon Creek Road. End the day with dinner at D'Agostino's Navajo Restaurant, Red Arrow Highway, Bridgman. Closed Sundays (465-3435).

DIRECTIONS: From the Lakeshore Visitor Center, turn left (west) on Rt. 12 and go 3 miles to Rt. 49. Turn left (south) on Rt. 49 for less than a mile to the I-94 East entrance ramp. Take I-94 for 44 miles to Benton Harbor. At Exit 23, turn right (north) into the Red Arrow Highway and proceed north for about 5 miles until the Red Arrow merges with Rt. 33 at traffic light. Proceed for about 6 blocks on Rt. 33. When the post office building is on your right, turn right on to Ship Street. Go a block and turn left and after another block turn right. Proceed until you have crossed 2 bridges. After another block, turn left at stoplight into Riverview Drive. Proceed on winding Riverview Drive for 1.3 miles to stoplight. Turn left on to Colfax Avenue and continue for .8 miles to Blossomtime Headquarters at 311 Colfax (925-7019). Pick up a Blossom Trail map there. To reach Trail 3, continue on Colfax .3 miles past overhead signals. Turn right into Territorial Road which jogs to the left in front of the Hotel Michigan. Take Territorial Road out of Benton Harbor (east) for about 6 miles. Turn right (south) on Hillandale Road and take Hillandale to Sodus. Stay on Hillandale for 2 miles more; turn left (east) into Pipestone Road. Take Pipestone approximately 5 miles to Eau Claire, turn right (south) on Claire Road for 2 miles. Then make a right (west) turn into Pokagon Road. Go about 2 miles to Berrien Springs and the University on Rt. 31. When you leave Andrews, turn left onto Rts. 31-33 and go on Rt. 33 for 2 miles. Here make a left into Lemon Creek Road. Go straight (west) on Lemon Creek for a beautiful 10 mile drive. At the Red Arrow Highway, make a left (south) turn and you will see the Navajo Restaurant. To return, head southwest on the Red Arrow Highway until it becomes Rt. 12 at the eastern end of New Buffalo. Continue on Rt. 12 to Kemil Road and the Visitor Center.

Rainy Day
(First Sunday in the Month)

MILES : 120
HOURS: Full Day

This is a day in South Bend which starts with a visit to the Studebaker Antique Car Collection (open only the first Sunday of each month 284-9051). After you're surfeited on beautiful old autos, take a leisurely ride down Washington Street and see the elaborate mansions, including the Clement Studebaker home. We suggest that you then jaunt over to the restored brewery, 100 Center, and tour its myriad shops, stay for lunch, and even take in some old time actors at the Boiler House Flix.

DIRECTIONS: From the Lakeshore Visitor Center, turn left (west) on Rt. 12 and go 3 miles to Rt. 49. Turn left into Rt. 49 and go south for 4.9 miles to Indiana Toll Road I-80–90. Take the Toll Road east 45 miles to South Bend.

Turn right (south) on to Rt. 31/33 and go 3¾ miles. At the 600 block turn right (west) for a block. Turn left (south) into Main Street. The Studebaker Museum is at 635 South Main. After your tour, go back to Rt. 31/33 (Michigan Avenue). Turn left (north) and continue for 5 blocks to Washington Street. Turn left (west) into Washington and drive west to see the splendid old houses. To reach 100 Center, 700 Lincoln Way West, return to Washington and Michigan. Turn right (south) onto Michigan which becomes Lincoln Way (Rt. 33). Follow Rt. 33 about 3 miles to 100 Center. To return to the Lakeshore Visitor Center, head north on Rt. 33 through South Bend to the Indiana Toll Road. Head west. Take Exit 5, Chesterton and turn north into Rt. 49. Continue on Rt. 49 to Rt. 12. Take Rt. 12 east to Kemil Road and the Visitor Center.

A Boating Day   MILES : 83
(A Friday in Spring)   HOURS: An Afternoon
                               an Early Evening

Take a leisurely drive to the Kankakee River. Start at English Lake, where the Yellow and the Kankakee Rivers meet. There will be wild flowers and good bird watching as well as fishing. Rent a flat bottomed "John boat" from Mrs. Wickizer (754-2174) in English Lake, and fish, float and have fun. Bring your own fishing gear. End the day with a Friday evening fish fry at John's Corner Tap in Kouts (766-9930).

DIRECTIONS: From the Lakeshore Visitor Center, go south .8 mile on Kemil Road to Rt. 20. Turn left (east) on Rt. 20 and go 6.7 miles to Rt. 421. Turn right (south) on Rt. 421 and go about 26 miles to LaCrosse. In LaCrosse turn left (east) on Rt. 8 and proceed 4 miles to 650W. At 650W, turn right (south). Road curves but keep left (south) for 3.5 miles to the double bridges at English Lake. Mrs. Wickizer lives in the first house on the left before you reach the bridges. For dinner, retrace your route into LaCrosse, and continue west on Rt. 8 for 6.6 miles into Kouts. After you eat, return north on Rt. 49 for 29 miles.

At Rt. 49 and Rt. 12 turn east for 3 miles to Kemil Road and the Visitor Center.

Rainy Day   MILES : 80
(Best during the week;   HOURS: Half a day
crowded on weekends)

A visit to the Cook Nuclear Center in Bridgman and a look at a remarkable facility, situated on lovely grounds, and telling the story of atomic power. This excellent propaganda show takes about an hour and fifteen minutes. Then to lunch at Hyerdall's (465-5546). Good country cooking. End the day with a tour of a Musselman cannery where you can see grapes, apples and endless other edibles canned for winter eating. Prior arrangements suggested (983-3901).

DIRECTIONS: From the Lakeshore Visitor Center, turn right (east) on Rt. 12 and continue through Michigan City and into New Buffalo. East of town take the Red Arrow Highway on to Bridgman, a total distance of approximately 27 miles. Go 3 miles beyond the stoplight in Bridgman until you see the Cook Nuclear signs. Make a left (west) turn off the Red Arrow into Center parking lot. After the show make a right turn (west) on to the Red Arrow and go back to Bridgman. Hyerdall's Restaurant (465-5546) is on the left side of the road in town. After lunch turn right on to the Red Arrow. Go northeast for 10 miles to the Musselman Cannery, 3515 Red Arrow (also called Lake Shore Drive at this point). To return to the Lakeshore Visitor Center, take the Red Arrow until it merges with Rt. 12 at the eastern end of New Buffalo and continue on Rt. 12 to Kemil Road and the Visitor Center.

Nature and Nurture   MILES : 140
(Any Wednesday, Thursday,   HOURS: A Full Day
or Friday in Summer)

First, a trip to Fernwood, the charming Michigan nature center which has trails, lectures, craft classes. Open 9 to 4:30, Tuesday through Saturday and from 10 to 4:30 on

Sunday (695-6491). Then lunch at Franky's in Niles (683-7474). End the day with a trip to Lakeside, Michigan for a look at John Wilson's Lakeside Studio. There are fine prints and paintings on display and for sale. Open Monday to Friday, from 9 to 5 (469-0675).

DIRECTIONS: From the Lakeshore Visitor Center, turn left (west) for 3 miles on Rt. 12 to Rt. 49. Turn left (south) on Rt. 49 and proceed a little less than a mile to I-94. Take I-94 east approximately 20 miles to the New Buffalo exit. Turn right (east) on to Rt. 12 and go through Three Oaks and Galien. At sign marked Buchanan, (there is also a blinker light), turn left (north) and go to the second stoplight. Turn left into River Street and cross bridge and take first paved street, Range Line Road, to left. Go 1½ miles on Range Line and Fernwood is on the left. To go to Franky's for lunch, Fernwood will direct you to Niles, a distance of 10 miles. When you get to Main Street in downtown Niles go south on Main to corner of 5th. Turn left (north) on 5th and go 2 miles to Lake Street. Turn right on Lake and go ½ mile. Franky's is on left side of road. After lunch return to 5th and Main. Take a right (west) on Main. Go over bridge and follow Main as it winds to left. Pass hospital to traffic light. Main turns right (west). Continue for 2 blocks to 2nd traffic light. Turn left (south) on Lincoln and continue past Catholic Church. Lincoln turns to right and becomes Chicago Road. Continue 2 miles further on Chicago where road becomes Rt. 12. Continue west on Rt. 12 (approximately 20 miles) to intersection with Red Arrow Highway. Turn right (north) on Red Arrow about 7 miles to Lakeside. Turn left (north) into Main Street in Lakeside, go past post office to Lakeshore Road. Turn left (west) on Lakeshore for 2 miles. The huge white frame inn, 150 South Lakeshore, is across the road from a pink stucco house with a blue tile roof. To return to Lakeshore Visitor Center, retrace the route to the Red Arrow. Turn right (southwest) and take the Red Arrow to the eastern end of New Buffalo where it merges with Rt. 12. Proceed on Rt. 12 to Kemil Road and the Visitor Center.

Garrets and Galleries   MILES : 27.7
(All Year, Any Day but Sunday)   HOURS: Morning
                                          and Lunch

For a day of art and crafts, start at the Hannell Pottery in
Furnessville. Then go on to Merle Fisher's home in
Chesterton where he makes elegant custom jewelry. For
the next stop, we suggest you pick an artist or craftsman
from the Categorical Guide, call and arrange for your
own studio visit. Next visit Michigan City's charming restored Brewery, and the Brewery Bookstore and Gallery.
Lunch at Tinker's Dam (879-7373).

DIRECTIONS: From the Lakeshore Visitor Center, take
Kemil Road .8 mile south to 1500N. Turn right (west) on
Furnessville Road and go .3 mile to the Hannell Pottery,
(down a long driveway to the right). Leaving the pottery,
make a left turn (east) to the corner, Schoolhouse Road.
Take Schoolhouse .1 mile to Rt. 20. Turn right (west) and
go 1.5 mile to Hadenfeldt Road. Turn right (north) and
continue .4 mile on Hadenfeldt. Merle Fisher's house is
on right side of street, set well back. When you leave, go
back to Rt. 20 and retrace course to Lakeshore Visitor
Center. (We presuppose the artist of your choice will direct you to his/her studio). From the Lakeshore Visitor
Center to reach the Brewery make a right turn (east) on
Rt. 12 and travel 7.2 miles to Michigan City. Turn right
(southeast) into Rt. 35 (East Michigan Boulevard) from
Rt. 12, and travel .6 mile to 8th Street. Make a right turn
into the Brewery parking lot. For lunch return to Rt. 12,
turn right (east) and travel 2.7 miles to Karwick Road.
Make a left turn (north) on to Karwick and go .3 mile.
Tinker's Dam will be on the right side of the road. To return, take Karwick Road south to Rt. 12. Turn right (west)
on Rt. 12 to Kemil Road and the Visitor Center.

Sleighs, Treats and Kids   MILES : 26
(A Saturday in Winter)   HOURS: 4

Arrange for a sleigh ride with Mr. Keith Simms in Burdick
(926-4883). Bump and chatter around the countryside.

Then on to Michigan City's Marquette Mall with its ice cream parlor, pet store, needle work shop, and several toy departments all under one roof. Have lunch at Robin Hood Restaurant in the Mall (872-8629) after you and your offspring have walked and gawked your fill.

DIRECTIONS: From the Lakeshore Visitor Center, turn left (west) on Rt. 12 to Rt. 49 for 3 miles. Turn left to Rt. 49 and continue south for 2.9 miles to Porter Avenue. Turn left (east) into Porter and go 1.2 miles to Friday Road. Turn right (south) on Friday .4 mile. At 250E, Burdick Road, turn left (east) for 1.9 miles. The road curves but you will see the Simms' name on mailbox (435). Turn left (slightly west) into his driveway. For Marquette Mall, retrace the route to Rt. 49, At Rt. 49 turn right (north) to Rt. 20. At Rt. 20 turn right (east) and travel to Marquette Mall (approximately 7.5 miles). The Mall is on the left (north) where Rts. 20 and 421 meet. To return to the Visitor Center, drive 6.7 miles on Rt. 20 to Kemil Road. Turn right (north) on Kemil Road .8 mile.

A Day in the Dunes　　　　　MILES : 36.3
(A Spring or Summer Day)　　　HOURS: Up to You

Getting a good look at the dunes requires some doing. We suggest you start in Beverly Shores with a look at the marsh, the foredunes, the beach, and the great Moon Dune (still moving). Then drive to the State Park where you pay, park, get a map. You can hike over trail 9 to see a blow out, or trail 10 to see a tree graveyard, or trail 2 through a marsh, or trail 8 to scale Mt. Tom, the highest dune. Have a picnic lunch in the park. The rangers will direct you to the picnic areas. With permission from the town clerk in Dune Acres (787-8800), you can take a look at the fragile and wonderful Cowles Bog. Then on to the interdunal ponds at West Beach, just west of Ogden Dunes. Check with the Lakeshore Visitor Center (926-7561) for parking instructions at West Beach.

DIRECTIONS: From the Lakeshore Visitor Center, cross

Rt. 12 and continue north on State Park Road for 1.1 miles to the National Lakeshore parking lot on east side of road. (Notice the marsh as you drive). Then walk to the beach. Return to your car and head south on State Park Road for .4 mile to Beverly Drive. Turn left (east) and take Beverly Drive for 4.8 miles to Rt. 12. At Rice Street, the first road on your left, turn north to see Moon Dune. Leave your car in the Lakeshore parking lot and walk about a hundred yards to Moon Dune. To get to the State Park, return to Rt. 12 and continue for 8.3 miles to Rt. 49. Turn at sign marked Indiana 49 and go north on Rt. 49 for .9 mile to entrance of Indiana Dunes State Park. Pay the admission fee, park and hike the trails. After lunch return to your car and go south on Rt. 49 to Rt. 12. Turn right (west) and travel for about 2 miles. At the Dunes Acres sign on your right, turn right (north) for .6 miles to Dune Acres entrance. Ask the guard for Cowles Bog information. For West Beach, go back to Rt. 12. Turn right (west) and go 4.7 miles to Ogden Dunes. Follow directions about parking given at the Lakeshore Visitor Center. Returning From West Beach in Ogden Dunes it will be 10 miles on Rt. 12 to the Lakeshore Visitor Center on Kemil Road.

All the Angles for the Anglers
(Any Day but Sunday)

MILES : 15
HOURS : Afternoon
and Evening

Michigan City calls itself the Coho Capital. Charter a boat, rent gear, or buy some fishing equipment and treat yourself to a shimmering day. If you don't haul in your quota, you can go to Ritter's Fish Store, 118 West Fifth Street, and make up for your deficiency. Ritter sends its own boats out every morning and has been selling fresh water fish to the area for decades. Later have dinner at Maxine and Heinies, 521 Franklin Street (879-9068). Then go on to a performance, just a few blocks away, at the Canterbury Playhouse, 907 Franklin Street (874-4269).

DIRECTIONS: From the Lakeshore Visitor Center, turn right (east) on to Rt. 12 and proceed 7.2 miles to Pine Street in Michigan City. Turn left (north) on Pine Street for .5 miles to the waterfront. Check at the Municipal Marina which is on your left for details about available charters and equipment. After your day on the Lake, to reach Ritter return to Rt. 12. Cross Rt. 12 and you will be on Washington Street. Proceed south on Washington Street and turn left (east) on to 5th Street. Ritter is on the right side of the street. For dinner, return to Washington Street, turn left (south) on Washington for a block. Turn left (east) on 6th Street and proceed a block to Franklin Street and parking for Maxine and Heinies. To reach the Canterbury Playhouse, return to Washington Street, turn left (south) and proceed for 3 blocks to 9th Street. Turn left (east) a block to Franklin Street. To return to the Visitor Center, go a block further east on 9th Street. Turn left (north) on Pine Street. Continue on Pine Street for 5 blocks to 4th Street. Turn left (west) on 4th Street for a block. Turn right (north) on Franklin Street for a block and turn left (west) on Rt. 12. Continue on Rt. 12 to Kemil Road and the Visitor Center.

Categorical Guide

In this section the reader can find everything listed by category. For example, if art galleries are your interest, look after architecture and before artists and you will find all of them from Gary to Benton Harbor. Only the name, address, town and telephone number is given. For detailed information look in the Community Guide under the town.

AIRPORTS (C=Charter Flights)

BENTON HARBOR: Ross Field, West Main Street (927-3194). Blue Star Aviation, 1681 Reeder (927-2954). C

GARY: Municipal Airport, Industrial Highway (944-1663). C

GRIFFITH: Griffith Airport, 1701 East Main (838-7110). C

HOBART: Sky Ranch, 3426 North Lake Park (962-1189). C

LAPORTE: Municipal Airport, 250S east of Rt. 39 (362-9925). C

MICHIGAN CITY: Municipal Airport, South Franklin Street (879-0291). C

Joe Phillips, Michigan Road (872-5571). C

NILES: Air Michiana, 191 Fir (683-2078). C

Niles Airways, 2020 Lake (683-3434). C

SOUTH BEND: St. Joseph County Municipal Airport, 22965 Rt. 20 (233-2185).

THREE OAKS: Oselka Field, Forrest Lawn Road (756-9252). C

VALPARAISO: Porter County Municipal Airport, 100N east of Rt. 30 (462-6508). C

AMUSEMENT PARKS

BENTON HARBOR: House of Daivd, Britain Avenue (926-6446).

CHESTERTON: Enchanted Forest, Rt. 20, west of Rt. 49 (926-1614).

COLOMA: Deer Forest, Paw Paw Lake (468-4961).

HIGHLAND: Wicker Park, Rts. 6 and 41 (839-9809).

SCHERERVILLE: Sauzer's Kiddie Land, Rts. 41 and 30 (865-8160).

ANTIQUES

COLOMA: Millstone Antiques, Martin Road (HO8-6667).

CHESTERTON: Antique Shop, Porter Avenue (926-1400).

CROWN POINT: Dan's Antiques, 8703 East 109th (663-4571).

EAST GARY: The Barn, East 33rd (962-9697).

FURNESSVILLE: Tree House Antiques, Furnessville Road (no phone).

HESSTON: Heston Gardens, 1000N and 215E (778-2421).

LACROSSE: Das Anttikaus, 2100S (754-2265).
Jackson Antiques, Rt. 421 (938-5018).

LAKESIDE: Heritage House, 15300 Red Arrow (469-1412).
What Not Shop, 15154 Lakeside Road (469-3113).

LAPORTE: Tulip Tree Antiques, 700N off Fail Road (778-2662).

LOWELL: Evergreen Shop, I-65 and Rt. 2 (696-0707).
Hitzeman's Country Haus, 135 West Commercial (696-7121).
The Livery Stable, Washington Street (696-9395).

MERRILLVILLE: Stagecoach Antiques, Broadway and Rt. 6 (769-5986).

MICHIGAN CITY: Five Gables Antiques, 217 Rice

(872-9315).

Gypsies of Canterbury, 110 West 9th (879-9713).

Phase II, 915 East Michigan (324-7881).

NILES: Lois Sherer, 1008 Oak (683-7224).

PORTAGE: Charlotte Curtiss, 6574 Sand (762-7441).

SCHERERVILLE: Landmark Antiques, 1619 Junction (322-4534).

SOUTH BEND: Thieves Market, 2309 Edison (233-9820).

THREE OAKS: Rainbow's End, 1000N (756-9291).

The Depot, Oak (756-9366).

VALPARAISO: Corner House, Franklin and Monroe Streets (462-3538).

Nielson's Country Shop, Old Suman Road (462-9812).

Uphaus, 300W west of Rt. 2 (462-2810).

ARCHITECTURE—Churches

BEVERLY SHORES: Old North Church, Beverly Drive.

COLOMA: Community Church, Church Street.

HESSTON: Greek Orthodox Chapel, Heston Gardens, 1000N and 215E.

LAPORTE: Methodist Church, Harrison and Clay Streets.

MISHAWAKA: St. Joseph Church, Third and Mill Streets.

NEW CARLISLE: Apostolic Church, Front Street.

Hamilton Church, Old Chicago Road.

Olive Chapel, Timothy Street.

PORTER: Augsburg Svenska Skola, Oakhill Road.

SOUTH BEND: Church of Loretta, St. Mary's College.

St. Paul Memorial Church, 1001 Colfax.

VALPARAISO: Chapel of Resurrection, Valparaiso University.

ARCHITECTURE—Homes, Inns, Courthouses (1830-1920)

BENTON HARBOR: Morton, 501 Territorial.

BERRIEN SPRINGS: Old Berrien County Courthouse, Cass and Union Streets.

CHESTERTON: Farr, 1050N and 350W.

Friday, Friday Road.

Holmes-Brown, 700 Porter.

Rhoda Barn, 1100N and 150E.

CROWN POINT: Lake County Courthouse, Courthouse Square.

Old Homestead, 227 South Court.

DOOR VILLAGE: Octagonal Barn, Rt. 35.

HEBRON: Stage Coach Inn, Main Street.

LAPORTE: 815 Division Street.

Garwood, 60N and 500W.

LaPorte County Courthouse.

Orr-Richter, Small Road.

Swan-Anderson, 1020 Indiana.

LONG BEACH: Bavarian, 2704 Lake Shore.

MICHIGAN CITY: Barker, 631 Washington.

Porter-Kerrigan, Washington and 10th Streets.

Waterford Inn, Johnson and Wozniak Roads.

MISHAWAKA: Beiger, 117 Lincoln Way West.

Hutcheson-Schindler, 810 Lincoln Way East.

Merrifield-Cass, 816 Lincoln Way East.

Niles-Weiss, 410 Lincoln Way East.

NILES: Chapin (City Hall), 508 East Main.

Lardner, 519 Bond.

NEW CARLISLE: Hubbard, Cherry and Front Streets.

ROLLING PRAIRIE: Foster-Shuck, Jimmerson Shores Road, north of Rt. 20.

Provolot-McGuire, Byron Road, north of Rt. 20.

PORTAGE: Wolf, 450N and East Cleveland Avenue.

SCHERERVILLE: Scherer, 33 Wilhelm.

SOUTH BEND: Bartlett, 720 West Washington.

Chapin-Willis, 407 West Navarre.

Cushing, 504 West Washington.

Navarre Cabin, Leeper Park.

Old St. Joseph County Courthouse, 112 South Lafayette.

Powell Home, Leeper Park.

Studebaker, 620 West Washington.

VALPARAISO: Barnard, 825E, north of Rt. 6.

Robbins, 800N and 800W.

Rose-Kuehl, 156 South Garfield.

WESTVILLE: Forrester, Rt. 2, east of town.

WHITING: Memorial Community House, 1938 Clark.

ARCHITECTURE—Modern

GARY: Gary-Hobart Water Tower, 7th and Madison Streets.

HOBART: Public Library, 100 Main.

MERRILLVILLE: Lake County Reference Library, Rt. 30 east of Rt. 55.

MICHIGAN CITY: Franklin Square, Franklin Street between 5th and 9th Streets.

Mullen Elementary School, 100 Manny Court.

SOUTH BEND: Convocation Center, Notre Dame University.

Library, Notre Dame University.

ARCHITECTURE—Restorations

MICHIGAN CITY: The Brewery, East Michigan Boulevard.

MISHAWAKA: 100 Center, 700 Lincoln Way.

VALPARAISO: Tratebas Mill, Tratebas Road.

ARCHITECTURE—World's Fair Houses

BEVERLY SHORES: Ben Franklin House, Pearson Street.

House of Tomorrow, Lake Front Drive.

Old North Church, Beverly Drive.

Paul Revere House, Pearson Street.

ARCHITECTURE—Frank Lloyd Wright Houses

GARY: 7th and Van Buren Streets.

GRAND BEACH: Station Street.

OGDEN DUNES: Cedar Trail, north of Ogden Road.

SOUTH BEND: 715 West Washington.

1404 Ridgedale.

ART GALLERIES

CHESTERTON: Gilbert Gallery, 115 4th (no phone).

CROWN POINT: Little Gallery, 321 Rose Ellen (663-1869).

Station Gallery, Goldsboro Street (663-8870).

EAST CHICAGO: Fine Arts Gallery, St. Joseph's College, 4721 Indianapolis (397-9197).

Municipal Art Center, Chicago and Kennedy Avenues (398-4200).

GARY: Richard Hatcher Art Gallery, 2137 Broadway (885-0591).

HAMMOND: Northern Indiana Art Center, 5446 Hohman (931-0018).

LAKESIDE: Lakeside Studios, 150 South Lakeshore (469-0675).

MICHIGAN CITY: Brewery Gallery, 600 9th (872-4395).

MILLER: Gard Gallery, 396 South Lake (938-6860).

Gary Artists League Gallery, 400 South Lake (938-3356).

MUNSTER: Town Gallery, 117 Ridge (836-6230).

NEW BUFFALO: The Atelier, 10 North Barton (469-1643).

ST. JOSEPH: St. Joseph Art Association, 600 State (983-0271).

SOUTH BEND: Baldoni Fine Arts, 1314 Mishawaka (287-6661).

Moreau-Hammer Galleries, St. Mary's College (284-4854).

O'Shaughnessy Hall Art Gallery, Notre Dame University (283-6011).

South Bend Art Association, 121 Lafayette (233-8201).

VALPARAISO: Sloan Gallery, Valparaiso University (462-5111).

ARTISTS

Macrame
MILLER: Toby Balter (938-8262).
LONG BEACH: Helen Miller (872-5767).

Painters
LAPORTE: Judith and Lee Rein (362-3738).
LONG BEACH: Gertrude Harbart (874-6394).
MICHIANA SHORES: Karl Warren (872-8550).
MICHIGAN CITY: Elizabeth Fleming (879-9446).
MILLER: Dale Fleming (938-3834).
VALPARAISO: Pamela and William Reddick (464-2757).
Harriet Rex Smith (462-4567).

Potters
FURNESSVILLE: Hazel Hannell (926-4568).
TREMONT: Loretta Cohn (926-4358).

Sculptors
MILLER: Belva and Clyde Ball (938-5580).
WESTVILLE: Antone Popp (785-2464).

Weavers
EAST CHICAGO: Helen and John Powers (397-1365).
VALPARAISO: Nancy Searles (462-7405).

AUCTIONS

HOBART: Mac's Auction, 150 Illinois (942-1915).
MICHIGAN CITY: Anxious Al's, Rt. 20 (874-4130).
  Nationwide Sales, Rt. 20 (879-5288).
  Twenty Grand, Rt. 20 (874-5054).
NILES: Niles Community Auction, 510 North Front
  (684-1263).
PORTER: Frye Barn, Old Porter Road (926-2501).
SOUTH BEND: Mayflower Auction, 55266 Rt. 23 (233-1021).

AUCTIONS—Livestock

MICHIANA SHORES: Michiana Riding Stables, 3848 Acade-
  my (872-2114). Horses.
WALKERTON: Walkerton Sales Barn, Rt. 23 (586-3159).
  Ponies.
VALPARAISO: Community Sales, Rt. 13 off Rt. 49
  (462-4570). Livestock and ponies.

BAND CONCERTS

MICHIGAN CITY: Washington Park, Pine Avenue at Lake
  Michigan.
MISHAWAKA: Battell Park, Mishawaka Avenue.
NILES: Ella Champion Park, Main and 5th Streets.
ST. JOSEPH: Lake Front Park, Lakebluff Avenue.

BEACHES on Lake Michigan
(*=admission fee **=parking fee)

BEVERLY SHORES
BRIDGMAN: Warren Dunes State Park*
  Weko Beach*
CHESTERTON: Indiana Dunes State Park*
  Johnson (Porter) Beach**

MICHIGAN CITY: Washington Park**
MILLER: Lake Street Beach**
NEW BUFFALO: Municipal Beach
PORTAGE TOWNSHIP: West Beach**
ST. JOSEPH: Public Beach

BICYCLE RENTAL

CROWN POINT: Crown Rental, 113 North Indiana (663-0164).
HOBART: Hobart Schwinn, 201 South Illinois (942-3942).
LAPORTE: Area Rental, 602 East Lincolnway (462-3594).
MERRILLVILLE: Area Rental, 5449 Broadway (887-7388).
SOUTH BEND: United Rent-All, 2022 South Bend (272-5482).
TREMONT: Dunes Lakeshore Hostel, Rt. 12 (926-1414).
VALPARAISO: United Rent-All, 906 Calumet (464-3594).

BOATS—Launching Ramps (P = Public $ = Pay)

BENTON HARBOR: Gardner's Favorite Sports, 741 Riverview (925-3247). $
Town Ramp, Riverview (925-7061). P
BENTON TOWNSHIP: St. Joseph River at 1725 Territorial (925-0616). P
BERRIEN SPRINGS: At St. Joseph River. P
BRIDGMAN: Weko Beach, one mile north of I-94 at Lake Michigan (465-5407). P
CEDAR LAKE: Lake Shore Drive and Cline Avenue. P
EAST CHICAGO: Jeorse Park, Michigan Avenue at Indiana Harbor. P
HAMMOND: Lake Front Park, Calumet at Lake Michigan (931-2760). P
Wolf Lake, 121st and Calumet (WE2-0093). P
HOBART: Lake George, South Lake Park. P
HUDSON: Hudson Lake, Rt. 20, east side of lake. P
LAPORTE: Holiday Boat Sales, 1270 Pine Lake Avenue (362-4423). $
Stone Lake, in Soldiers Memorial Park, Rt. 35 (362-9746). P
MICHIGAN CITY: B & E Marine, 500 Center (879-8301). $
MILLER: Lake Street at Lake Michigan. P

MISHAWAKA: Marine Stadium, East Jefferson (255-6610). P

Merrifield Park, East Mishawaka (255-6610). P

NEW BUFFALO: Galien River at Red Arrow Highway. P

NILES: St. Joseph River and Marmont Street. P

PORTAGE: Doyne's, Burns Ditch off Rt. 249 (938-3551). $

Lefty's Coho Landing, Route 12 (762-1711). $

ROLLING PRAIRIE: Hog Lake, 300E east of Rt. 2 (778-2241). P

SCHNEIDER: LaSalle State Game and Fish Area, Rt. 41 and 150N (992-3019). P

SHELBY: Rt. 55 at Kankakee River. P

SOUTH BEND: Bass Lake, Rt. 20 (232-7026). $

Darden Road. P

Memorial Park, North Drive. P

Szmanda Lake, north of Rt. 2. $

VALPARAISO: Flint Lake, off Rt. 49 (464-1441). $

Loomis Lake in Harold Rogers-Lakewood Park, Burlington-Beach Road (462-5144). $

Wahob Lake, off Rt. 49. $

WESTVILLE: Clear Lake, Porter-LaPorte County Line Road (872-9363). $

BOATS—Marinas

BENTON HARBOR: Gardner's Favorite Marina, 741 Riverview (925-3247).

CEDAR LAKE: Pine Crest Marina, 14415 Lauerman (374-5771).

EAST CHICAGO: Jeorse Park, Michigan Avenue at Lake Michigan (398-4200).

HOBART: Bowman's Landing, 603 Wisconsin (942-7765).

LAPORTE: Holiday Boat Sales, 1270 Pine Lake Avenue (362-4423).

Pine Lake Marina, 816 Pine Lake Avenue (362-8455).

MICHIGAN CITY: B & E Marine, 500 Center (879-8301).

Georg Boat and Motors, 83 Franklin (872-8608).

Great Lakes Marine, 6th Street (872-7201).

Michigan City Municipal Marina, Washington Park Basin (872-1712).

NEW BUFFALO: New Buffalo Marina, 245 Whittaker (469-0010).

Oselka Snug Harbor Marina, 514 West Water (469-2600).

PORTAGE: Burns Harbor Marine, 1700 Marine (762-2304).

Doyne's, Burns Ditch off Rt. 249 (938-3551).

Lefty's Coho Landing, Rt. 12 (762-1711).

ST. JOSEPH: Whispering Willow Marina, 2383 Niles (983-9963).

Chaney's Wharf, Industrial Island (983-3681;.

West Basin Marina, 273 Prospect (983-5432).

BOATS—Rental

BENTON HARBOR: Gardner's Marina, 741 Riverview (925-3247).

BUCHANAN: Bear Cave, Red Bud Trail (OX5-3050).

Clear Lake, Clear Lake Road (695-3785).

Wagner Lake, Madron Road (695-9895).

CEDAR LAKE: Chuck's Pier, 13947 Huseman (374-5791).

Ernie's Canoes, 133rd Street (663-2809).

Pinecrest Marina, 1445 Lauerman (374-5771).

Shell Harbor, 133rd Court (374-9833).

ENGLISH LAKE: Wickizer (754-2174).

HOBART: Bowman's Landing, 603 Wisconsin (942-7765).

HUDSON: Hudson Lake, Rt. 20.

KOUTS: Donna Jo Campground, 1200S and 350E (462-1545).

LACROSSE: Miller's Landing, Rt. 421 at Kankakee River.

LAPORTE: D & D Boat Mart, 908 Pine Lake Avenue (362-1491).

Holiday Boat Sales, 1270 Pine Lake Avenue (362-4423).

Lower Fish Lake, Rt. 4 (324-6401).

Stone Lake in Soldier's Memorial Park, Rt. 35 (362-9746).

Upper Fish Lake, Rt. 4 (325-8385).

NEW BUFFALO: Skipper's Landing, 244 Whittaker (469-1120).

ROLLING PRAIRIE: Hog Lake, 300E east of Rt. 2 (778-2241).

Saugany Lake, east of Rt. 2 (778-2936).

St. Joseph: Whispering Willow Marina, 2383 Niles (983-9963).

Walt Wolf Enterprises, 205 Wayne ((983-1008).

Shelby: Ballard, Rt. 55 (552-0188).

South Bend: Bass Lake, Rt. 20 (232-7026).

Goodman Lake, Myrtle and Kern Roads.

Szmanda Lake, Quince Road, north of Rt. 2.

Valparaiso: Lake Eliza, Rt. 30 (462-1953).

Loomis Lake in Harold Rogers-Lakewood Park, Burlington-Beach Road (462-5144).

Long Lake, Edgewater Beach Road, west of Rt. 49.

Mink Lake, Rt. 49 (462-2585).

Westville: Clear Lake, Porter-LaPorte County Line Road (872-9363).

BOWLING

Benton Harbor: Blossomlanes, 2305 M-139 (927-3174).

Bridgman: Bridgman Country Club, 9794 Jericho (465-5611).

Buchanan: Poorman's Recreation, 708 Front (695-5521).

Chesterton: Gateway Lanes, 535 West Broadway (926-9036).

Westchester Lanes, 8th (926-2523).

Crown Point: Fricke's Recreation, 519 North Grant (663-0529).

East Gary: Ray's Lanes, 3221 Central (962-1297).

Gary: Tri-City Bowl, 4255 Tri-City Plaza (949-1541).

Griffith: Bowl Arena, Broad Street (838-4123).

Hammond: Bowl-Era, 6530 Calumet (WE1-4800).

Calumet Bowling Center, 5851 Calumet (WE1-2641).

Kenwood Lanes, 6311 Kennedy (TI5-0980).

Pin Bowl Lanes, 6716 Kennedy (844-9810).

Stardust Bowl, 167th and Columbia Avenue (932-5010).

Highland: Plaza Lanes, 8101 Kennedy (WA3-3800).

Hobart: Cressmoor Bowling Lanes, Wisconsin Avenue (942-1212).

Hobart Lanes, Rt. 130 (942-6248).

Kirk's Cressmoor Lanes, 620 Wisconsin (942-3213).

New Chicago Pla Bowl Lounge, 3617 Michigan (962-9059).

LaPorte: Idle Hour Lanes, 610 Colfax (362-1751).

LaPorte Civic Auditorium, Ridge Road (362-7422).

Thunderbird Lanes, 1251 Pine Lake Avenue (362-3555).

Lowell: American Legion Post, 1108½ East Commercial (696-7401).

Merrillville: Merri-Bowl, 7610 Broadway (769-2449).

Michigan City: Rose Bowl Lanes, 2309 Franklin (872-9930).

Suburban Lanes, 2820 East Michigan (879-9445).

Mishawaka: Jefferson Manor Lanes, 1504 North Chestnut (255-5424).

Parkway Lanes, 2806 Lincoln Way West (255-4277).

Regal Lanes, 1121 West 8th (259-5209).

Munster: Munster Lanes, 8000 Calumet (TE6-9161).

New Buffalo: Theo's Lanes, Rt. 12 (469-0400).

Niles: Shula's 31 Bowling, 2732 South 11th (684-2276).

Timber Lanes, 517 North 2nd (683-6122).

White's, 530 South 11th (683-8484).

St. Joseph: Gersonde, 2705 Cleveland (983-3034).

Temple Lanes, 520 Broad (YU3-9071).

Stevensville: Lakeshore Lanes, 6201 Red Arrow (429-5421).

Three Oaks: Three Oaks Bowling, 17 South Elm (756-9131).

Valparaiso: Inman's Bowling Lanes, 711 Calumet (462-9250).

Wellman's, Rt. 30 (462-5681).

BRIDGES—Unusual

Hobart: Pennsylvania Railroad at Deep River.

Kouts: Baum's, Baum's Bridge Road.

Dunn's, 500S and 600E.

Wheeler: Railroad Bridge, Rt. 130 west of town.

CAMPING

Benton Harbor: House of David, Britain Avenue (927-3302).

BRIDGMAN: Weko Beach, one mile north of I-94 (465-5407).

Warren Dunes State Park, Red Arrow Highway (426-4013).

BUCHANAN: Bear Cave, Red Bud Trail (695-3050).

Fuller's Campground, Clear Lake (695-3785).

Three Braves Campground, Wagner Lake (695-9895).

CEDAR LAKE: Lemon Lake County Park, 133rd and Cedar Lake Road (663-6804).

Pinecrest Resort, 14415 Lauerman (374-5771).

CHESTERTON: Camp Farr, 1050N and 350W (926-4900).

Indiana Dunes State Park, Rt. 49 (926-1215).

DeMOTTE: KOA Campground, I-65 at Rt. 10 (987-3132).

HANNA: KOA Campground, Rt. 30 (797-2395).

HOBART: Robinson Park, 53rd and Liverpool Road (942-5498).

KINGSBURY: Kingsbury State Fish and Wildlife Area, Rt. 6 (393-3612).

KOUTS: Donna Jo Campground, 1200S and 350E (462-1545).

LaCROSSE: Kankakee State Fish and Game Area, Rt. 8 (754-2237).

LaPORTE: Cutty's Campground, Rt. 39 (362-5111).

MEDARYVILLE: Jasper-Pulaski Fish and Wildlife Area, Rts. 421 and 143 (843-3641).

MICHIGAN CITY: KOA Campground, Rt. 421 (872-7600).

MISHAWAKA: Marine Stadium, East Jefferson Road (255-6610).

NEW CARLISLE: Mini-Mountain Campground, Rt. 2 (654-3302).

NILES: Spaulding Campground, Bell Road (684-1393).

ROLLING PRAIRIE: Hog Lake, 300E, three miles north of town (778-2241).

SCHNEIDER: Duncan's Lake, Rt. 41 and Schneider Road (696-7328).

LaSalle Fish and Game Area, Rt. 41 and 150N (992-3019).

VALPARAISO: Lake Eliza, Rt. 30 (462-1953).

Mink Lake, Rt. 49 (462-2585).

Harold L. Rogers-Lakewood Park, Campbell Road (402-5144).

CAR RACING

GRIFFITH: G and G Model Raceway, Broad Street (838-2686). Slot cars.

PORTAGE: K and R Raceway, McCool Road (762-3422). Go-Karts.

SCHERERVILLE: Illiana Speedway, 7211 Lincoln (322-5311).

SOUTH BEND: South Bend Motor Speedway, Rt. 2 (287-1704). Stock and midget cars.

VALPARAISO: Harold L. Rogers-Lakewood Park, Campbell (482-5141). Soap box derby.

CAVES

BUCHANAN: Bear Cave, Red Bud Trail (695-3050).

CEMETERIES

BUCHANAN: Oak Ridge Cemetery, Front Street.

CEDAR LAKE: Indian Mound Cemetery, Marquette Street.

CROWN POINT: Civil War Cemetery, Iowa Street off Rt. 8.

DOOR VILLAGE: Door Village Cemetery, Joliet Road.

FURNESSVILLE: Furnessville Cemetery, Furnessville Road.

GARY: Pioneer Cemetery, Grant and 19th Street.

HESSTON: Posey Chapel Cemetery, 1000N.

KNOX: Crown Hill Cemetery, East Lake Road.

LAPORTE: Union Chapel Cemetery, Rt. 6.

NEW CARLISLE: Hamilton Cemetery, Old Chicago Road. Town Cemetery, Rt. 20.

NILES: Bertrand Catholic Cemetery, Madalene Street.

OTIS: Eight Square Cemetery, LaPorte-Porter County Line Road.

PORTER: Bailly Cemetery, Oakhill Road.

SOUTH BEND: Highland Cemetery, 255 Portage.

VALPARAISO: Quakerdom Cemetery, Rt. 6 east of Jackson Center.

CHAMBERS OF COMMERCE

BENTON HARBOR-ST. JOSEPH: 777 Riverview, Benton Harbor (925-0044).

BUCHANAN: 119 Main (695-3291).

CHESTERTON-PORTAGE: 209 Calumet, Chesterton (926-5513).

CROWN POINT: 150 Joliet (663-1800).

EAST CHICAGO: 20001 Columbus (EX8-1600).

EAST GARY: no office (962-1196).

GARY: 538 Broadway (885-7407).

GRIFFITH: no office (923-2200).

HAMMOND: 429 Fayette (931-1000).

HIGHLAND: 8536 Kennedy (WA3-3666).

HOBART: 18 Ridge (942-5774).

KOUTS: 406 Main (766-2228).

LAPORTE: 509 State (362-3178).

LOWELL: 603 East Commercial (696-7321).

MERRILLVILLE: 47 67th Place (769-3180).

MICHIGAN CITY: 719 Franklin (874-6221).

MUNSTER: 719 Ridge (836-5096).

NILES: 103 North 4th (683-3720).

PORTAGE: Portage Mall (762-3300).

SOUTH BEND-MISHAWAKA: 320 West Jefferson, South Bend (234-0051).

VALPARAISO: 106 Franklin (462-1105).

WHITING: 1905 New York (659-0292).

COLLEGES AND UNIVERSITIES

BENTON HARBOR: Lake Michigan College, 2755 East Napier (927-3571).

BERRIEN SPRINGS: Andrews University, Rt. 31 (471-7771).

EAST CHICAGO: St. Joseph's College, 4721 Indianapolis (397-9197).

GARY: Indiana University—Northwest Campus, 3400 Broadway (887-0111).

   Indiana Vocational and Technical College, 1440 East 35th (887-9646).

HAMMOND: Purdue University—Calumet Campus, 2233 171st (844-0520).

MISHAWAKA: Bethel College, 1001 McKinley (259-8511).

SOUTH BEND: Indiana University, 1825 Northside (282-2341).

Indiana Vocational and Technical College, 534 West
Sample (289-7001).

St. Mary's College, Rt. 31 (284-4854).

University of Notre Dame, Rt. 31 (283-6011).

VALPARAISO: Valparaiso Technical Institute, West Chestnut Street (462-2191).

Valparaiso University, 651 College (462-5111).

WESTVILLE: Purdue University—North Central Campus,
Rt. 421 (872-0527).

DANCING (S = Square P = Polkas F = Folk B = Ballroom)

BENTON HARBOR: House of David, Britain Avenue (926-
6446). S

BUCHANAN: Clear Lake Campground, Clear Lake Road
(695-3785). S

CROWN POINT: Presbyterian Church, 218 Court
(663-2476). S

MERRILLVILLE: Promenade Hall, Rt. 55 north of Rt. 30
(769-5074). S

MICHIGAN CITY: Polka Dot, 926 Chicago (879-9017). P

St. Joseph's Hall, 2001 Franklin (879-9454). P

Side Door, 5518 Rt. 421 (879-7388). B

NEW BUFFALO: Blue Chip lounge, Red Arrow Highway
(469-9828). P

ROLLING PRAIRIE: 2 Maple (778-2669). F

VALPARAISO: Stone Balloon Tavern, 1409 Lincolnway
(462-9363). B

EMERGENCY MEDICAL CARE

BENTON HARBOR: Mercy Hospital, 960 Agara (925-8811).

BERRIEN CENTER: Berrien General Hospital, 1250 Deanhill
(471-7761).

BUCHANAN: Buchanan Community Hospital, 1301 Main
695-3851).

DYER-ST. JOHN: Our Lady of Mercy Hospital, Lincoln
Highway (365-2141).

EAST CHICAGO: St. Catherine Hospital, 4321 Fir (392-1700).

GARY: Methodist Hospital, 600 Grant (882-9461).

St. Mary Mercy Hospital, 540 Tyler (882-9411).

HAMMOND: St. Margaret Hospital, 25 Douglas (932-2300).

HOBART: St. Mary's Medical Center, Lake Park Avenue (942-5015).

LAPORTE: LaPorte Hospital, Lincolnway (362-7541).

MICHIGAN CITY: Memorial Hospital, 5th and Pine (879-0202).

St. Anthony Hospital, 301 Homer (879-0661).

MISHAWAKA: St. Joseph Hospital, 215 West 4th (259-2431).

NILES: Pawating Hospital, 34 North St. Joseph (MU3-5510).

SOUTH BEND: Memorial Hospital, 615 West Michigan (234-9041).

St. Joseph's Hospital, 811 East Madison (234-9191).

ST. JOSEPH: Memorial Hospital, 2611 Morton (983-2151).

VALPARAISO: Porter Memorial Hospital, Monroe Street (462-1121).

ENTERTAINMENT CENTERS

HAMMOND: Civic Center, Sohl Avenue (WE2-0093).

SOUTH BEND: Notre Dame Athletic and Convocation Center (283-7354).

FAIRS

BERRIEN SPRINGS: Berrien County Youth Fair, Fairgrounds (473-4251).

CROWN POINT: Lake County Fair, South Court and West Greenwood Avenue (663-0428).

LAPORTE: LaPorte County Fair, Rt. 2 at 150N (362-2647).

SOUTH BEND: St. Joseph County 4-H Fair, Jackson and Lakewood Avenues (291-3400).

VALPARAISO: Porter County Fair, Evans and Indiana Streets.

FARM PRODUCE

BENTON HARBOR: Benton Harbor Fruit Market, 1891 Territorial (925-0681).

CROWN POINT: Rinkenberger, 109th Street (663-5019).

DEMOTTE: Eenigenburg, Rt. 231 (987-3500).

HOBART: Johnson Rt. 6 (926-5045).

LAPORTE: Bernacchi Farm Market, 2429 Monroe (362-7416).

Garwood Orchards, 50S north of Rt. 2 (Pinola) (362-4385).

John Hancock, Fail Road (778-2096).

MICHIGAN CITY: Arndt's Orchards, Wozniak Road (872-0122).

Kintzele, Earl Road (874-4779).

N.W.D. Blueberry Ranch, Fryar Road (872-7477).

Radke, 200N (872-3140).

OGDEN DUNES: Ewen, Stagecoach Road (762-2339).

ROLLING PRAIRIE: Sunacre Orchard, 300E north of Rt. 20 (778-2483).

SOUTH BEND: Farmers Market, 760 Eddy (282-1259).

VALPARAISO: Anderson Orchards, Rt. 6 (462-8568).

Esserman, 75W north of Rt. 6 (926-2749).

WHEELER: Cochran, 475W west of Rt. 30 (759-2980).

FARMS

LACROSSE: Lavern Kruger Angus Farm, 2100S (754-2402).

MEDARYVILLE: Jasper-Pulaski Tree Nursery, Rt. 421 (843-4827).

MICHIGAN CITY: Great Lakes Duck Farm, Rt. 2.

NEW CARLISLE: Homer Fitterling, Rt. 2. Buffalo.

SOUTH BEND: Martin Blad Mint Farm, Rt. 23 (287-9022).

VALPARAISO: Strongbow Turkey Farm, Rt. 30 (462-3311).

WANATAH: Pinney-Purdue Experimental Farm, Rt. 30 at 100N (733-2379).

FISH HATCHERIES

KINGSBURY: Kingsbury State Fish and Game Area, Rt. 35 (393-3612).

KNOX: Bass Lake, Lake Road (772-2353).

FISHING—Boat Charters

BENTON HARBOR: Gardner's Marina, 741 Riverview (925-3247).

MICHIGAN CITY: B & E Marine, 500 Center (879-8301).

Bob's Sport Shop, 1705 Franklin (872-1720).
NEW BUFFALO: New Buffalo Marina, 245 Whittaker (469-0010).
ST. JOSEPH: Whispering Willow Marina, 2383 Niles (983-9963).

FISHING-Information

LAKE COUNTY: Conservation Officer, Larry Hunter (374-6124).
LAPORTE COUNTY: Conservation Officer, Mickey Rosenbaum (325-3961).
MICHIGAN CITY: Hot line for coho (872-7311).
PORTER COUNTY: Conservation Officer, Jim Weeks (926-1807).
ST. JOSEPH COUNTY: Conservation Officer, Russell Sherwood (288-3772).

FISHING—Private Sites

CEDAR LAKE: Chuck's Pier, 13947 Huseman (374-5791).
   Pinecrest Marina, 14415 Lauerman (374-5771).
GRIFFITH: Wild Lake, Broad Street.
HOBART: Robinson Park, 53rd and Liverpool Road (942-5498).
HUDSON: Hudson Lake, Rt. 20.
KOUTS: Donna Jo Campground, 1200S and 350E (462-1545).
LAPORTE: Clear Lake, Truesdale Road (362-2434).
   Fish Trap Lake, McClurg Road (325-0290).
   Lower Fish Lake, Rt. 4 (324-6401).
   North and South Pine Lakes, Waverly Road (362-9746).
   Stone Lake in Soldiers' Memorial Park, Rt. 35 (362-9746).
   Upper Fish Lake, Rt. 4 (325-8385).
ROLLING PRAIRIE: Rolling Timbers Lake, south of Rt. 2 (778-4107).
   Saugany Lake, off Rt. 2 (778-2936).
ST. JOHN: Stan's Fish Lake, Rt. 41.
   Bingo Lake, Rt. 41.
SCHNEIDER: Duncan's Lake, Rt. 41 and Schneider Road (696-7328).

SOUTH BEND: Bass Lake, Rt. 20 (232-7026).
  Goodman Lake, Myrtle and Kern Roads.
  Szmanda Lake, Quince Road.
VALPARAISO: Loomis Lake in Harold Rogers-Lakewood
    Park, Burlington-Beach Road (462-5144).
  Lake Eliza, Rt. 30 (462-1953).
  Mink Lake, Rt. 49 (462-2585).
WESTVILLE: Clear Lake, Porter-LaPorte County Line Road
    (872-9363).

FISHING—Public Sites

CEDAR LAKE: Cline Avenue at Lake Shore Drive.
DYER: Bingo Lake, Rt. 51.
  Stan's Fish Lake, Rt. 51.
EAST GARY: Riverview Park, Rt. 51 and Deep River.
HAMMOND: Dowling Park, Kennedy and Bohrman Ex-
    pressway.
  Lake Front Park, Calumet at Lake Michigan.
  Riverside Park, Calumet and Bohrman Expressway.
  Wolf Lake, 121st and Calumet avenue.
HOBART: Lake George, South Lake Park Avenue.
KINGSBURY: Kingsbury State Fish and Wildlife Area, Rt. 6.
LACROSSE: Kankakee State Fish and Game Area, Rt. 8.
MEDARYVILLE: Jasper-Pulaski State Fish and Wildlife Area,
    Rts. 421 and 143.
MICHIGAN CITY: Breakwater, Washington Park.
MISHAWAKA: Marine Stadium, East Jefferson Road.
  Merrifield Park, East Mishawaka Avenue.
PORTAGE: Port of Indiana, Rt. 12.
ROLLING PRAIRIE: Hog Lake, 300E, three miles east of
    town.
SCHNEIDER: LaSalle State Game and Fish Area, Rt. 41 at
    150N.
SOUTH BEND: Memorial Park, North Drive.
  Pleasant Lake
VALPARAISO: Flint Lake, off Rt. 49 (464-1441).
  Wahob Lake, 700N off Rt. 49.
WHITING: Lake Front Park, 117th Street at Lake Michigan.

GARDENS

CHESTERTON: Cook (926-4029). Roses.

EAST CHICAGO: Washington Park Conservatory, 141st and Grand Boulevard (398-4200).

GARY: South Gleason Park Conservatory, 3400 Jefferson.

HESSTON: Heston Gardens, 1000N and 215E (778-2421). Wild flowers.

MICHIGAN CITY: International Friendship Gardens, Liberty Trail (874-3664).

MISHAWAKA: Battell Park, Mishawaka Avenue (255-6610). Rock garden.

NEW BUFFALO: David Holmes (469-2330). Geraniums.

SOUTH BEND: Fragrance Garden, Leeper Park, 900 North Michigan (284-9405).

Morris Conservatory and Mussell-Ellison Tropical Gardens, 2105 Mishawaka (284-9442).

VALPARAISO: Podresky (462-3531). Roses.

GOLF COURSES

BENTON HARBOR: Blossom Trails, 1565 Britain (925-4951).

BRIDGMAN: Bridgman Country Club, 9794 Jericho (465-5611).

BUCHANAN: Brookwood, Niles-Buchanan Road (695-9193).

CEDAR LAKE: Cedar Lake, 9728 129th (374-7750).

South Shore, Lake Avenue (374-6070).

CROWN POINT: Golden Key Golf Center, 7611 Lincoln (942-8929).

Oak Knoll, Rt. 8 (663-3349).

Pheasant Valley, 3834 141st (663-5000).

EAST CHICAGO: MacArthur, Todd Park, 142 Henlock (398-4200).

GARY: North Gleason, 3200 Jefferson (944-0607).

South Gleason, 3400 Jefferson (944-6417).

GRIFFITH: Colonial, 1901 Cline (923-3223).

HIGHLAND: Wicker Memorial Park, Rts. 6 and 41 (838-9809).

HOBART: Cressmoor, 601 Wisconsin (942-7424).

Indian Ridge, 6363 Grand (942-6850).

LaPorte: Beechwood, Woodlawn Drive (362-2651).
  Char-Mar Hills, Rt. 39 (no phone).
Merrillville: Broadmoor, Rt. 30 and Whitcomb (769-5444).
  Turkey Creek, 6400 Harrison (887-9479).
Michigan City: Michigan City Municipal, Wolf and Michigan Boulevard (872-2121).
Mishawaka: Eberhart Petro Municipal, State Street (255-0550).
Niles: Kelly's Sport Land, 2107 11th (MU3-5421).
  Plym Park Municipal, east of Rt. 2 (684-1928).
Rolling Prairie: Valley Hills, Rt. 2 (778-2823).
St. John: Lake Hills, Rt. 41 (365-8601).
St. Joseph: Sport-O-Rama, 33 Rt. 33 (429-3800).
  Wyndwicke, 3711 Niles (429-7007).
Schererville: Sherwood, 600 Joliet (865-2554).
South Bend: Elbel Park Municipal, 26595 Auten (272-4048).
  Erskine Park, 4600 Miami (291-0156).
  Playland, 1721 Lincoln Way East (288-0033).
  Robin Hood, 20099 New Road (291-2450).
  Studebaker, 718 East Calvert (289-0041).
Valparaiso: Forest Park, Harrison at Yellowstone Avenue (462-4411).
  Mink Lake, Rt. 49 (462-2585).

GRAIN ELEVATORS

Boone Grove: Heinold (462-1284).
Kouts: Heinold (766-2234).
LaCrosse: LaCrosse Grain (754-2113).
Malden: Farm Bureau Coop (462-4861).
Valparaiso: Pennsy Elevator, 352 Washington (462-2873).
Wanatah: Thompson Grain, 1050 West (733-2430).
Wheeler: Farm Bureau Coop Elevator (759-3105).

HAY RIDES (H) and SLEIGH RIDES (S)

Berrien Springs: Country Hideaway, Range Line Road (683-7290). H

Red Bud Trails, 3 miles north of town on Red Bud Trail (695-6405). H

CHESTERTON: Theodore Groszek, 1400N west of Brown Road (926-1051). H

Keith Simms, Burdick Road (926-4883). H and S

EAST GARY: Remus Farm, Rt. 6 (962-2213). H

MICHIANA SHORES: Michiana Riding Stables, 3848 Academy (872-2114). H and S

NILES: Diamond D Ranch, 3232 Dunning (683-5892). H

ST. JOHN: Trails Bend Ranch, 14620 West 93rd (365-5789). H

SCHERERVILLE: Logal's Rt. 41, one mile north of Rt. 30 (865-3131). H

WESTVILLE: Red Rock Ranch, Snyder Road (785-2622). H

HORSEBACK RIDING

CEDAR LAKE: Willowdale Farm, Rt. 41 (374-9876).

CHESTERTON: Camp Farr, 1050N and 350W (926-4900).

CROWN POINT: Walk Away Stables, 709 East 101st (663-6865).

LAPORTE: Colonial Stables, 100W (362-3675).

Richard Fritz, Fail Road (778-2614).

LEROY: Bill Cottingham, 5507 East Rt. 8 (663-4647).

LOWELL: Candlestick Farm, 15807 Morse (696-8650).

Barbara Henry Stables, 12708 West 165th (696-8655).

MICHIANA SHORES: Michiana Riding Stables, 3848 Academy (872-2114).

NILES: Daimond D Ranch, 3232 Dunning (683-5892).

Laughin' Place Stable, 2140 Niles-Buchanan Road (683-8813).

Wild Bill Plott Riding Stables, 3165 Portage (683-2923).

SCHERERVILLE: Lakehill Downs Riding School, 85th Street and Cline (365-8253).

Logal's Rt. 41, one mile north of Rt. 30 (865-3131).

ST. JOHN: Pleasant Hill Farm, 9300 Sheffield (365-5984). Boarding only.

Trails Bend Ranch, 14620 West 93rd (365-5789).

ST. JOSEPH: Stockbridge Farms, 1955 Dickerson (492-9892).

WESTVILLE: Red Rock Ranch, Snyder Road (785-2622).

HOSTEL

TREMONT: Dunes Lakeshore Hostel, Rt. 12, (926-1414).

HUNTING

KINGSBURY: Kingsbury State Fish and Wildlife Area, Rt. 6 (393-3612).

LACROSSE: Kankakee State Game and Fish Area, Rt. 8 (754-2237).

MEDARYVILLE: Jasper-Pulaski State Wildlife Area, Rts. 421 and 143 (843-3641).

SCHNEIDER: LaSalle State Game and Fish Area, Rt. 41 and 150N (992-3019).

MILLS (O=operating)

DEEP RIVER: Deep River Mill, County Road 330.

LAPORTE: Garwood Cider Mill, north of Rt. 2 (362-4385). O

MICHIGAN CITY: Arndt Cider Mill, Wozniak Road (872-0122). O

NEW TROY: New Troy Grist Mill (426-3422). O

VALPARAISO: Tratebas Mill, Tratebas Road.

MOVIES

BENTON HARBOR: Fairplain Cinema 1 and 2, Fairplain Plaza (927-4862).

Liberty, 212 Main (WA6-2216).

Starlite Drive-In, M-139 (WA5-3682).

State, 148 Main (925-7002).

BERRIEN SPRINGS: Berry, Ferry Street (471-1931).

CROWN POINT: Crown, 19 Court (663-1616).

EAST GARY: Dunes Outdoor, Rt. 51 (962-1307).

GARY: Dunes Plaza Cinema I and II, Rts. 20 and 51 (938-0700).

Ridge Plaza I and II, 5900 Ridge (923-9100).

GRIFFITH: Ridge Road Drive-In, Ridge Road (TE8-1600).

HAMMOND: Hammond 41 Outdoor, 2500 Calumet (WE2-2180).

Hammond Outdoor, Indianapolis Boulevard (844-0219).

Kennedy, 6735 Kennedy (TI4-9769).

Paramount, 5404 Hohman (WE2-8168).

Parthenon, 5144 Hohman (WE2-0431).

HIGHLAND: Jerry Lewis, 3022 45th (838-1417).

HOBART: Art, 230 Main (942-1670).

LaPORTE: LaPorte DeLuxe Drive-In, Rt. 2 (362-4013).

MERRILLVILLE: Y and W Twin, 6600 Broadway (769-2203).

MICHIGAN CITY: Lido, 814 Franklin (872-3414).

Marquette, Marquette Mall (872-9101).

212 Outdoor, Rt. 212 (872-1472).

MISHAWAKA: Boiler House Flix I and II, 100 Center, 700 Lincoln Way (255-9575).

Cinema Art, 208 Main (255-0697).

Town and Country, 2340 Hickory (259-9090).

NILES: Outdoor 31, 2131 South 11th (683-4272).

Ready, 420 Main (683-7272).

PORTAGE: Jerry Lewis, 6224 Central (762-7979).

SOUTH BEND: Avon, 307 South Michigan (288-7800).

Colfax, 213 West Colfax (233-4532).

Moonlight Drive-In, 4000 South Main (291-5191).

River Park, 2929 Mishawaka (288-8488).

State, 214 South Michigan (233-1676).

Western Drive-In, 56445 Peppermint (288-1727).

ST. JOSEPH: Southtown Twin, 815 St. Joseph (983-3233).

St. Joseph Auto Theatre, Rt. 12 (GA9-3946).

VALPARAISO: 49'er Drive-In, Rt. 49 (462-3609).

Premier, 6911 Lincolnway (462-3012).

MUSEUMS and LIBRARY COLLECTIONS

BENTON HARBOR: Josephine Morton Memorial House, 501 Territorial (WA5-7011).

CROWN POINT: Old Homestead, 227 South Court (663-0456).

GARY: Indiana Room, Gary Public Library, 220 West 5th (886-2484).

HAMMOND: Calumet Room, Hammond Public Library, 566 State (931-5100).

HEBRON: The Stage Coach Inn, Main Street (996-2700).

HESSTON: Heston Steam Museum, 1000N east of Rt. 35.

HOBART: Hobart Historical Museum, 4th and East Streets (942-2724).

LACROSSE: Miller's Museum, Rt. 421 (754-2255).

LAPORTE: LaPorte County Historical Museum, Courthouse (362-7061).

MERRILLVILLE: Lake County Reference Library, Rt. 30 (769-3540).

MICHIGAN CITY: Lighthouse Museum, Harbor (872-6133).

MISHAWAKA: Mishawaka Children's Museum, 410 Lincoln Way East (259-3475).

NILES: Fort St. Joseph Historical Museum, 508 East Main (MU3-4702).

SOUTH BEND: Northern Indiana Historical Museum, 112 South Lafayette (284-9664).

Studebaker Antique Car Collection, 635 South Main (234-4121).

VALPARAISO: Porter County Historical Society Museum, County Court House (462-2233).

MUSIC

CEDAR LAKE: Moody Bible Institute, 137th Street.

MERRILLVILLE: Northwest Indiana Symphony Orchestra, Merrillville High School, 276 East 68th (769-2401).

MUNSTER: Northwest Indiana Symphony Orchestra, Munster High School, 8808 Columbia (836-1450).

MICHIGAN CITY: International Friendship Gardens, Liberty Trail (874-3664).

MISHAWAKA: Bethel College, 1001 McKinley (259-8511)

SOUTH BEND: Notre Dame University (283-7367).

St. Mary's College (284-4176).

South Bend Symphony Orchestra, Morris Auditorium, 211 North Michigan (282-1392).

VALPARAISO: Valparaiso University (462-5111).

NATURE CENTERS

BENTON HARBOR: Sarett Nature Center, Benton Center Road (927-4832).

HOBART: Deep River Nature Center, 3100 Liverpool (962-1579).

MISHAWAKA: South Bend Audubon Society Nature Sanctuary, Clover Road (291-2830).

NEW CARLISLE: Bendix Woods Park Nature Center, Rt. 2 (654-7658).

NILES: Fernwood Nature Center, 1720 Range Line Road (695-6491).

STEVENSVILLE: Grand Mere Nature Study Preserve, (381-1574).

ORCHARDS

DeMOTTE: Eenigenburg, Rt. 231 (987-3500).

HOBART: Johnson, Rt. 6 (962-1383).

LaPORTE: Garwood Orchard, off Rt. 2 (362-4385).

John Hancock, Fail Road (778-2096).

MICHIGAN CITY: Arndt, Wozniak Road (872-0122).

N.W.D. Blueberry Ranch, Fryar Road (872-7477).

ROLLING PRAIRIE: Sunacre Fruit Farm, 300E north of Rt. 20 (778-2483).

ST. JOSEPH: Nye's Apple Barn, 4716 Hollywood (983-6602).

VALPARAISO: Anderson, Rt. 6 (462-8568).

Esserman, 75W (926-2749).

WANATAH: Siegesmund, 900W (733-2259).

Tidholm, 1050W (733-2560).

PARKS

BRIDGMAN: Warren Dunes State Park, Red Arrow Highway (462-4013).

CEDAR LAKE: Lemon Lake County Park, 133rd and Cedar Lake Road.

CHESTERTON: Indiana Dunes State Park, Rt. 49 (926-1215).

CROWN POINT: Fancher Lake Park, South Court and West Greenwood Avenue (663-1672).

EAST CHICAGO: Joerse Park, Michigan Avenue (398-4200).

Washington Park, 141st Avenue (398-4200).

EAST GARY: Riverview Park, Rt. 51 and Deep River.

GARY: Gateway Park, 4th and Broadway.

South Gleason Park, 3400 Jefferson.

HAMMOND: Dowling Park, Kennedy and Bohrman Expressway.

Lake Front Park, Calumet at Lake Michigan (931-2760).

Riverside Park, Calumet and Bohrman Expressway. Wolf Lake Park, 121st and Calumet Avenue (WE2-0093).

HIGHLAND: Wicker Park, Rts. 6 and 41 (838-9809).

HOBART: Lake George, South Lake Park Avenue (942-7765).

Robinson Park, 53rd and Liverpool Road (942-5498).

KNOX: Bass State Park, off Rt. 35 (772-2243).

LEROY: Stoney Run County Park, 450S (663-6804).

MICHIGAN CITY: Washington Park, North Franklin at Lake Michigan (879-8393).

MILLER: Marquette Park, Marquette and Grand Boulevards (944-6677).

MISHAWAKA: Battell Park, Mishawaka Avenue (255-6610). Izaak Walton League Park, 2400 Darden (372-3660). Marine Stadium, East Jefferson Road (255-6610). Merrifield Park, Mishawaka Avenue (255-6610).

NEW BUFFALO: Warren Woods State Park, 735N east of Red Arrow Highway

NEW CARLISLE: Bendix Woods County Park, Rt. 2 (654-7658).

PORTAGE: Woodland Park, 2100 Willow Creek (762-1675).

SOUTH BEND: Leeper Park, 900 North Michigan (284-9405).

Pottawattomie Park, 2000 Wall (284-9438).

ST. JOSEPH: Lake Front Park, Lake Bluff Avenue. Riverview Park, Rt. 31 (983-6341).

VALPARAISO: Harold Rogers-Lakewood Road, Campbell Road (462-5144).

Womar Woods, 750N.

WHITING: Whiting Park, 117th Street at Lake Michigan.

RELIGIOUS SITES

CEDAR LAKE: Franciscán Retreat, Parrish Road (374-5741).

CROWN POINT: Capuchin Seminary of St. Mary, 8400 Burr (365-8522).

MUNSTER: Carmelite Monastery, 1628 Ridge (838-5050).

SCHERERVILLE: Hyles-Anderson Bible College, 134 Joliet (865-3350).

SOUTH BEND: Lourdes Grotto, Notre Dame (283-6011).
VALPARAISO: Seven Dolors Shrine, 700N (759-2521).

RESTAURANTS

BARODA: Bill's Tap, 1st Street (422-1141).
BENTON HARBOR: Vegetarian Restaurant, House of David, Britain Avenue (926-9710).
   Bill Knapp's, M-139 at I-94 (925-3212).
BEVERLY SHORES: Red Lantern, Lake Front Drive (874-6201).
BRIDGMAN: D'Agostino's Navajo, Red Arrow Highway (465-3434).
   Hyerdall, Red Arrow Highway (465-5546).
BUCHANAN: Meadowbrook, 1207 Red Bud (695-3811).
CEDAR LAKE: Hanover House, 133rd and Parrish Avenue (374-5232).
   Heritage House, Wicker and 133rd Street (374-6200).
   Tobe's Steak House, 7301 138th (374-9605).
CROWN POINT: Lighthouse South, 101 Courthouse (663-7141).
DEMOTTE: Forest River Lodge at Ramsey's Landing, Kankakee River off Rt. 231 (996-3363).
DYER: Dick's Tap, Rts. 8 and 41 (365-5041).
EAST CHICAGO: Puntillo, 4905 Indianapolis (397-4952).
GARY: Lighthouse, 644 5th (886-1922).
   Miner-Dunn, 301 Ridge (887-5124).
   Pete's Grecian Cafe, 612 5th (886-9491).
GRIFFITH: San Remo, 112 Ridge (838-6000).
HAMMOND: Barton's Pizza, 6819 Indianapolis (844-1000).
   Cam-Lan, 132 Sibley (931-5115).
   Purdue University Cafeteria, 2233 171st (844-0520).
HEBRON: Country Kitchen, Main Street (996-5241).
   Old Heritage Inn, Main Street (996-9010).
HESSTON: Heston Bar, 1000N and Fail Road (778-2938).
HOBART: Country Lounge, 37th Street (942-6074).
KOUTS: Hilliard's, Main Street (766-3851).
   John's Corner Tap, Main Street (766-9930).
LAPORTE: Oriental, 610 Colfax (362-1571).
   Timbers, 444 Pine Lake Avenue (362-4585).

LONG BEACH: Tinker's Dam, Karwick Road (879-7373).

MICHIGAN CITY: Canterbury Playhouse Inn, 110 West 9th (874-4269).

Maxine and Heinie's, 521 Franklin (879-9068).

Robin Hood, Marquette Mall (872-8629).

MILLER: Golden Coin, Rt. 20 and Clay Street (989-5357).

MISHAWAKA: 100 Center, 700 Lincoln Way West (259-7861).

MUNSTER: New Moon, 8250 Calumet (836-5464).

Vince's, 1734 45th (838-6660).

NEW BUFFALO: Czech Haspudka Villa, Red Arrow Highway (469-3330).

Golden Door, Rt. 12 and I-94 (469-1191).

Little Bohemia, 115 Whittaker (469-1440). ·

Redamak's Tavern, Rt. 12 (469-9866).

Scotty's Place, Rt. 12 (469-1353).

Theo's, Rt. 12 (469-0400).

NEW CARLISLE: Miller's Cafe, 110 East Michigan (654-3431).

NILES: Franky's, 1033 Lake (683-7474).

Portofino's, Rt. 12 31 (683-5000).

PORTER: Meltz's, 112 Lincoln (926-9967).

The Spa, Mineral Springs Road (926-1654).

SAWYER: Anderson's, Red Arrow Highway (426-4904).

SCHERERVILLE: Teibel's, Rts. 41 and 30 (865-2000).

SOUTH BEND: Boar's Head, 52855 Rt. 31 (277-5478).

Eddie's, 1345 North Ironwood (232-5861).

Morris Inn, Notre Dame Campus (234-0141).

Wooden Keg, 1611 South Main (289-4824).

ST. JOSEPH: Flagship, 100 Main (983-3212).

Holly's Landing, 105 Main (983-2334).

Lobster Lounge, 221 Wayne (983-5031).

STEVENSVILLE: Ritter's, Red Arrow Highway (GA9-3591).

Win Schuler, 5000 Red Arrow (429-3273).

Tosi, 4337 Ridge (429-3689).

VALPARAISO: Hotel Lembke, 15 Lafayette (462-1141).

Old Style Inn, 5 Lincolnway (462-9196).

Strongbow Turkey Inn, Rt. 30 (462-3311).

The Fishery, 714 Calumet (462-0436).

Wellman's Rt. 30 (462-6141).
WHITING: Condes, 1440 Indianapolis (659-1052).
  Fonda Del Lago, 1423 Indianapolis (659-4738).
  Phil Smidt, 1205 Calumet (659-0025).
  Vogel's, 1250 Indianapolis (659-1250).

ROLLER SKATING RINKS

CHESTERTON: Skateland Arena, 878 Indiana (926-1791).
GRIFFITH: Twilight Skating Club, 135 West Main (838-9882).
HAMMOND: Roller Dome Rink, 730 Goslin (933-9407).
HOBART: Oak Ridge Roller Dome, 143 Hobart (942-2416).
LAPORTE: LaPorte Casino, 115 McClurg (362-6765).
MISHAWAKA: Mishawaka Roller Rink, 506½ Main (255-0451).
  Rainbow Roller Rink, 1705 East 12th (259-9642).
NEW BUFFALO: Scotty's Roller Bowl, 27 North Whittaker (469-3750).

SHOOTING RANGES

HIGHLAND: Hansen's Sports, 3750 Ridge (838-7495). (Indoor range.)
KINGSBURY: Kingsbury State Fish and Wildlife Area, Rt. 6 (393-3612). (Outdoor range.)
MEDARYVILLE: Jasper-Pulaski State Fish and Wildlife Area, Rts. 421 and 143 (843-3641). (Skeet shooting.)

SHOPS—Craftsmen

BERRIEN SPRINGS: College Wood Products, Andrews University, Rt. 31 (473-5511). Woodworking shop.
BRUNSWICK (near Cedar Lake): Ericson Violin Shop, 13321 Calumet (374-7864). Violin maker.
CHESTERTON: W. Merle Fisher, Hadenfeldt Road (926-2555). Jewelry maker.
LAPORTE: Elwin Ames, 400N off Fail Road (325-8368). Blacksmith.
PORTER: Gem Tree Rock Shop, Rt. 12 (926-1919).
  Sanders Wood Engraving Company, 212 Lincoln (926-4929).

UNION MILLS: Ed Klein, Rt. 39 (767-2640). Saddlemaker.

SHOPS—Craft Supplies

LAKESIDE: Arts and Crafts of Lakeside, 14876 Red Arrow (469-2771).

MICHIGAN CITY: Old Towne Crafts, 1410 Franklin (874-7588).

VALPARAISO: Artists' Den, 203 Jefferson (462-3883).
  Wooden Shoe Crafts, 504 Lincolnway (462-7455).

SHOPS—Discount and Salvage

CEDAR LAKE: Flea Market, 9600 151st (696-8855).

KNOX: Toto's, Toto Road (772-4533).

MICHIGAN CITY: Junk Shop, 1620 Columbia (874-3161).
  Nationwide Flea Market, Rt. 20 (879-5288).

NEW CARLISLE: Railroad Salvage, East Michigan Street (654-3533).

SAN PIERRE: Railroad Salvage, 2300S (285-2515).

STEVENSVILLE: Paris Flea Market, Red Arrow Highway (429-7501).

VALPARAISO: Fetla's, Rt. 2 (462-5221).

SHOPS—Flowers and Seeds

BENTON HARBOR: Grootenhorst, 2450 Red Arrow (925-2535).

BRIDGMAN: Rainbow Gardens, 9394 Red Arrow (465-3191).

CHESTERTON: Chesterton Feed and Garden Center, 400 Locust (926-2790).

LAPORTE: Bernacchi Greenhouse, 1010 Fox (362-6202).

MEDARYVILLE: Jasper-Pulaski Tree Nursery, Rt. 421 (843-4827).

MICHIGAN CITY: Allison, LaPorte-Porter County Line (872-5004).
  Tuholski, 519 Chicago (874-4188).

STEVENSVILLE: Emlong, off Red Arrow Highway (429-3431).

VALPARAISO: McMahan, 6 Michigan (462-1411).

WALKERTON: Carl Webb, Rt. 104 (325-9659).

SHOPS—Foods

BARODA: Tabor Hill Winecellar, Mt. Tabor Road (422-1515).

BERRIEN SPRINGS: Andrews University Grocery Store, Rt. 31 (471-7442). Vegetarian foods.

GARY: Oriental Bakery, 28 Ridge (981-2020).

HARBERT: Harbert Bakery, 13746 Red Arrow (469-1777).
  Molly Pitcher Wines, 13581 Red Arrow (469-0700).
  Swedish Bakery, Red Arrow Highway (469-4202).

KOUTS: Horn's Chocolate Factory Shop, Rt. 8 (766-2241).

MICHIGAN CITY: Great Lake Duck Farm, Rt. 35 (874-6642).
  Ritter Fish Company, 118 5th (872-3912).

MILLER: Wilco, 6300 Miller (989-6631). Greek bakery.

NILES: Paris Candy, 220 East Main (683-9792). Ice cream.

SOUTH BEND: Farmers Market, 760 South Eddy (282-1259).

STEVENSVILLE: Mrs. Halby's Jams and Jelly Kitchen, Red Arrow Highway.
  A Bit of Swiss Bakery, 4337 Ridge (429-1661).

THREE OAKS: Drier's Meat, 14 South Elm (756-3101).

VALPARAISO: The Fishery, 714 Calumet (462-0436).

SHOPS—Guns

BURNS HARBOR: Jack's Gun Shop, Rt. 20 (787-8311).

LAPORTE: Gun Shop, 925 Lincolnway (362-3038).

MICHIGAN CITY: Heritage Gun Shop, 105 Barker (879-5714).

SHOPS—Miscellaneous

BENTON HARBOR: Heath Company Factory Store, Hilltop Road (983-3961). Electronic kits.

CHESTERTON: Casa Morena, 216 Grant (926-6916). Imports.

FURNESSVILLE: Schoolhouse Shop, Furnessville Road (926-1875). Every sort of gift.

HAMMOND: Indiana Botanic Gardens, 626 177th (WE1-2480). Herbs.

MICHIGAN CITY: Eastmoor Factory Store, Chicago and Ford Streets (874-5231). Women's clothes.
  Hayloft, 909½ Franklin, (874-6833). Gifts.

Indiana State Prison Store, Chicago Avenue (874-7258). Handcrafts.

Patchwork Shop, Deutscher Road (874-7054). Handcrafts.

Society Lingerie Factory Store, Roeske Avenue (872-7206).

MISHAWAKA: 100 Center, 700 Lincoln Way West (259-7861). Shopping complex.

NEW BUFFALO: Decor, Red Arrow Highway (469-2745). Imports.

SAWYER: Haalga's, Red Arrow Highway (426-4233). Swedish Imports.

SCHERERVILLE: Schererville Clock Shop, 105 Joliet (322-5433).

VALPARAISO: Hans and Fritz Antique Clocks, 9 Lincolnway (464-2010).

SHOPS—Sporting Equipment

BENTON HARBOR: Jim's Bait and Tackle, 942 Crystal (926-2544).

BUCHANAN: Gambles, 226 East Front (695-6891).
Thompson's Archery, 315 Liberty (695-3379).

CEDAR LAKE: Cedar Lake Sport Shop, 7926 Lake Shore (374-6133).
Kiefer's Sports, Lake Shore Drive (374-9601).

CHESTERTON: Chesterton Sporting Goods, 104 Calumet (926-5526).

CROWN POINT: Henderlong Lumber, 500 Foote (663-0600).

EAST CHICAGO: A. P. Davis Sports, 4532 Indianapolis (397-0274).
Main Sporting Goods, 3822 Main (EX7-5870).

GARY: Archer's Lodge, 560 5th (939-8444).
Mike's and Tom's, 739 41st (981-3123).
Westforth Sport, 4704 Roosevelt (884-8680).

GRIFFITH: Blythe's, 138 Broad (838-2203).

HAMMOND: Hessville Sporting Goods, 6637 Kennedy (844-2205).
Johann, 6942 Indianapolis (844-8000).

J. W. Millikan, 449 State (WE1-2760).

Pla-Time, 441 State (We1-3512).

Sportsmen's Store, 7112 Calumet (WE1-6999).

HIGHLAND: Arctic Ski Shop, 9636 Forest (923-8700).

C-K, 9553 Indianapolis (923-6809).

Hansen's Sports, 3750 Ridge (838-7495).

Highland Sports Center, 2820 Highway (838-2212).

HOBART: Hobart Sports, 437 3rd (942-4014).

LaPORTE: Garr Hardware, 505 State (362-3474).

LaPorte Sporting Goods, 816 Lincolnway (362-3447)

Lee Jax, 910 Lincolnway (362-2332)

LOWELL: Blythe's, 1330 Commercial (696-7010).

MERRILLVILLE: Merrillville Sporting Goods, 7119 Broadway (769-7031).

MICHIGAN CITY: Bob's, 1705 Franklin (872-1720).

Michigan City Sport Center, 1716 Franklin (879-0907).

MUNSTER: Rothstein, 4937 White Oak (838-9734).

NEW BUFFALO: Skipper's Landing, 244 Whittaker (469-1120).

NILES: Hully's Bait and Tackle, 12215 11th (684-1444).

W. S. Leisure Center, 2607 South 11th (684-0750).

Twelve Oaks Sports, 2610 South Rt. 31 (684-1743).

PORTAGE: Brandt's, 5700 Central (762-3421).

Coast-to-Coast, 2565 Portage Mall (762-7717).

Sport Port, 2548 Portage Mall (962-3387).

SOUTH BEND: Midwest Athletic, 517 West Hill (232-9550).

Sonnenborn's, 115 West Colfax (232-11451).

Sportsmen's Paradise, 254 Dixie Way West (272-9755).

ST. JOHN: Schererville Bait and Sports, Rt. 41 (365-5158).

ST. JOSEPH: Midwest Athletic, 507 Pleasant (983-7905).

VALPARAISO: Johnston's Sports, 119 Lincolnway (462-2671).

Triangle Sporting Goods, 2608 Calumet (462-5041).

WHITING: Whiting Sport Shop, 1601 121st (659-2600).

SKIING

BUCHANAN: Royal Valley, Main Street (695-3847).

LaPORTE: Ski Valley, Rt. 2 (362-1212).

NEW CARLISLE: Bendix Woods Park, Rt. 2 (654-7658).

VALPARAISO: Pines Ski Area, Meridian Road (462-1465).

SKI RENTAL

BENTON HARBOR: Gardner's Favorite Sports, 741 Riverview (925-3247).
HIGHLAND: Arctic Ski Shop, 9636 Forest (923-8700).
VALPARAISO: Pines Ski Area, Meridian Road (462-1465).

SLEDDING and TOBOGGANING

MILLER: Marquette Park, Marquette and Grand Boulevards.
NEW CARLISLE: Bendix Woods Park, Rt. 2 (654-7658).
VALPARAISO: Forest Park, Harrison Avenue (462-5144).
   Mink Lake, Rt. 49 (462-2585).

SWIMMING POOLS (I = Indoor O = Outdoor)

Check YMCA's and high schools in communities for hours and fees for public swimming.
HIGHLAND: Wicker Park, Ridge Road (839-9809). O
MISHAWAKA: Merrifield Park, Mishawaka Avenue (255-6610). O
   Mary Gibbard Park, 1024 Somerset (255-0854). O
NEW CARLISLE: Bendix Park, Rt. 2 (284-9424). O
SOUTH BEND: Natatorium, 1044 West Washington (284-9413). I
   Pinhook Park, 2801 Riverside (284-9421). O
   Pottawattomie Park, 2000 Wall (284-9438). O
PORTAGE: Woodland Park, 2100 Willow Creek (762-1675). O

THEATERS

LONG BEACH: Barlo Playhouse, North Karwick Road (872-0941).
MICHIANA SHORES: Dunes Art Foundation Summer Theater, Oakdale Road (879-9782).
MICHIGAN CITY: Canterbury Playhouse, 907 Franklin (874-4269).
   Dunes Art Foundation, East Michigan Boulevard (872-3912).

NEW BUFFALO: Scotty's Dinner Theater, Rt. 12 (469-1353).
SOUTH BEND: Civic Theater, 701 Portage (233-0683).
   Laughlin Theater, St. Mary's College (284-4141).
   Morris Civic Auditorium, 211 North Michigan (232-6954).
ST. JOSEPH: Twin City Players, 4681 South Red Arrow (429-9402).
VALPARAISO: Opera House, South Franklin Avenue (462-3704).
   Wellman's Bridge-Vu, Rt. 30 (462-0563).
WHITING: Marion Theater Guild, 1844 Lincoln (695-2118).

TOURS

BENTON HARBOR: Blossom Time, 311 Colfax (925-7019).
   Heath Company, Hilltop Road (983-3961).
   Whirlpool, Upton Road (926-5000).
BRIDGMAN: Cook Nuclear Plant, Red Arrow Highway (465-6101).
BURNS HARBOR: Bethlehem Steel, Rt. 12 (787-3241).
BUCHANAN: Clark Equipment Company, Automotive Division, 324 East Dewey (697-8385).
CROWN POINT: Old Homestead, 220 South Court (663-0456 or 663-0590).
KINGSBURY: LaPorte Egg Ranch, Industrial Park (393-3531).
KOUTS: Heinold Fertilizer, Rt. 8 (766-2234).
   Heinold Hog Yards, off Rt. 49 (766-2221).
   Heinold Grain, off Rt. 49 (766-2234).
MICHIGAN CITY: Barker Mansion, 631 Washington (872-0159).
MISHAWANA: Southhold Restoration, 112 Lafayette (232-4284).
NILES: Clark Equipment Company, Tyler Refrigeration Division (683-3720).
SOUTH BEND: Associated Investment Company, 1700 Mishawaka (288-9141).
   Avanti Corporation, 765 South Lafayette (287-1836).
   Martin Blad Mint Farm, Rt. 23 (287-9022).
   Notre Dame Campus (283-7367).

Southhold Restoration, 112 South Lafayette (232-4284).

St. Joseph: Musselman's Cannery, 3515 Red Arrow (983-3901).

Nye's Apple Barn, 4716 Hollywood (983-6602).

Valparaiso: Strongbow Turkey Farm, Rt. 30 (462-3311).

WILDLIFE AREAS

Kingsbury: Kingsbury State Fish and Wildlife Area, Rts. 6 and 35 (393-3612).

LaCrosse: Kankakee State Game and Fish Area, Rt. 8 (754-2237).

Medaryville: Jasper-Pulaski State Wildlife Area, Rts. 421 and 143 (843-3641).

Schneider: LaSalle State Game and Fish Area, Rt. 41 and 150N (992-3019).

ZOOS

Michigan City: Michigan City Zoo, Washington Park, Lakefront (872-8628).

South Bend: Pottawattomie Park, 2000 Wall (288-8133). Storyland Zoo, 1304 West Ewing (284-9434).

Benediction:

Now that you've done the Dunes and trekked the countryside beyond, you've probably found five markers we've missed or that perfect little restaurant which serves home-grown pheasant exquisitely cooked and served under glass. Tear out this page and add your discoveries to ours. When we publish the next edition of DOING THE DUNES, we'll probably include your recommendations and acknowledge your help.

Send your comments and additions to:
Dunes Enterprises
Box 371
Beverly Shores, Indiana 46301.

DOING THE DUNES

The FIRST
  Guidebook to the Indiana Dunes National Lakeshore
  Compendium to the area from Lake Michigan to the
    Kankakee River

A lively account of where to go and what to see for all
    ages and interests

18 months of researching, writing and photographing

Fits into your glove compartment or your knapsack for
    ready reference

Photographs   Maps   Tours   History   Fun

240 pages $2.50

_____ Order By Mail Today _____

Dunes Enterprises
Box 371
Beverly Shores, Indiana 46301

Please send my copy of DOING THE DUNES. I am
enclosing $_____ in check or money order. (Indiana
residents add 4% sales tax.)

Name _____

Address _____

City _____ State _____ Zip Code _____

Buy copies for your friends, relatives, or neighbors who
are dune lovers at heart. Send your check and list and
we'll do the rest!